THE
Principle of Reason

Studies in Continental Thought

GENERAL EDITOR
JOHN SALLIS

Martin Heidegger

THE
Principle of Reason

TRANSLATED BY

Reginald Lilly

Indiana University Press

BLOOMINGTON AND INDIANAPOLIS

First Paperback Edition 1996

Preparation of this book was aided by a grant from the Program for Translations of the National Endowment for the Humanities, an independent federal agency.

Published in German as *Der Satz vom Grund* ©1957 by Verlag Gunther Neske, Pfullingen

The paper used in this publication meets the minimum requirements of American
National Standard for Information Sciences—Permanence of Paper for Printed
Library Materials, ANSI Z39.48–1984.

Manufactured in the United States of America

Library of Congress Cataloging-in-Publication Data
Heidegger, Martin, 1889–1976.
   [Satz vom Grund. English]
   The principle of reason / Martin Heidegger ; translated by Reginald Lilly.
      p.   cm. — (Studies in Continental thought)
   Translation of: Der Satz vom Grund.
   Includes bibliographical references.
   ISBN 0–253–32724–5 (hard : alk. paper)
   1. Reason.   2. Metaphysics.   I. Title.   II. Series.
B3279.H48513   1991
110—dc20   90–25454
   ISBN 0-253-21066-6 (pbk.)

2 3 4 5 6 00 99 98 97 96

Contents

Contents

TRANSLATOR'S INTRODUCTION

In 1955–56 Martin Heidegger gave a one-hour lecture course at the University of Freiburg under the title "Der Satz vom Grund." In 1957 he published the manuscript of that lecture course, together with an address having the same title that he delivered twice in 1956, as *Der Satz vom Grund*. *The Principle of Reason* is a translation of *Der Satz vom Grund*, originally published by Verlag Gunther Neske, Pfullingen.

Heidegger remarked on several occasions that a translation is always an interpretation, and it would be disingenuous to claim here that the present translation is an exception. Yet if it is an interpretation, it is different from interpretations that take the form of exegetical and critical analyses. The latter call upon a text and, in doing so, presume that readers can, if they wish, have independent access to that text. However, a translation presumes, to some extent, that readers (ostensibly for linguistic reasons) do not have (satisfactory) access to the original text. So if Hegel rightly ridiculed introductions because they presume to convey what one would learn if one were to read the text which is there for the reading, the present case is quite different: it is precisely the absence of Heidegger's German text that gives this introduction whatever *raison d'être* it may have; for my purpose is not to summarize what one would learn if one read *The Principle of Reason* in the original German, but to compensate for the displacement that inevitably has occurred in the translation of that text.

Heidegger himself, in *The Principle of Reason*, discusses an example of such a translation-displacement and its significance.[1] This displacement is all the more pronounced and significant the more the text being translated draws its sense from the peculiarities of the language in which it was composed. Poetry is, of course, an exemplary case of such a text. There is no question that Heidegger's text is philosophical rather than poetic, but the displacement that has occurred in translating it is nevertheless significant, and for many of the same reasons that displacement occurs in literary, especially poetic, texts. By pointing to some of the specific instances of displacement, this introduction seeks to help readers make better use of the translation and to encourage them, if linguistic ability permits, to consult the original German text; for *The Principle of Reason* is also certainly no exception to the rule that a translation, as an interpretation, can at best be an introduction to the original text.

Without presuming to summarize, I will nevertheless start with some general remarks concerning my understanding of the text, for this understanding has been important in identifying and dealing with problems of translation and has shaped the translation itself.

In the *Principle of Reason*, as elsewhere, Heidegger is concerned with the question of being. However, the way he approaches this question in the present text is unique in his published corpus: he takes up a statement—the principle of reason, which says "nothing is without reason"—and considers the notion that this principle first came into being as an explicit statement at a particular moment in history, namely with Leibniz. Heidegger explains that this principle has its own history, a history that cannot be said to begin with Leibniz's formulation of it but that in fact preceded it by some two thousand years. This odd history of the principle of reason can be recognized once one sees that the principle of reason is an utterance of being and that Leibniz's formulation of this principle was a response to being as it was proffered to him. Heidegger's text on the whole seeks to bring the reader to this insight.

Thus, to understand the principle of reason requires that one see it in terms of a response to a proffering of being, a proffering which is the essence of history, of the history of being. And indeed *The Principle of Reason* contains Heidegger's most extensive reflection on the history of being (*Seinsgeschichte*) and its essence, which he calls "Geschick." Because of their importance as well as their resistance to translation, I have devoted the greatest effort to those passages and words which deal with the various facets of the *Geschick* of being. They have greatly influenced my translation of terms more "remote" to Heidegger's discussion. I would like to turn briefly to these difficulties.

PRINCIPLES AND DIFFICULTIES OF TRANSLATION

In 1969 in an interview with Richard Wisser Heidegger addressed the issue of the complex relationship of thinking to the tradition of philosophy. He commented, "And it requires a new attentiveness to language, not the invention of new terms, as I once thought; rather, it requires a return to the original contents of our own language as it has been conceived, which is constantly decaying."[2] Heidegger's great sensitivity to the rhetorical and conceptual resources of the German language in *Der Satz vom Grund* has led many to remark that this work, perhaps better than any other, shows Heidegger as a master of the German language. From a linguistic point of view, Heidegger's text is unstrained and frequently makes use of idioms. And even where Heidegger uses words or phrases in an unusual or antiquated manner, it is clear that he does so to occasion reflection in his reader. He is able to accomplish this without these uses getting in the way of what he is saying. In short, the German text is rhetorically fluid and elegant while being philosophically rigorous. It is, so to speak, linguistically "easy to read."

It is possible to imagine many texts of foreign origin having been written in one's own language. Translating such texts is often relatively easy. But it is difficult if not impossible to imagine *Der Satz vom Grund* having been written in English, for at least one important reason: contemporary philosophical English is, for the most part, Latin in origin. To the extent that this is the case, the terminology we employ stems directly and seamlessly from the philosophical discourse stretching from the medieval philosophers to modernity. Hence, linguistically our relation to this tradition is, for the most part, one of continuity. Such is not the case with German philosophical discourse. As Heidegger points out,[3] the Latinate terms of the tradition went through a process of translation into German, and though these translations attempted to establish and maintain a continuity with the tradition of Latin philosophical discourse, an important conceptual transformation occurred. Although the German translations of the Latinate terms of the tradition were conceived to be the German equivalents for those terms and were "correct" translations, they say something more and something different from those terms of the tradition that they were to translate. This identity and difference means that these German philosophical terms harbor a conceptual richness as well as the rhetorical possibility for bringing this richness to light: the way Heidegger says what he says cannot be separated from the meaning of what he says, and the way he says what he says—and hence what he says—is deeply rooted in the character and history of the German language.

Heidegger's rhetoric—and here we understand *rhetoric* to mean the composition of a text such that the reader is led by the character of the discourse to insights, a discourse composed such that it deploys itself as the gradual revelation of the richness and depth of meaning harbored in its basic words—takes advantage of this tension between the intended continuity and the often forgotten difference of German philosophical discourse vis-à-vis that of the tradition in order to with seeming effortlessness develop his philosophical exposition. Herein lies the intimacy of concept and rhetoric in *The Principle of Reason*. This tension or intimacy cannot be reproduced in English precisely because of the much greater continuity of English philosophical discourse with that of the tradition. Therefore, whereas the relation of rhetoric and concept in Heidegger's text is intimately rooted in the language of the German philosophical tradition, because we have a different philosophical tradition, in translating the text I have had to strike a balance between them, one which is inevitably imperfect.

Thus, I constantly risked erring in either of two directions: translating too literally risks destroying the rhetorical character of the text, reducing it to a mass of more or less disconnected statements. This would, ironically, undermine the clarity of meaning to which literal translations aspire. But there has been the pendant risk of attempting to produce a text that is as graceful and rhetorically well constructed as the original. To do so one must inevitably depart from the conceptual specificity inherent in the language of the original in order to take advantage of the rhetorical resources of one's own language; one thereby risks rendering a paraphrase rather than a translation of the original. This dilemma is familiar to translators of Heidegger, whose texts are exceptionally difficult to translate because the sense of an entire passage often depends upon the relations evoked by and among various words. In many of Heidegger's early works it is perhaps easier to strike a balance in English between fluidity of prose and conceptual precision because Heidegger's rhetoric is often relatively traditional. The difficulty in translating these works stems not so much from the structure and development of his exposition, but, as he himself suggests, from the fact that he tended to use the well-known possibility of the German language to construct unprecedented words and meanings, imposing them, as it were, upon the German language; often he uses common German philosophical terms in an uncommon manner. Therefore his translator may decide to sacrifice fluidity for the sake of conceptual precision through the employment of neologisms, for example, which often are no more disturbing to the rhetoric of the English than Heidegger's neologisms are for the rhetoric of the German. In some of his later works Heidegger uses an untraditional philosophical vocabulary and rhetoric, and indeed these lead to philosophical insights that seem to be ones that cannot be reached if one were to approach them through traditional philosophical prose; this may be why those for whom philosophical insights cannot be reached except through a traditional philosophical rhetoric are incapable of understanding these works as philosophical. In the case of these later works, it is perhaps more practical for a translator to depart from traditional philosophical English, its vocabulary and rhetoric, in order to take advantage of the rhetorical resources of English.

No text of Heidegger is easy to translate, but the dilemma becomes particularly acute in *The Principle of Reason*, which goes to the very heart of modern philosophy in taking up one of its basic notions: the principle of reason. And at least at the outset, its exposition seems quite traditional—the ideas and the vocabulary used to discuss them are relatively straightforward. But Heidegger develops his reflection upon traditional (German) philosophical terms, phrases, and ideas and upon the way they have been understood in and by the tradition not through a traditional tour de force of presenting a thesis and supporting arguments. Instead he allows the language of traditional German philosophy to suggest more than it can when it is pressed into the service of such a traditional rhetoric and prose, that is, when it is taken as a mere translation of Latin philosophical terms and ideas. This manner of allowing traditional German philosophical prose to say more than it can be heard to say when one listens to it in the traditional way constitutes the unique—and for his translator, difficult—rhetorical character of *Der Satz vom Grund*. It is difficult because Heidegger takes up and discusses some of the most traditional terms and ideas, and it is necessary for the reader to hear these terms in a traditional way; hence, one is justifiably inclined to preserve this connection to the tradition by rendering the text in traditional philosophical English. Yet the text as a whole has a structure that rhetorically —and philosophically—is *not* traditional, precisely because Heidegger hears and allows his reader finally to hear something in traditional philosophical German that cannot be heard if one persists in hearing it only in a traditional manner; hence, one is also justifiably inclined *not* to render the text in traditional philosophical English lest this obscure what Heidegger means to bring into view.

Thus, in *Der Satz vom Grund* Heidegger discovers *within* traditional German philosophical prose rhetorical possibilities that enable him to bring forward the identity and difference of this discourse with that of the tradition of Western philosophy and thereby to bring into view insights into the philosophical tradition and its discourse. The dilemma of translating Heidegger's text is to arrive at an English translation of the tradition that is not simply traditional.

If *Der Satz vom Grund* is in need of at least a double reading, and hence a double translation, this is unfortunately not feasible, and thus the translator's challenge is to try in a single text to accommodate the complex structure of Heidegger's text. So where concept and rhetoric are essentially united in the German text, I can only try to simulate this unity through the rather artificial means of striking a balance between them. When considering possible translations I have paid close attention to the way Heidegger develops his discussion from beginning to end, specifically the way he coordinates the basic words of his exposition with a view to their philosophical and rhetorical character. The terms Heidegger coordinates are not always found together in the same passage, nor even in the same lecture, nor are they always cognates. Indeed what is coordinated is not always two different words, but often two or more different senses of the same word. Therefore one must constantly keep in view the way Heidegger's use of a term in a given instance contributes to the developing unity of the text as a whole. Though the movement of thought in *Der Satz vom Grund* often requires that a single word be given different rendering, it also affords a structure for ordering these different renderings. Generally, one proceeds from a traditional understanding of a term to a "nontraditional" understanding of the terms of the tradition.

The most obvious example of this developmental unity as it bears on the translation of the text is seen in Heidegger's use of the terms *Satz* and *Grund*. *Satz vom Grund* is the common German term for "principle of reason," and indeed it is clear from the opening pages of the text that Heidegger means the reader to hear *Satz vom Grund* in the traditional manner as the German translation of Leibniz's *principium rationis*. As his discussion progresses, Heidegger brings forward senses of *Satz* beyond that of "principle," among them "proposition," "leap," "sentence," and "movement." And beyond *Grund* as "reason" he brings forward the senses of "ground" and "foundation." However—and Heidegger makes this explicit—these further senses of *Satz* and *Grund* are not meant to displace the senses of "principle" and "reason"; *Satz* and *Grund* are not incorrectly grasped when understood in the traditional senses of "principle" and "reason." Rather the senses he gradually brings forward aim to augment the sense of *Satz* as "principle" and *Grund* as "reason" and thereby to bring more clearly and essentially into view what "principle" (*Satz*) and "reason" (*Grund*) mean as basic words of the tradition. These first or ordinary senses are not abandoned, but come to be seen from a new point of view. So, when Heidegger uses the word *Grund*, he sometimes means the reader to hear it more saliently in the sense of "reason" and at other times in the sense of "ground." At other points in the text it is clear that he intends the reader to hear both senses in the single word *Grund*. Our translation has sought to strike a balance that allows for this semantic movement.

The greatest difficulties in translating arise when he clearly means to evoke more than one sense of a single word. Faced with this conundrum, I have drawn my principle of translating from the contextual, structured dynamic of the text; in those instances where no single sense seems to have the upper hand but it is necessary to choose one, I have favored the traditional philosophical sense inasmuch as this is the initial sense and, philosophically speaking, the sense that must be retrieved and rethought according to Heidegger.

SPECIFIC DIFFICULTIES

Many of the words Heidegger uses are extremely difficult to translate, and although it is impossible here to mention all of them or to fully discuss the ones I do mention, I believe it will be helpful to point out some of the most important ones and indicate the richness they bear.

Satz: Above I suggested that the title of Heidegger's book *Der Satz vom Grund* presents many difficulties. At various points in the text I have rendered *Satz* as "principle," "sentence," "proposition," "movement," "leap," and "vault." Since *Satz vom Grund* is the German translation of Leibniz's *principium rationis*, it is usually and at least initially necessary to translate *Satz* as "principle" or "sentence," especially when Heidegger is discussing the traditional and immediately understood sense of *Satz vom Grund*. In the course of his exposition, it becomes clear that *Satz* must also be understood in the sense of "leap," such as when he speaks of the *Satz vom Grund* as a *Satz in das Sein*, a leap into being. Given this, it becomes more difficult when Heidegger speaks of the *Satz vom Grund* as a *Satz über das Seiende*. Understood in the traditional way, a *Satz über das Seiende* means a "principle about beings." But inasmuch as the principle of reason as leap into being is concerned with being rather than beings—a fact that Heidegger holds has been obscured in the traditional understanding of the principle of reason—the *Satz über das Seiende* could be correctly translated as the "leap over beings" into being. As such a leap over beings into being, the *Satz vom Grund* is a *Satz vom Sein*, which could be rendered as a "principle of being," as well as a "leap of being," a "leap from being," or even an "address from being." As important as it is to keep these senses in mind, it would often be extremely awkward, if not potentially misleading, to give *Satz vom Sein* one of the latter renderings, for they tend to obscure the traditional understanding of *Satz*, and it is an insight into the traditional understanding of *Satz* as "principle" that Heidegger is trying to bring forward *especially when departing from* this understanding. Thus I have generally translated *Satz vom Sein* as "principle of being."

Grund: The exact origin of *Grund* is unknown, but among its earliest meanings are "bottom," "base," and "the lower lying level," as in the level at which sediments come to rest in wine. When the medieval theologians and mystics thought of *Grund* in reference to the human condition, it was seen to be God: humans have their "ground" in God. Later, especially with Leibniz, when God is interpreted as reason, *Grund* likewise took on this sense, which is one of its primary senses in modern German.

Although *Grund* does not require as many different renderings as *Satz*, in a sense it is often more difficult to translate. I have used "reason," "foundation," "ground," "grounds," and finally "ground/reason" to translate it. As part of the traditional German translation of the *principium rationis*, it is necessary to translate it as "reason," especially in the first several lectures. One of the senses of *Grund* that Heidegger takes great effort to bring forward is its sense as "ground." Often, for instance in Lecture Five, it is clear that *Grund* must be translated as "ground" and not as "reason." However, it is equally clear that one must understand *Grund* in both senses, of "reason" and "ground." In fact, Heidegger's discussion in Lectures Twelve and Thirteen treats the fact that *Grund* as the translation of *ratio* has two distinct senses, namely "ground" and "Reason." Where both these senses are implied but neither seems more salient given the context of the discussion, I have rendered it as "ground/reason" hoping with this virgule to indicate not so much alternatives as a unity or convergence of senses.

We then see that *Der Satz vom Grund* could be translated as *The Principle of Ground(s), The Leap of Reason, The Leap from Reason, The Leap of Ground, The Leap from Ground(s), The Sentence of Reason, The Principle of Ground/Reason*, as well as others.

Geschick: Because of its great importance in Heidegger's text, coupled with the extreme difficulty of translating it into English, I have decided to leave only one word untranslated: *Geschick*. There are three common translations of *Geschick* —the rather theological rendering of it as "destiny," and the more neutral "sending" and "mittence." In the case of the former, Heidegger explicitly states that *Geschick* should not be understood in its ordinary German sense of "destiny."[4] Although what Heidegger means by *Geschick* certainly has some bearing on the notion of destiny, Heidegger states that destiny is a derivative notion of *Geschick*. In addition, the translation of *Geschick* as "destiny" would tend to necessitate specific translations of other words which, when taken together, are of not inconsiderable philosophical significance. For instance, if *Geschick* were translated as "destiny," then one would be inclined to translate *die Beschickten* as "the appointed ones" rather than as "the bestowed ones," emphasizing thereby the hegemony of being over man. Likewise, one would then be inclined to translate *brauchen* as "use" instead of "engage" (in reference to the relation of being to man). All these translations are possible, but they seem to introduce too great a difference between man and the *Geschick* of being. By overemphasizing the hegemony of being, one virtually hypostatizes being—clearly an incorrect reading of Heidegger —and leads to the danger of suggesting facile and hackneyed political readings of Heidegger's text. Therefore, even if one were to warn the reader against reading metaphysical, theological, and political notions into the word *destiny*, it seems almost impossible not to do so.

The translation of *Geschick* as "sending" does have its merit, for *schicken* means "to send, dispatch." Heidegger often uses the prefix *Ge-* in a very specific manner: *Ge-* is a way in which a collective or totality can be signified in German, such as *Gebirge* (mountain range), which is built from the root *Berg* (mountain), or *das Gewährte*, which means "all that has lasted" or "been vouchsafed." *Ge-* also is the prefix used to form the past participle of many German verbs, such as *geschickt* ("sent") from *schicken*. Thus *Geschick* can be understood to mean "all that has been sent." Though this, like "destiny," is not an altogether incorrect translation, "sending" conveys little of the richness of *Geschick*, as well as having some unfortunate connotations that do not hold for what Heidegger means by *Geschick*. For instance, sending implies that one sends something from one place to another, hence that there is some means of conveyance as well as a sender and receiver. It also implies a process, and Heidegger explicitly proscribes this sense from *Geschick* as well as *Geschichte* (history).[5]

Heidegger discusses the meaning of *Geschick* at several places in the text and it is one of the more frequently used words. Since one of the central issues in *Der Satz vom Grund* is to think what is said in the word *Geschick*, I hope to foster such a reflection by not translating it.

In *Der Satz vom Grund* there is a group of important words that are etymologically related to *schicken*, all of which bear directly on the meaning of the term

Geschick.[6] Among the more important are *beschicken, die Beschickten, Geschichte, geschicklich, das Geschickliche, sich in (etwas) schicken, das Schickliche, Schicksal, Schickung,* and *sich zuschicken.* The reflexive verb *sich in (etwas) schicken* means "to adapt oneself to (something), to fit (oneself) in." Hence the adjectives *schicklich,* which means "what is fitting, suitable, appropriate," and *geschickt,* which means "skillful, dexterous, practiced, adroit." If "what is fitting, suitable and appropriate" (*das Schickliche*) is understood as having come about through a transitive action, as the *be-* of *beschicken* implies, then it can be seen as having been bestowed, appointed, arranged, put in order—all senses of *beschicken.* If what is well-appointed, suitably arranged, and fittingly ordered comes about as though on its own, then what is thus arranged—as well as the arrangement itself—"proffers itself" (*sich zuschickt*). "The offering of what is arranged and the arranging of the arrangement," *Schickung,* is thus "a bestowing" (*Beschickung*), and the ones who find themselves in and through what is bestowed are "the bestowed ones" (*die Beschickten*). The self-proffering of what is arranged in the suitable arranging of the arrangement in which we are the bestowed ones is, when taken together, the *Geschick.* Most fundamentally, what is proffered in the *Geschick* is being, hence the *Geschick* is a *Seinsgeschick.* One can begin to think the *Geschick* of being by thinking upon history (*Geschichte*) as the history of being (*Seinsgeschichte*), whose essence is *Geschick.* Naturally, if one were to think of *Geschick* metaphysically, then one would of course take what is dispatched (*Schickung*) in and as history (*Geschichte*) to be providence or fate (*Schicksal*), and we, who must be who are as the ones dealt (*beschickt*) a fate, would be the ones appointed (*die Beschickten*) to meet destiny (*Geschick*)—all of which of course would be a misunderstanding.

What I offer here as a "discussion" of these terms cannot be mistaken for definitions, for each and every one of these words admits of a broader range of meanings than those given here. I offer this only as an indication of the richness of the texture of the text Heidegger has composed in terms of *Geschick,* as well as of the understanding that has guided my translation.

Machten: Macht is a noun which means "power" or "might." In *Der Satz vom Grund* one finds this neologized in a verbal form as *machten,* as well as the compound form *durchmachten.* Though *machten* itself does not exist in common German usage, it is incorporated into three common compound verbs: *bemächtigen* (to take possession of something [violently]), *ermächtigen* (to empower), and "*entmachten*" (to enervate); the only one Heidegger uses in his text is *bemächtigen.*

Heidegger uses forms of *machten*[7] in reference to the principle of reason as well as the relation of this principle to the modern age. Specifically, the issue is of the might or power of this principle. There are at least two ways to understand the power of this principle which bear on its translation. On the one hand, the principle of reason can be seen as that which, in governing all modern thought and action, makes this thought and action—as well as all its consequences—possible. In this sense, the principle of reason could be understood as *empowering* the modern age to be the mighty age that it is. On the other hand, as that principle which pervades all modern thought and action, making it difficult if not impossible to think and act except in the manner prescribed by the principle of reason, the power of this principle could be understood as *overpowering* the modern age. Both these senses are at issue when Heidegger discusses *das Machtende im Satz vom Grund*. Since no English term plausibly renders *machten* and its cognates in these senses, and since *machten* indeed strikes the German reader as unusual, we have chosen to coin the term "bepower," using such extant English words as "bespeak," "betroth," "befog," and "befriend" as guides. It is hoped that the specific sense of this "word" can accrue to it through its contextual usage.

Stellen: There are a number of words that are built on the verb *stellen*, which has numerous meanings, including "to put, place, stand, arrange," and which has an etymological and semantic relation to *stehen*, "to stand, etc." Originally *Stelle* meant "the place where something stands."[8] Among the *stellen* words, the most difficult to render is *vorstellen*, which has the general meaning of "to put forward; present." In common usage it can mean "to introduce (one person to another)." Used reflexively it can mean "to think, imagine," as in "Imagine that!" as well as "to become familiar with (something)." It has a number of other common usages.

Vorstellung is certainly one of the most important terms in German philosophy and admits of a broad range of technical understandings. It was first used in its philosophical sense by Christian Wolff, who was a student of Leibniz and was responsible for translating many Latin philosophical terms into German. Wolff used *Vorstellung* to translate the Latin *notio*, and *vorstellen* to translate *cogitare*. As a verbal noun, *Vorstellung* stands "for the intellectual processes in consciousness,"[9] which is inseparable from its contents. Of course for Leibniz as well as for Wolff, the intellectual processes in consciousness—even perception —is a matter of representation, and therefore to translate *Vorstellen* with "representational thinking" is quite justifiable. I have done so on a number of occasions.

However, sometimes it is awkward and even misleading to translate *Vorstellen* as "representational thinking"; Hegel sought to go beyond representational thinking—*Vorstellen*—to conceiving—*begreifen*. But for Heidegger, *begreifen* also counts as a *vorstellendes Denken*,[10] and hence Hegel marks not an end of the tradition and a new beginning in Science, as he himself would have it, but he is the completion and fruition of that tradition. Since for Heidegger *Vorstellen* is that manner of thinking characteristic of the modern (philosophical) tradition up to, including, and beyond Hegel, I have sought out a translation for it which indicates a solidarity with this traditional manner of thinking without giving it an overly restrictive interpretation, such as "representational thinking." To do so I have often used the word "cognition." "Cognition" can indicate the representational thinking which is generally conceived in terms of the philosophy of the subject: the *cogito* thinks a thought, a *cogitatum*, which is a representation of an object by and for a subject. So if it is misleading to speak of such a representational thinking in Hegel as well as in the age of technology where the subject–object distinction in a certain manner has been overcome, it is not misleading to speak of an (intellectual) processing of (intellectual) contents, namely, of "cognition."

Überlieferung: This word is commonly translated as "tradition" and indeed it has this sense. However, Heidegger often uses *Überlieferung* as a verbal noun; the verb *überliefern* means "to hand down, transmit, deliver, pass on." *Überlieferung* is closely connected to *Übersetzung* and *Übertragen*. *Übersetzung*, which is translated as "translation," literally means "to place or set across, over." *Übertragen* means "to carry over, across; convey." As Heidegger explains,[11] a tradition occurs where something is preserved and passed along from one epoch to another. This happens, for instance, in the translations of basic words which convey to us a legacy, a tradition. Where Heidegger emphasizes the character of the tradition as that-which-has-been-preserved-in-being-passed-on, I have translated *Überlieferung* as "legacy"; when he means to emphasize the movement that constitutes a tradition or legacy, I translate it simply as "passing along." Otherwise I have used the traditional translation for *Überlieferung*: "tradition."

Er-: Heidegger uses a number of words that bear this prefix, one of whose most important senses is the effecting or inauguration of an action. Some of the most important of these in *Der Satz vom Grund* are *erblicken, ergründen, Erinnerung, erkennen, erklingen, Erörterung*, and *erhören*. For instance, since *blicken* means "to glance, look," I have in most cases translated *erblicken* as "to bring into view." Particular difficulties arise when it comes to the translation of *erhören*. *Hören* means "to hear," and generally one would also translate *erhören* as "to hear." Not only does Heidegger explicitly draw a connection between *erblicken* and *erhören*, thereby stressing its *er-* prefix, but he further emphasizes the peculiar sense of *erhören* by distinguishing it from *hören*. Unfortunately there is no English word or phrase one could use with any consistency that captures the sense of *erhören*, an attentive hearing in which one begins to listen to what one hears but to which one had previously not been attentive, a hearing that implies a responsiveness.

This sense of *erhören* is crucial to the reading of *Der Satz vom Grund* inasmuch as the development of Heidegger's exposition depends on our coming to hear the principle of reason in a different manner than we usually do. Though my translation of *erhören* as "to listen" captures some of its sense, it does not do it full justice; in any case, the connection to *un-erhört*—"unheard of" or "unprecedented"—is lost. One should generally pay attention to constructions in the translation that convey the sense of an inauguration of an action, especially in the case of "listening" and "seeing."

Wahren/währen and *weilen: Wahren* means "to preserve, protect" and is etymologically related to *warten* (to wait) and probably also to *wahr* ("true"). *Währen,*
which means "to last, abide," is related to the Old High German *wesan* ("to
be"), from which the modern word *Wesen* ("essence; essential being; nature,
coming-to-be") comes. *Währen* is commonly used in its prepositional form *während,* which is translated as "while, during." These senses of "preserving," "true,"
"lasting," and "essential being" are evoked in a number of words Heidegger uses
that have *wahren* and/or *währen* as their root, for instance *gewähren* ("vouchsafe,
provide").[12] For its part, *gewähren* poses a special translation problem. *Gewähren*
is commonly rendered as "to provide, grant, bequeath," and indeed Heidegger
wants these senses to be conveyed to the reader. But he also explicitly means
the reader to hear the temporal sense of "to last." Though "vouchsafe" is a rather
antiquated word, we have used it to render *gewähren,* for it seems to convey
best the senses of lasting, preserving, and granting. In any case, Heidegger's
use of *gewähren* is one of the words in this text that strikes the German reader,
as does "vouchsafe," as unusual and, hopefully, thought-provoking. Likewise,
das Gewährte, which means "all that is bequeathed, granted, preserved, and
that lasts," has been translated as "what is vouchsafed." In this regard, the reader
should note that *das Gewährte* is essential to Heidegger's understanding of the
concrete constitution of history, *Geschichte,* and hence *Geschick.*

As complex as this group of words is, it becomes even more complex, especially
for the translator, when Heidegger brings these words into relation with another
group of words that have *weilen* as their root. *Eine Weile* means "a (short) while,
period of time," and the verbs *weilen* and *verweilen* mean respectively "to spend
time, tarry, abide" and "to linger." Hence *das Jeweilige* means "that which, for
the time being, is." These senses of *weilen* and its cognates are carefully coordinated by Heidegger with those of *wahren* and *währen* and their cognates. Particular
difficulties arise with the word *weil,* which is one of the most common causal
conjunctions in German and is normally translated as "because" or "since." Heidegger uses this causal sense of *weil* in reference to the principle of reason
that states every being has a cause or, more broadly, a reason for being. In
this regard it is clear that *weil* qua "because" is one of the central terms in
the philosophical tradition and its propositional manner of thinking. On the
other hand, he uses poems by Angelus Silesius and Goethe to bring forward
the verbal sense of *weilen,* the abiding and lingering of a being in its being,
which is "without why" qua reason. Heidegger thereby points out a *contresense*
in the word *weil,* not to disprove and eliminate one of the senses, but to gain
insight into its traditional philosophical use. In *weil* we have an excellent example
of Heidegger using a basic, traditional German word both in a traditional manner
and as a word that says something about the Western philosophical tradition
that the tradition has, for its part, left unthought.

Capitalization: In German there are so-called *Fremdwörter,* words that do not stem from German but, as is usually the case, from Latin. Heidegger often uses these words to emphasize a connection with the Western philosophical tradition. Occasionally he points out this fact by noting that a word he has used is a "foreign word," in which case we have used "not of German origin." It would have been possible to capitalize these terms to draw attention to them as Heidegger means to do in employing them, but this seemed exaggerated. There are, however, a few exceptions. Heidegger uses the Latinate *Prinzip* and the German *Satz*, both of which are commonly translated "principle." These words are among the most important in Heidegger's text and have distinctly different senses—they are even specifically opposed to one another on a number of occasions. Since it is essential not to confuse these terms, I have capitalized "Principle" to render *Prinzip*. Along the same lines it has been necessary to preserve the distinction between *Vernunft* and *Grund*, both of which are commonly translated as "reason." I have reserved the capitalized "Reason" for the translation of *Vernunft*. On the few occasions that Heidegger uses the Latinate *rationale* I have capitalized it as "Rational" to preserve the relation to the tradition. Heidegger likewise distinguishes between *Gegenstand* and *Objekt*; I rendered both by "object," capitalizing it when it translates *Objekt*.

CRITICAL APPARATUS

Heidegger employs no footnotes or endnotes but includes bibliographical information in the body of the text, usually within parentheses. I have placed this information in the Bibliographical Notes, designated by superscripted Arabic numbers. Heidegger did not always give full bibliographical information—on a few occasions, he provided only an author's name or the title of a work. When I have been able to find fuller information, I have included it in the endnotes. Whenever an English translation for these various works could be found, the appropriate information is given in brackets. Notes on the Translation, designated by bracketed numbers, reproduce a German phrase or sentence when this may be helpful for the reader, or point out some element of a word or passage that is significant and whose translation seems to need clarification.

In his published text, Heidegger includes material which he did not present in the lecture course. This material has been placed between braces ({ . . . }) in the present translation. Material found in brackets ([. . .]) is of two sorts. First, if the word or words are German, they are drawn from Heidegger's text. These interpolations are offered either when the specific German word or phrase being translated is particularly important, or to call attention to plays on words.

A good example of the latter occurs on pages [33–34] where Heidegger uses the terms *Gegen-standlose, Standlose, Gegenstände, Ständigen, zuständigen,* and *Beständigung.* An attempt has been made to reflect these sorts of word-plays in the English, but usually it is not possible to do so fully.

The second type of material appearing in brackets is in English. These interpolations are included not to translate a specific German word but because they are implied by the text; their addition has enabled me to formulate a more clearly constructed sentence. I have kept additions of this kind to a minimum. Page numbers of the German edition appear in the running heads.

In addition to German–English and English–German glossaries, I have included a Glossary of Cognate Words. The latter presents groups or families of words whose etymological relations Heidegger often draws upon in order to develop his exposition.

ACKNOWLEDGMENTS

I must first thank John Sallis for his unflagging interest and support from the moment I got it into my head to undertake the present translation, as well as Janet Rabinowitch of Indiana University Press for her Zenlike patience and editorial savoir faire. The National Endowment for the Humanities provided a full-year grant at the most opportune moment, which enabled me to finish this translation in a timely manner. I offer special thanks to Martha Chomiak of NEH for her encouragement and good humor. A fellowship from the University of Louvain, Belgium, provided financial and collegial support for the preparation of this translation. Several of the NEH reviewers were also generous and helpful in their comments. William Richardson, who attended Heidegger's lecture course "The Principle of Reason" in 1955–56, invited me to teach a graduate seminar at Boston College on Heidegger's text. He and the students in that seminar contributed more to the quality of the final translation than they probably suspect. During the course of translating, I have benefited from the thoughts of, among those too numerous to mention, John Caputo, Edward Casey, Klaus Held, Samuel IJsseling, David Kolb, Werner Marx, Reiner Schürmann, Thomas Sheehan, Joan Stambaugh, and Jacques Taminiaux. I am indebted to Richard Findler for his work in preparing the critical apparatus. Michael Heim performed the tedious job of vetting the translation, and I am grateful for his many excellent suggestions. Though the presence of my wife, Betsy Braun, may find no mark in the text that others can discern, it is gratefully evident to me.

Notes

1. See Lecture Twelve, p. 97ff.
2. *Martin Heidegger im Gespräch* Richard Wisser, ed., (Verlag Karl Albert: Freiburg, 1970), p. 77.
3. See, for example, p. 14ff. What Heidegger has to say concerning translation is certainly relevant to what is at issue here. See pp. 98–99, 81.
4. See pp. 61–62.
5. See pp. 61, 95.
6. See Glossary of Cognate Words: *schicken*.
7. See Glossary of Cognate Words: *machten*.
8. See Glossary of Cognate Words: *stellen* and *stehen*.
9. Christian Wolff. *Vernünftige Gedanken I* §220, 232, 749, 774.
10. See p. 16 on the connection between *vorstellen* and *begreifen*.
11. See p. 91.
12. See Glossary of Cognate Words: *wahren/weilen*.

THE
Principle of Reason

FOREWORD

The thoughts imparted here concerning the principle of reason belong to the broader horizon of an endeavor whose exposition requires other forms.

The unaltered text of a lecture course (read during the Winter Semester 1955–56 at the University of Freiburg in Bresgau) has intentionally retained the repetitions of the same course of thought.

The address was delivered on May 25, 1956, at "The Bremen Club" and on October 24, 1956, at the University of Vienna.

Portions that were not delivered, as well as subsequently added references, are placed in braces { . . . }.

Freiburg in Bresgau, March 1957

LECTURE COURSE

Lecture One

The principle of reason reads: *nihil est sine ratione*. One translates it: nothing is without a reason. What the principle states is illuminating. When something is illuminating, we understand it without further ado. Our understanding doesn't labor on in order to understand the principle of reason. How is this so? It is because human understanding, whenever and wherever it is active, always and everywhere keeps on the lookout for the reason why whatever it encounters is and is the way it is. Understanding looks for reasons insofar as it requires a specification of reasons. The understanding demands that there be a foundation for its statements and assertions. Only founded statements are intelligible and intelligent. Yet understanding requires reasons not only for its statements, but human cognition is already looking for reasons as soon as it dabbles in those things about which it might then make statements. In all that surrounds and concerns it, human cognition seeks reasons, often only the most proximate ones, sometimes even the more remote reasons, but in the end it seeks the first and last reasons.

This quest for reasons pervades human cognition even before it bothers with the founding of statements. The ubiquitous quest for reasons requires that one get to the bottom of what is encountered. Whenever we are getting to the bottom and founding things we find ourselves on the path to reason [*Grund*]. Without exactly knowing it, in some manner we are constantly addressed by, summoned to attend to, grounds and reason.

We are, in our conduct and cognition, on the way to reason as though this came about on its own. We constantly have, as it were, the principle of reason in view: *nihil est sine ratione*. Nothing is without reason. Our conduct everywhere takes into account what the principle of reason says.

Thus, in every instance where human cognition proceeds not only intelligently but with forethought, it cannot come as a surprise that eventually human cognition becomes explicitly aware that it follows what is stated in the principle of reason, a principle which is only later expressly posited. It only gradually dawns on humans that they stand and fall in the train of the principle of reason.

To the extent that human cognition reflects on the fact that in some manner it always gets to the bottom and founds everything, the principle of reason resounds in human cognition as the motive of its conduct.[1] We say with caution: the principle of reason resounds. This principle is by no means as easily and straightforwardly put into words as one would like to suppose on the basis of its contents. Even where human cognition embarks upon a reflection on its own proper activity and fosters this reflection; even where this reflection rises up to what was, for a long time, identified with the Greek word φιλοσοφία; even in philosophy the principle of reason has just begun to resound, and this for some time now. Centuries were needed for the principle of reason to be stated *as a principle*. The short formulation mentioned earlier speaks in Latin. This formulation of the principle of reason was first mentioned and specifically discussed in the course of those meditations Leibniz carried out in the seventeenth century.[1]

In the West, however, philosophy has been reigning and transforming itself ever since the sixth century BC. Hence it took two thousand three hundred years until Western European thinking actually discovered and formulated the simple principle of reason.

How odd that such an obvious principle, which always directs all human cognition and conduct without being stated, needed so many centuries to be expressly stated as a principle in the formulation cited above. But it is even odder that we never wonder about the slowness with which the principle of reason came to light. One would like to call the long time it needed for this its "incubation period": two thousand three hundred years for the positing [*Setzen*] of this simple principle [*Satz*]. Where and how did the principle of reason sleep for so long and presciently dream what is unthought in it? It is not yet the correct moment to ponder this. It is likely that we are still not awake enough to take in the oddity we would encounter if, for once, we began to give due attention to the uncommonly long incubation period of the principle of reason.

At first we find nothing provocative about it. Now, the statementlike formulation of the principle has already once remained unformulated for a long time. And when the principle was finally stated, apparently nothing essential changed in the course of thinking. So why all the amazement about the odd history of the principle of reason? Let us not kid ourselves. The principle of reason and its history hardly entice us to linger over it. We already have plenty of things that provoke us: the discovery of new elements in the natural sciences, the discovery of new kinds of clocks that can calculate the age of the earth, a book about *Gods, Gravediggers, and Scholars*,[2] or news about the construction of space ships.

But the principle of reason—this obvious statement and the fact that its equally obvious short formulation could not be found for such a long time! Why does this sort of thing not touch us, even upset us? Why not? Answer:⟨because our relation to the obvious is always dull and dumb⟩ The path to what lies under our nose is always the furthest and hence the most difficult path for us humans.

So we have hardly an inkling of how close what the principle of reason says is to us. No wonder we are not in the slightest touched by the odd history of this principle.

Why should we trouble ourselves at all with such vacuous principles as the principle of reason? Vacuous indeed, because there is evidently nothing in it to bring into view, nothing we can grasp with our hands, and indeed nothing more to be grasped by the understanding. We are finished with the principle of reason as soon as we hear it. Nevertheless, perhaps the principle of reason is the most enigmatic of all possible principles. If this is the case, then we would do well to treat it more attentively than we have till now. If we are prepared to do that, then it is necessary that for once we listen thoughtfully to what the principle says and how it says what it says.

Nihil est sine ratione. Nothing is without reason. There is nothing—and here that means everything that in some manner is—that is without reason. What immediately strikes us about this formulation of the principle of reason is that it contains two negations: *Nihil—sine*; nothing—without. The double negation yields an affirmation: nothing that in any manner is, is without a reason. This means that everything that is, every being whatsoever, has a reason. The Latin formulation of this reads: *omnes ens habet rationem*.

Normally we prefer, both substantively and linguistically, the affirmative form of a principle over the negative form. The situation is different when it comes to the formulation of the principle of reason just mentioned. To what extent?

The affirmative statement "Every being has a reason"[2] sounds like an assessment. It notes that every being is equipped with a reason. An assessment can be tested as to whether and to what extent it holds true. Now, can we verify whether every being has a reason? To verify this we would have to parade before us every being wherever and whenever it is, was, or will be in order to check the extent to which it comes equipped with a reason for itself. Such a process of verification remains proscribed to humans. At any given time we know only samplings from the various realms of beings and even these we know only in limited regards, within particular ranges and at specific levels. Our assessment "Every being has a reason" therefore rests, as one says, on unsure footing. Assuming we were in the position to test whether all actual beings have a reason, there would still always remain that open field of what is not actual but nevertheless is, insofar as it possibly—is. Even the possible—beings in the mode of possibility—belongs to beings in the broader sense and has a reason for its possibility. But who can presume to oversee everything that is possible and possibly actual?

Nevertheless many will already have said to themselves that the principle of reason formulated as "Every being has a reason" is hardly a mere assessment, and therefore it does not need to be checked in the manner that is usual for assessments. If the principle of reason were merely a principle that makes an assessment, it would have to be given in the precise formulation: "Every being, so far as and as long as beings can be observed, has a reason." But the principle of reason intends to say more, namely, that generally, and that means as a rule, every being has some sort of reason for being, and for being the way it is. But to what extent is the rule valid? The validity of a rule isn't much easier to verify than the correctness of an assessment. And besides this, to the rule there belongs the exception. Nevertheless, the principle of reason simply says that every being has a reason. What the principle posits, it posits as being without exception. The principle of reason is neither an assessment nor a rule. It posits what it posits as something necessary. It articulates this as something unavoidable through the double negation "Nothing . . . without."

The negative form of the principle speaks more clearly than the affirmative form. Apropos of the matter at hand it must read: every being *necessarily* has a reason. Yet what kind of necessity is this? On what is it based? What reason is there for the principle of reason? Where does the principle of reason have its own ground? With these questions we touch upon what is insidious and enigmatic about this principle. In a single stroke one can of course set aside what is enigmatic about the principle of reason by decree. One can aver that what the principle states is immediately illuminating; it needs neither verification nor demonstration. When it comes to such principles philosophy is, of course, all too readily inclined to appeal to what is immediately illuminating. But no one will hazard that the principle of reason is unconditionally immediately illuminating in what it states. In order for something to be illuminating, and that means luminant, there must of course be a light that shines. The shining of this light is a decisive condition for what is said in the principle to luminate such that it occurs to us, enlightens us.[3]

In which light, then, is the principle of reason an illuminating principle? Which light does the principle need in order to luminate? Do we see this light? And in the event that we see it, is it not always dangerous to look into the light? Evidently we are able to find the light in which the principle of reason illuminates only if we first clarify to what kind of principles this principle of reason belongs.

A few things have already been mentioned about the principle-character of the principle of reason. We distinguished between the negative and affirmative forms of its formulation. Many will think that by now we have already said enough about the form of this principle, that it is high time to stop beating around the bush and to go straight into the content of the principle of reason. It will be claimed that observations about the form of principles belong to grammar and logic.

This position seems justified. Indeed it is, especially wherever it is a question of statements and principles in which all that matters is the content of the sentence, and above all wherever the content of the sentence refers to itself. Such is the case with all those statements that figure in our considerations, plans, discussions, and calculations. The statements one finds in scientific observation and research also prove to be of this sort. They remain immediately related to the domain of objects in question. Even where the sciences expressly include the relation they have to their objects as they do in a scientific-methodological reflection, the relationship to these objects is conceived of as something immediately given. This even holds for the realm in which the relation of the cognizing subject to the object essentially changes, as in modern atomic physics. Parenthetically it should be mentioned that in modern atomic physics a transformation in the relation to objects is underway that, on the way through modern technology, completely changes the manner of human cognition.

Nevertheless even this transformed cognition and the type of statement-making associated with it still remain far removed from the manner of speaking that the principle of reason harbors. With regard to its principle-character, this principle never lets itself be reduced to the level of commonplace sentences, nor even to the level of scientific principles. However, at first sight and upon first hearing it, this principle [*Satz*] also seems like all other sentences [*Sätze*]: every being necessarily has a reason. Every tree has its roots. Five and seven make twelve. Goethe died in 1832. Migratory birds fly south in the fall.

The sentences we mention are, taken roughly, grammatically built in the same manner. They are simple statements. We also first hear the principle of reason from this perspective. So long as this perspective is established as the only normative one, we cannot unfetter the principle of reason from the compass of this sentence-form.

What the principle of reason posits, and how it posits it—the manner in which it is, strictly speaking, a principle—is what makes it incomparable to all other sentences. This we assert. If our assertion is true, then we cannot help but wonder whether the principle of reason is at all a sentence understood in the grammatical sense of a statement. Presumably what it says and how it says it can remove us to an entirely different manner of speaking. Therefore, with the first groping attempt to discuss the principle of reason we must now refer more clearly, even if still rather crudely, to what is peculiar to it. Just a moment ago this meant the principle of reason is not merely an assessment; it also meant it does not simply articulate a rule which would admit of exceptions. The principle of reason declares a state of affairs that necessarily is the way it is: each and every being necessarily has a reason. The principle says something from which we cannot escape. The principle says something unconditional. The principle articulates, as we are wont to say, something fundamental. The principle of reason is a fundamental principle. Perhaps we may even assert something further and say that *the principle of reason is the fundamental principle of all fundamental principles*. Saying this ushers us, with a hardly noticeable jolt, into something enigmatic about the principle, and that means about what it says.

The assertion that the principle of reason is *the* fundamental principle most immediately means that the principle of reason is not just one fundamental principle among many others. It is rather the highest, the one which ranks first among all fundamental principles. We may wish to ask straight away, Which fundamental principles? We adhere to fundamental principles in various realms of cognition, willing, and feeling. If the principle of reason is supposed to be the highest of all fundamental principles, then by this multitude of fundamental principles we mean the various first fundamental principles that are directive and normative for all human cognition. One is familiar with the principle of identity, the principle of difference, the principle of contradiction, and the principle of excluded middle as such first principles. The traditional doctrine of philosophy since Leibniz also explicitly ranks the principle of reason among these principles. However this principle does not count—not even for Leibniz—as the highest principle, much less as the fundamental principle, period. The principle of identity counts as the highest of all fundamental principles. One often formulates this principle as A = A. But equality is something other than identity. What identity really means is by no means univocally and unanimously determined. Identity can mean that something is the same and nothing more than the same: the self itself, the self-same. Instead of this, one often says, imprecisely, that "identical" means "being equal to itself." But something is equal only where there is a multitude. However, every individual, every single thing, can be self-same with itself, for itself.

On the other hand, others define identity in another way. Identity may mean the belonging-together of distinct things in the same. More clearly: the belonging-together of distinct things on the basis [*Grund*] of the same. On the basis? Here the same plays the role of a reason or basis for belonging-together. In identity, reason shows itself to be the basis upon which and in which the belonging-together of distinct things rests.

Here we see, if only roughly, that the nature of identity cannot do without a reason. But the principle of reason deals with reasons. Thus the principle of identity could be grounded in the principle of reason. So the highest fundamental principle of all fundamental principles would not be the principle of identity, but the principle of reason.

Or perhaps the principle of reason is only the *primus inter pares*, the first among the first fundamental principles which among themselves are basically [*im Grunde*] of equal rank. In any case the assertion that the principle of reason is the highest fundamental principle isn't completely pulled out of the thin air. Nevertheless the assertion certainly contests the traditional doctrine of fundamental principles. So, as for its presumed clarity and validity, this doctrine is backed up more by a long-standing cognitive habit than by a thinking that engages in, and lingers with, what is worth questioning. In order to find what is worth questioning here we need not first meander to some remote outpost of thinking.

The question of the supreme fundamental principles and their hierarchy certainly stumbles around in the fog as long as we are unclear about what a fundamental principle is. To answer this question requires that we are sufficiently clear about what a fundamental reason is and, secondly, what a principle is. Where and how do we come by reliable information about what a reason is? Ostensibly through the principle *of* reason. But remarkably enough, the principle of reason doesn't deal at all with reason as such. Rather, the principle of reason says: every being necessarily has a reason. For its part the principle of reason already presupposes that what a reason is has already been determined, that it is clear wherein the essence of reason lies. The principle of reason is grounded on this presupposition. But is a principle that presupposes something so essential to be taken seriously as a fundamental principle, much less as the supreme one? The principle of reason does not help us much when we try to clarify what the essence of reason is. Yet it is necessary to know this if, when discussing fundamental principles, we do not want to have a blurred notion of what a principle-reason [*Grund-Satz*] is.

It is indeed equally necessary to clarify what a sentence [*Satz*] is. According to grammar, a simple sentence consists of the connection of the subject of a sentence with a predicate. The predicate is to agree with the subject and is predicated of the subject. But what is meant by "subject"? The Latin *subjectum*, the Greek ὑποκείμενον means "that which is at the basis," "that which is lies present as the ground for statements about something." Hence even this —what a sentence is—can only be brought to light if we have clarified beforehand wherein lies the essence of ground/reason.[4]

What a principle-reason is remains obscure. What for us remains worth questioning is the principle of reason as the supreme fundamental principle. We can continue questioning only if we break ourselves of the habit of precipitously and cavalierly conceiving what is treated under the term "fundamental principles" so as to pass on to more important matters.

Wherever we may look, the discussion[5] of the principle of reason becomes obscure with its very first steps. And that is how it should be. For we would like to elucidate the principle of reason. What is lucid and light needs the obscure and the shadowy, otherwise there would be nothing to elucidate. Goethe once mentioned a sentence of Johann Georg Hamann, the friend of Herder and Kant. Hamann's sentence reads: "Lucidity is a suitable apportionment of light and shadow." Goethe added to this briefly and concisely: "Hamann—listens!"[3]

Lecture Two

It might be useful if, with the first steps we must take on the path of this lecture, we pay attention to which clue we are following and into what province this leads us. The path moves towards the principle of reason, towards what the principle says, whereof it says what it says and how it says it. The principle of reason reads: *Nihil est sine ratione*; nothing is without reason. We did not go into the content of the principle. The path immediately turned away from this obvious tack. Rather, we reflected on what sort of principles to which the principle of reason might belong. Philosophy includes it among the supreme fundamental principles that are also called Principles.[6] Since we are thinking about the principle of reason as a fundamental principle, the next clue leads us, so to speak, along the periphery of the principle. We avoid straightaway touching its interior, the content of the principle. What is disconcerting about this principle is that the path around its outside has already given us more than enough to think about. Later we will have to see whether this procedure has served us well, which means, to what extent this procedure has brought us closer—and perhaps even in a better way—to the content of the principle than if we were now to attempt straightaway a discussion of its contents.

Therefore we do not want to let the thread grasped in the first session fall by the wayside prematurely. It should lead us to a position from which we obtain a more intimate knowledge of how the principle of reason shows up in the field of Western thinking.[7] We thus make a first acquaintance with the principle of reason as a fundamental principle. From this comes an insight into our customary relationship to the principle of reason. But this insight into our relationship to the principle of reason sheds a light both on ourselves and on our customary way of thinking. So it may be that the principle of reason, when considered in this way, will also disclose something to us about our own essence, and this without our being preoccupied with ourselves.

We may or may not know it, we may or may not pay particular attention

10

to what we know, but our stay in this world, our sojourn on earth, is constantly under way to grounds and reason. We get to the bottom of what we encounter, often really only getting to the foreground; sometimes we even venture into the background, and seldom enough up to the edge of the abysses of thinking. Yet we require that the statements we make about what surrounds and concerns us be founded. Getting to the bottom and founding define our modus vivendi.

Why is this the case with us? Is it only a fact to which we need not turn? The world and life get along without our reflecting on the principle of reason. As things stand, our modus vivendi is motivated to somehow get to the bottom and found everything. Yet solely and precisely because our modus vivendi is thus motivated we can also ask: For what reason is our modus vivendi a getting to the bottom and a founding?

The principle of reason holds the answer to this question. It holds the answer but it does not give it, rather it conceals the answer in that about which it speaks. In its short formulation the principle of reason reads: *Nihil est sine ratione*; nothing is without reason. In the affirmative formulation this means: everything that in any manner is necessarily has a reason. One understands without further ado what the principle says. We agree with what it states, yet we do not do so just because we believe that so far the principle has proved true everywhere and from now on will always prove true. We agree with the principle of reason because we, as they say, feel sure that the principle itself must be true.

But does it suffice if we lend credence to the principle of reason in such a feeble manner? Or is this crediting, in truth, the grossest neglect of the principle itself? Indeed the principle of reason is, as a principle, not nothing. The principle is itself something. Therefore, according to what the principle itself tells us, it is the sort of thing that must have a reason. What is the reason for the principle of reason? The principle itself behooves us to ask this question. On the one hand we bristle at continuing to question in this way because it seems to be a twisted and cavilling question in contradistinction to the simple principle of reason. On the other hand we see that the principle of reason itself compels us, in a manner apropos of the principle of reason, to ask about reasons even in relation to the principle of reason. How do we save ourselves from this embarrassment?

We are faced by two possibilities, both of which equally provoke our thinking. Either the principle of reason is that principle, generally that "something," which alone is not affected by what the principle says: Every thing, which in any manner is, necessarily has a reason. In this case something most odd would follow, namely, that precisely the principle of reason—and it alone—would fall outside its own jurisdiction; the principle of reason would remain without reason.

Or else, even the principle of reason has—and necessarily so—a reason. But if this is the case, then presumably this reason cannot be just one among many others. Rather, when it speaks in its full scope we might expect that the principle of reason makes the greatest claim to a foundation. The reason for the principle of reason would then be the most eminent of all reasons, something like the reason of reasons.

But what are we getting ourselves into if we take the principle of reason at its word and move towards the reason of reasons? Does not the reason of reasons press forward beyond itself to the reason of reason of reasons? If we persist in this sort of questioning, where can we find a respite and a perspective on reason? If thinking takes this path to reason, then surely it can't help but fall intractably into groundlessness.[8]

So one might like to make a cautionary note here: whoever takes such a path to reason is one whose thinking runs the danger of going to ruin. This warning may harbor a deep truth. But it may also be just a pathetic defense against the claim of thinking. In either case we see that there is something special about the principle of reason and its foundation, the principle as a fundamental principle. According to one view, we understand the principle without further ado and, without scrutiny, lend credence to it. According to the other view, the principle seems to thrust our thinking into groundlessness as soon as we take what the principle says seriously in relation to the principle itself.

Thus the principle of reason casts an odd light on the path to reason and also shows us that if we meddle with fundamental principles and Principles, we reach a remarkably ambiguously lit, not to mention perilous, province.

This province is familiar to many thinkers, even though they justifiably seldom speak of it. To know a little about a few of them might be of some help to us, who stand at the beginning of the path to the fundamental principle of reason and are strangers in this province. In discussing the principle of reason we are on guard as much against hasty and inflated claims as against a thought-weary modesty.

It is well known that Descartes wanted to bring all human knowing to an unshakable ground (*fundamentum inconcussum*) by first doubting everything and acknowledging only what presented itself clearly and distinctly as secure knowledge. Leibniz remarked that Descartes' procedure neglected to specify what was entailed in the clarity and distinctness of cognition that count as his leading principles. According to Leibniz, Descartes had at this point doubted too little. Concerning this, Leibniz said in a letter to Johann Bernoulli on August 23, 1696: *sed ille dupliciter peccavit, nimis dubitando et nimis facile a dubitatione discedendo*; "but he (Descartes) failed in a two-fold manner, by his doubting too much and by too easily desisting from doubting."[4]

What do we learn from these words of Leibniz? Two things are needed simultaneously for the path to reason and for residing in the province of fundamental principles and Principles: cleverness of thinking and reticence—but both always at the right place.

Therefore, in the fourth chapter of the fourth book of the *Metaphysics*, where he deals with what later is called the fundamental principle of contradiction and its foundation, Aristotle made the following remark: εστι γαρ απαιδευσία τὸ μὴ γιγνώσκειν τίνων δεῖ ζητεῖν 'απόδειξιν τίνων οὐ δεῖ· "There is present a lack, namely of παιδεία, when one does not know for what one is to seek proof and for what not."[5]

The Greek word παιδεία—still half alive in our word "pedagogy," which is not of German origin—cannot be translated. What it means here is the circumspect and vigilant sense for what at any time is appropriate and inappropriate.

What do we learn from the words of Aristotle? Whoever sets out into the province of fundamental principles needs παιδεία in order not to overestimate or undervalue them; we could also say, what is needed is the gift of distinguishing between what is pertinent and impertinent when it comes to simple states of affairs.

If we were able to think about the words of Leibniz and Aristotle still more reflectively, we would have to consider the possibility that it is a commonplace but dubious opinion which alleges that the first fundamental principles and supreme Principles need be immediately illuminating, clear as day, and patently stabilizing for thinking.

Novalis, the poet who was also a great thinker, knew otherwise. In a fragment he says:

> Should the highest principle contain the highest paradox in its task? Being a principle that allows absolutely no peace, that always attracts and repels, that always anew would become unintelligible as soon as one had understood it? That ceaselessly stirs up our activity—without ever exhausting it, without ever becoming familiar? According to old mystical sayings, God is something like this for the spirits.[6]

What do we learn from Novalis's words? We learn that in the province of the highest Principles, things apparently have a very different look than the widespread doctrine of the immediate evidence of the supreme fundamental principles would like to admit.

Everywhere we use the principle of reason and adhere to it as a prop for support. But it also immediately propels us into groundlessness without our hardly thinking about it in its genuine meaning.

So we already see that plenty of shadows are cast over the principle of reason. The shadows become darker as soon as we maintain that the principle of reason is not just any principle among others. It counts as a fundamental principle. According to our assertion, it is supposed to be the principle of all principles. Taken to its extreme, this means that the principle of reason is the ground/reason of principles. The principle of reason is the ground/reason of the principle.[9]

Let us pause for a bit, if we may: the principle of reason—the ground/reason of the principle. Here something turns in on itself. Here something coils in on itself but does not close itself, for it uncoils itself at the same time. Here is a coil, a living coil, like a snake. Here something catches [*fängt*] itself at [*an*] its own end. Here is a commencement [*Anfang*] that is already completion.

The principle of reason as the ground/reason of the principle—this odd relationship confuses our ordinary cognition. This should not surprise us, given that the confusion now surfacing has a genuine origin. One could of course doubt this and suggest that the confusion springs from our playing with the words *Grund* [ground, reason] and *Satz* [principle] which make up the title: the *Grundsatz* [fundamental principle] of reason. Yet the word game immediately comes to an end if we refer to the Latin formulation of the principle of reason. It reads: *Nihil est sine ratione*. But how does the corresponding Latin title read? Leibniz names the principle of reason the *principium rationis*. What *principium* means here can best be learned through the succinct definition that the most industrious student of Leibniz, Christian Wolff, gives in his *Ontology*. There he says: *principium dicitur id, quod in se continet rationem alterius.*[7] According to this, a *principium* is what contains in itself the *ratio* for something else. Hence the *principium* is nothing other than the *ratio rationis*: the reason of reason. The Latin title of the principle of reason also plunges us into the same confused tangle: the reason of reason; reason turns back upon itself just as it did when the principle of reason declared itself the ground/reason of the principle. So it is not because of the wording of the principle—neither in the German nor the Latin—that we cannot proceed in a straight line along the principle of reason but are immediately drawn into a coiling movement. Yet we must still consider the fact that the German title *Der Satz vom Grund* [the principle of reason] is anything but the literal translation of the Latin title *principium rationis*, even when we more appropriately say *Grundsatz des Grund* ["fundamental principle of reason"] instead of *Satz vom Grund* ["principle of reason"]. For neither is the word *Grund* the literal translation of the word *ratio* (*raison*), nor is the word *Grundsatz* the literal translation of the word *principium*. That the principle and the Principle confuse us already by the mere title, without our giving a thought to content, is exactly what belongs to the enigma of the principle of reason as *principium rationis*. The enigma does not lie in the title, as though we were playing an empty game with words. The enigma of the principle of reason lies in the fact that the principle under discussion is the principle which has the rank and role of a Principle.

The translation of the Latin *principium* with the newly coined word *Grundsatz* first came into use [in German] at the beginning of the eighteenth century— only an insignificant event in linguistic history, or so it seems. Commonplace [German] words such as *Absicht* for *intentio*, *Ausdruck* for *expressio*, *Gegenstand* for *objectum*, *Dasein* for *praesentia* were also first coined in the eighteenth century.

Who would want to dispute that these German words are firmly rooted locutions? Today nothing in us takes root any more.[10] Why? Because the possibility of a thoughtful conversation with a tradition that invigorates and nurtures us is lacking, because we instead consign our speaking to electronic thinking and calculating machines, an occurrence that will lead modern technology and science to completely new procedures and unforeseeable results that probably will push reflective thinking aside as something useless and hence superfluous.

Nothing of what the [German] word *Grund-Satz* says is apparent in the meaning of the Latin word *principium*. Nevertheless we go ahead and indiscriminately use the terms *principium*, "Principle," and "fundamental principle" in the same sense. This also goes for the term "axiom," which comes from the Greek. We speak of the axioms of geometry. In his *Elementa* Euclid catalogued groups of ἀξιώματα. For him, the following sentence is an example of an axiom: "What are equal to the same are equal to each other." The Greek mathematicians did not understand axioms as fundamental principles. What they had in mind can be seen in their paraphrase of the word: ἀξιώατα are κοιναὶ ἔννοιαι. Plato used the word often; it means "insight," "to have an insight" and indeed with the mind's eye. The paraphrase of ἀξιώματα by ἔννοιαι is usually translated *allgemeine angenommene Vorstellungen* [universally assumed ideas]. In a certain manner even Leibniz held to this interpretation of what an axiom is, of course with the essential difference that he defines an axiom as a principle: *axiomata sunt propositiones, quae ab omnibus pro manifestis habentur*, and Leibniz adds: *et attente considerata ex terminis constant*. "Axioms are principles that are held by everyone as being obvious and—scrupulously viewed—as consisting of limit-concepts.[8] The *principium rationis*, the fundamental principle of reason, is for Leibniz such an axiom.

It is crucial to note: axioms and Principles have the character of principles. They are supreme principles insofar as they have a separate standing in the derivation of principles and somehow stand at the top in proofs and syllogisms. Aristotle already knew what belongs within the compass of axioms. But even today we lack an adequate illumination of the deeper insights Aristotle developed, though not immediately but mediately, concerning the essence of axioms. This takes place in connection with the previously mentioned treatment of the principle of contradiction.[9]

Why are we referring to the terms "axiom," "Principle," and "fundamental principle"? We need to be reminded that these terms have been used interchangeably for a long time in philosophy and the sciences, despite the fact that each of them stems from a different conceptual domain. And nevertheless they must, even if superficially, mean the same thing—otherwise they could not be translated from one language into another. The Greek ἀξίωμα comes from ἀξιόω, "I find something worthy." But what does "find something worthy" mean? We contemporaries are quick to the draw and say: "to find worthy," that means "to value something," "to esteem its value." But we would like to know what ἀξιοῦν means when understood in the Greek sense of "to find worthy." We must contemplate what "finding worthy" could mean when thought in a Greek way, for the Greeks were not familiar with the idea of valuing and the concept of value.

What does "to find something worthy" mean, especially in the sense of the original Greek relation of humans to what is? "To find worthy" means "to bring something to shine forth in that countenance in which it finds its repose, and to preserve it therein." An axiom shows what has the most noble countenance, and has this not as a consequence of an evaluation emanating from humans and conferred by them. What has the most noble countenance composes this regard on its own. This countenance is based in its own particular look. That which enjoys having the most noble countenance opens the lookout towards that stature from whose look everything else always receives its look and possesses its countenance.[11] When an axiom is thought in a Greek way, the concealed sense of what it refers to is simple. For us, of course, this sense is difficult to grasp. Above all this is because we have become quite accustomed to understanding "axiom" in the sense of a Principle and of a fundamental principle, an understanding moreover that is abetted by the late Greek comprehension of axioms as principles. But then again, even the Latin *principium* says nothing directly about what speaks in the Greek ἀξίωμα. *Principium—id quod primum cepit*: that which has grasped, captured, and thus contains what is first, and in this manner is that which stands first in rank. Then again, nothing of what the German word *Grund-Satz* says is heard in the Latin *principium*. If we wanted to translate this word back into Greek, then the Greek word for *Grund-Satz* would have to be ὑπόθεσις. Plato used this word in a sense that is essential for the whole of his thinking. Of course it does not mean what is intended by our word *Hypothese* [hypothesis], which is not of German origin, namely, a supposition that has not yet been proven. Ὑπόθεσις means that which already lies at the basis of something else and which always already has come to light through this other, even if we people do not immediately or always expressly notice it. In the event we were to finally hear our German word *Grund-Satz* as a pure, literal echo of the Platonic word ὑπό-θεσις, then there would be another tone and emphasis in the term *Grundsatz*. Our discussion of the fundamental principle of reason would thereby come, in a flash, to have a different footing.

The θέσις in Plato's ὑπόθεσις must, however, be thought in a Greek sense.[10]

Lecture Three

Nihil est sine ratione. Nothing is without reason, says the principle of reason. Nothing—which means not even this principle of reason, certainly it least of all. It may then be that the principle of reason, that whereof it speaks, and this speaking itself do not belong within the jurisdiction of the principle of reason. To think this remains a grave burden. In short it means that the principle of reason is without reason. Said still more clearly: "Nothing without reason" —this, which is something, is without reason. If this is the case, then we face a state of affairs that is extremely alienating, but only for a moment, for in such cases we know a way out. What is the case at hand? "Nothing without reason"—itself groundless—is an obvious contradiction. But what in itself is contradictory cannot *be*. So says the fundamental principle of contradiction. Formulated briefly, it reads: *esse non potest, quod implicat contradictionem*; whatever implies a contradiction cannot *be*. Whenever and wherever we want to get at what can be and actually is, we must avoid contradictions—which means, we must adhere to the fundamental principle of contradiction. Thus, every effort to gain secure knowledge about what is aims not only at avoiding contradictions, but also at resolving contradictions that are present by adopting appropriate new suppositions. The sciences endeavor methodically to eliminate the contradictions that now and again surface in theories and the conflicts that crop up in observed facts. This style of cognition defines the passion of modern science. The fundamental principle of contradiction—its demand to unconditional adherence—is the hidden prod that goads modern science onward. But how do things stand in our case, which we can formulate thus: the supreme fundamental principle of reason is groundless? The fundamental principle of contradiction prohibits our thinking of such a thing. But in a case such as this, where it is a matter of discussing the supreme fundamental principle, may one thoughtlessly import another fundamental principle, that of contradiction, as a normative, principle-reason? How valid is the fundamental principle of contradiction? Can

17

we rate it as a fundamental principle [*Grundsatz*] without discussing what a reason [*Grund*] is and what a principle [*Satz*] is?

The constant appeal to the principle of contradiction may be the most illuminating thing in the world for the sciences. But whoever knows the history of the principle of contradiction must concede that the interpretation of its content really remains questionable. Over and above that, for the last one hundred and fifty years there has been Hegel's *Science of Logic*. It shows that contradiction and conflict are not reasons against something being real. Rather, contradiction is the inner life of the reality of the real. This interpretation of the essence and effect of contradiction is the centerpiece of Hegel's metaphysics. Ever since Hegel's *Logic* it is no longer immediately certain that where a contradiction is present what contradicts itself cannot be real. So within the context of our considerations of the fundamental principle of reason in many respects it remains an overhasty procedure if, without hesitation and without reflection, we appeal to the fundamental principle of contradiction and say that the principle of reason is without reason, that this contradicts itself and therefore is impossible. Of course —but what are we supposed to make of [*vorstellen*] this state of affairs: the principle of reason without reason? That is to say, as soon as we conceive [*vorstellen*] of something, we represent [*vorstellen*] it *as* this and *as* that. With this "as this, as that" we lodge what is represented somewhere; we deposit it there, so to speak; we give it a ground. Our cognition [*Vorstellen*] everywhere takes refuge in some reason. The principle of reason without reason—for us this is inconceivable. But what is inconceivable is by no means also unthinkable, given that thinking does not exhaust itself in conceiving.

If we nevertheless insist that the principle of reason—and it above all others —has a reason, then we are faced with the question: what reason is the reason for the principle of reason; what sort of reason is this most odd reason?

The principle of reason counts as a fundamental principle. We even assert it is the supreme fundamental principle; it is the ground/reason for all principles and that means for what a principle is per se. The following is imbedded in this assertion: the principle of reason—which means, that about which it speaks —is the ground/reason for what a principle is, for what a statement is, for what an utterance per se is. That about which the principle of reason speaks is the ground of the essence of language. A wide-ranging thought. Therefore, in order to follow it we must start with what is most obvious. If the principle of reason were the most supreme of all principles, then it would also be, in every case, the ground/reason for principles. The principle of reason is the ground/reason for principles. Here we fall into a vortex. But have we really gotten into this vortex? Or are we only making an assessment from afar: the principle as the ground/reason for principles—this looks like a whirlwind? It would be gratifying and useful if we could be swept up so swiftly into the whirlwind and especially into its eye. For in the eye of a hurricane, as they say, calm is supposed to ‖ prevail.

But for the time being the province of the principle of reason is not familiar to us, just as little is the course into this province. Take note: the course and province lie in shadows, and the light there is limited. It consists simply in the fact that one says the principle of reason is an illuminating principle. This —that such principles are immediately illuminating—holds for the fundamental principles that are also called Principles or axioms. Ultimately we see that this glib talk—superficially and off the cuff—of *axioms, principia,* and fundamental principles in a homologous sense is indeed precarious, for the three terms— the Greek word ἀξίωμα, the Latin word *principium,* the German word *Grundsatz* —speak from out of completely disparate conceptual domains. To all appearances, behind this harmless disparity of word-meanings is concealed the basic trait of the history of Western thinking—history not as something bygone, rather history as the still pending *Geschick*[12] that determines us today as hardly ever before.

In the meantime people have become accustomed over the centuries to a trite way of speaking and thinking. In regard to other principles below them, axioms are the supreme fundamental principles found more worthy than all others. One pays no attention to the extent to which and the sense in which axioms are things found inherently worthy, things that find something worthy without looking to derivative principles—in Greek, that means to let something repose in its countenance and preserve it therein. *Principia* are the sort of things that occupy the first place, that stand first in line. *Principia* refer to a ranking and ordering. The term "principle-reasons" already implies that the ordering-realm (which according to popular opinion deals with axioms and Principles) is the realm of principles. We hold this to be self-evident and think nothing of it. But this comprehension of axioms apropos of principles has most recently developed into the notion of axioms according to which the sole role of axioms *qua* suppositions and stipulations is to secure the construction of a system of principles free of contradiction. The axiomatic character of axioms consists exclusively in this role of eliminating contradictions and safeguarding against them. What "axiom" could mean when taken on its own lacks objective meaning. The axiomatic form of scientific thinking that lacks an object in this sense today stands before unforeseeable possibilities. This axiomatic thinking already circulates without our noticing it or fathoming its import in so changing human thinking that it adapts itself to the essence of modern technology. Whoever meditates on this event will discern right away that the frequent talk of the human mastery of technology arises from a cognitive mode that still moves only on the fringes of that which now *is*. The assessment that contemporary humanity has become the slave of machines and mechanisms is also superficial. For it is one thing to make such an assessment, but it will be something quite different to ponder the extent to which the human being today is subjugated not only to technology, but the extent to which humans must respond to the essence of technology, and the extent to which more original possibilities of a free and open human existence announce themselves in this response. The technico-scientific world-construct deploys its own specific claims on the shaping of all available resources which, in such a world, throng into its daylight. What one names with the ill-suited title "abstract art" thus has its legitimate function in the domain of this technico-scientific world-construct. In making this observation I intentionally make use of words understood around the globe [which are not of German origin.][13]

If we now refer to the homologous use of axioms, Principles, and fundamental principles and thereby take into consideration the fact that this use serves the axiomatic securing of calculative thinking, then we move towards a reflection in which a few things must be resolved.

It would be both short-sighted and presumptuous if we wanted to disparage modern axiomatic thinking. But it would also be a childish and pathetic notion if we were to believe that this modern thinking would let itself be bent back upon its great and open origin in the thinking of the Greeks. The only fruitful path leads through and beyond modern axiomatic cognition and its concealed grounds. First of all, this cognition persists in the commonplace representation of axioms, Principles, fundamental principles, and their roles. We must reflect upon how we relate to the supreme fundamental principles. It is clear: we adhere to them without reflection.

We hardly give a second thought to where there might be things like axioms, Principles, and fundamental principles, where they may reside, where they come from. Principles—that seems to be a matter of Reason,[14] and fundamental principles to be what pertains to our understanding, that is, the sort of thing that we carry around in our heads. Besides, the formulae of these fundamental principles show their apparent universal validity; yet these principles also remain hollow as long as we are not capable of thinking about their contents on the basis of the essential plentitude of that about which they speak.

About what does the fundamental principle of reason speak? To what does it belong? From where does it speak?

These questions are not completely irrelevant, although they give the impression that their discussion can contribute little to the promotion of the sciences, and that their discussion will even seduce philosophy into overlooking the pressing needs of the contemporary era.

Such apprehensions are justified. Therefore, before we attempt a discussion of the principle of reason, we might give one more of those characterizations that only hovers, as it were, around the exterior of the principle. The following

should make it still clearer where we stand and where we are going in the event that we set out to discuss the principle of reason.

Leibniz calls the principle of reason a *principium grande*, a mighty Principle. What this honorific distinction means can become clear in its full significance only if we are already in a position to enter into a thoughtful conversation with Leibniz. But this remains barred to us as long as we do not have the benefit of a discussion that sufficiently situates the principle of reason. Schelling initiated the first and truly metaphysical conversation with Leibniz, a conversation that stretches up to and includes Nietzsche's doctrine of the will to power.

But surely what is mighty about the principle of reason will also open itself to us if we simply pay attention to a formulation of the *principium rationis* that one often finds in Leibniz. He says: *Nihil est sine ratione seu nullus effectus sine causa*. "Nothing is without reason, or no effect is without a cause." One calls the principle "no effect is without a cause" the Principle of causality. By using *seu* (or)[14a] in the formula cited here, Leibniz obviously posits the principle of reason and the principle of causality as being equivalent. One is tempted to find fault with this equation, for it makes one wonder: every cause is indeed some sort of reason, but not every reason has the character of being a cause that has an effect as a consequence. For instance, we think of the axiom quoted from Euclid's *Elementa*: "What are equal to the same are equal to each other." When it has the role of a major premise in a syllogism, this axiom can serve as the ground. Two determinate magnitudes prove to be equal to each other in accordance with this ground. But the axiom does not first cause the two determinant magnitudes to be equal to each other in the way that rain causes the roof of a house to become wet. Reason and consequence are not equivalent to cause and effect.

These comments are correct in a certain regard. But one is reluctant to instruct Leibniz in this matter. Such instruction might even block us from the way into the peculiar character of Leibniz's thought. Therefore we leave open the question of the relationship between the principle of reason and the Principle of causality. This much becomes clear: the Principle of causality belongs within the orbit of the principle of reason. But now, does what is mighty about the principle of reason consist in the fact that it also includes the Principle of causality? In referring to this inclusion, which often looks like an equation of both Principles, we have at most only determined the range of the dominion of the mighty principle. But we would like to know wherein consists the power of the mighty principle. We would like to bring into view what in this Principle really is bepowering and how it bepowers.[15]

Till now we have spoken of only one formulation of the principle of reason, which we called the short formulation. The short formulation is an abbreviated one compared to those which for Leibniz counted as the authentic, strict, and hence solely normative formulations.

In one of his later pieces Leibniz writes: *duo sunt prima principia omnium ratiocinationum, Principium nempe contradictionis . . . : et principium reddendae rationis*, "there are two supreme Principles for all proofs, the Principle—it goes without saying—of contradiction and the Principle *reddendae rationis*."[11] This principle, mentioned second says, *quod omnis veritas reddi ratio potest*, "that for every truth" (which means, according to Leibniz, every true proposition) "the reason can be rendered."[12] Strictly speaking, for Leibniz the *principium rationis* is the *principium reddendae rationis*. *Rationem reddere* means "to give back the reason." Why "back," and "back" to where? Because in proofs—generally speaking, in knowledge—where it is a matter of the cognition of objects, this "back" comes into play.[16] The Latin language of philosophy says it more clearly: cognition is *repraesentatio*. What is encountered is presented to a cognizing I, presented back to and over against it, made present. According to the *principium reddendae rationis*, cognition must render to cognition the reason for what is encountered—and that means give it back (*reddere*) to cognition—if it is to be a discerning cognition. In a discerning cognition a reason is rendered to the discerning I. The *principium rationis* requires this. Therefore, for Leibniz the principle of reason is the fundamental principle of rendering reasons.

Leibniz made the following remark about the definition of the *principium rationis* as the *principium reddendae rationis: vel ut vulgo ajunt, quod nihil fit sine causa*; "or as one ordinarily says, that nothing happens without a cause."[13] Leibniz brings the ordinary formulation of the *principium rationis* into relief against the formulation thought philosophically. From the quoted passage as well as from similar ones we see that the strict formulation is only reached when the principle is represented as the fundamental principle of demonstrations, which in the broader sense means represented as the fundamental principle of statements. *Duobus utor in demonstrando principiis*. "I use two Principles in demonstrations."[14] Leibniz means the principle of contradiction and the principle of reason. For Leibniz the principle of reason is a Principle for sentences and statements, in the first place for those of philosophical and scientific knowledge. The principle of reason is the fundamental principle of the possible and necessary rendering of reasons for a true sentence. The principle of reason is the fundamental principle of the necessary founding of sentences and principles. What is mighty about the Principle is that it pervades, guides, and supports all cognition that expresses itself in sentences or propositions.

But the strict formulation of the *principium rationis* as the *principium reddendae rationis* also apparently contains a restriction. What must be added to the term *principium reddendae rationis* to fill it out is *cognitioni*—the principle of reason insofar as [reason] must be rendered to cognition for it to be a founded and thus a true knowledge-yielding cognition. So it may seem that the *principium reddendae rationis* thereby concerns only knowledge, but *not* those things which *are* in some other manner. Is the validity of the *principium reddendae rationis* limited to cognition? On the contrary, the *principium rationis* in its ordinary formulation is valid for everything which in any manner *is*.

So the *principium rationis* in the form of the *principium reddendae rationis* is not in the slightest a restriction of the Principle to cognition. Much depends on seeing this clearly from the very beginning. For it is only this insight that enables us to fully understand in what sense the *principium rationis* is the *principium grande*, the mighty Principle. Only by having grasped this sense can we more clearly bring into view what is bepowering about the principle of reason.

Cognition is a kind of representational thinking [*Vorstellen*]. In *this presentation* [*Stellen*] something we encounter comes to stand [*Stehen*], to a standstill [*Stand*]. What is encountered and brought to a standstill in representational thinking is the *object* [*Gegenstand*]. For Leibniz and all modern thinking, the manner in which beings "are" is based in the objectness of objects. For representational thinking, the representedness of objects belongs to the objectness of objects.

But then again the *principium rationis* as the *principium reddendae rationis* says that this representational thinking and what it represents, that is, the object in its obstancy [*Gegenstehen*], must be a founded one. The obstancy of the object amounts to the manner in which the object as such stands, which means, *is*. So the strict formulation of the *principium rationis* as the *principium reddendae rationis* is not a restriction of the principle of reason; rather, the *principium reddendae rationis* is valid for everything that is an object, which means here everything that "is." Accordingly, the strict formulation of the *principium rationis* as the *principium reddendae rationis* contains a very specific and decisive explanation of what the unrestricted principle of reason says: nothing is without reason. This now says: something "is," which means, can be identified as being a being, only if it is stated in a sentence that satisfies the fundamental principle of reason as the fundamental principle of founding. What is mighty about the principle of reason displays its power in that the *principium reddendae rationis*—to all appearances only a Principle of cognition—also counts, precisely in being the fundamental principle of cognition, as the Principle for everything that *is*.

Leibniz could finally discover the principle of reason—a principle adhered to for centuries because it was ever resounding—because he had to articulate the *principium rationis* as the *principium reddendae rationis*; we say "had to" and of course do not thereby mean an irresistible, blind compulsion under which Leibniz stood. We mean the freedom and openness with which Leibniz, a man of his times, managed to hear the decisive claim[17] in the already resounding verdict of the principle of reason and who brought it—in the literal sense—to the language in which the content of the principle (which had not yet been posited as a fundamental principle) articulates itself. The exacting claim of the principle speaks in the word *reddere*: "to give back," "to bring along," "to re-nder" [*zu-stellen*]. We speak of "rendering unto Caesar what is his."[18] *Ratio* is *ratio reddenda*. This means that reason is what must be rendered to the representing, thinking person. What is great and constant in the thinking of a thinker simply consists in its expressly giving word to what always already resounds. What stirs in the thinking of Leibniz easily and fully shows itself in the insertion of a single, moreover commonplace, word: the *principium rationis* is the "principium *reddendae* rationis." The *reddendum*, the demand that reasons be rendered is what bepowers the principle of reason as the mighty Principle. The *reddendum*, the demand that reasons be rendered, now speaks unabatedly and without surcease across the modern age and out over us contemporaries today. The *reddendum*, the claim that reasons be rendered, has insinuated itself between the thinking person and their world in order to take possession of human cognition in a new manner.

Have we—we, who are here now—been on the trail of what is bepowering about the mighty principle of reason, or even expressly experienced and thought it through with sufficient thoroughness? If we are not to fool ourselves, we must all be in agreement: no. And I say *all*—including those who now and again have given some thought to the "essence of reasons."

How do things stand? We pursue the study of the sciences with the greatest zeal. We get to know their various fields down to every wayside nook and minute cranny. We rehearse the procedures of the sciences. We even have an ear out for the particular disciplines and take note of the whole of the sciences. We let ourselves go on about how the realms of nature and history are not so sharply separated from each other as it may seem from the arrangement of the diverse university faculties. Everywhere a nimble, gratifying spirit is at work in the study of the sciences. But if we reflect for a moment on the question posed a moment ago, we must still say that in all our endeavors in the sciences we haven't ever stumbled on the principle of reason. Yet, without this mighty Principle there would be no modern science, and without such a science there would be no university as we have it today. The university is grounded on the principle of reason.

How are we supposed to conceive this: the university grounded on a principle? May we venture such an assertion?

Lecture Four

We hear the principle of reason: *Nihil est sine ratione*. Nothing is without reason. We subscribe to this principle as soon as we hear it, for we find nothing that seems to speak against the principle. But initially we also find nothing that inclines us to ponder the principle in a special manner.

Thus the principle belongs among the many obvious and trivial things through which we daily make our way. By this we also mean that the principle must have always already been familiar. In a certain sense this is true. Shortly we will experience more clearly to what extent the principle of reason not only factually always already resounds, but necessarily resounds, and in which sense of necessity. In the meantime we must at the very beginning of our path let ourselves be instructed by the fact that the principle of reason was first discovered as a principle by Leibniz in the seventeenth century. One is inclined to say that the spirit of the seventeenth century led to the discovery of the principle of reason as a Principle. But one can say with equal right that the discovery of the *principium rationis* as one of the first axioms of all cognition and conduct first molded the spirit of the seventeenth century and the centuries following it up to, including, and beyond our own. Perhaps both opinions are correct. Yet neither of them suffices for the calm circumspection needed here to fathom that history reigning in the long absence and sudden emergence of the principle of reason. In any case, it has been established that the discoverer of the principle of reason as a fundamental principle—Leibniz himself—gave the *principium rationis* a name with the distinction of *principium grande*, the mighty Principle.

We are, within the bounds of a preparatory reflection, ready to clarify the extent to which the principle of reason is the mighty Principle. From what perspective must we understand its mightiness? The sense of the mighty would be much too restricted if we were to connect what is mighty about the *principium rationis* only to the role ascribed to it within the philosophy of Leibniz, which, like every modern philosophy, has the character of a system—even if it does not stand there as a finished conceptual edifice.

25

The principle of reason is a normative Principle within the Leibnizian system only because this Principle is related to everything that is. Hence, in the formulation that Leibniz himself calls vulgar it reads: *Nihil fit sine causa*. Nothing happens, that means, nothing becomes a being, without a cause. The vulgar formulation of the principle of reason is not false—it is, however, imprecise in Leibniz's sense. The *principium rationis*, which is valid for everything that in any way is, pervasively reigns not only over the realm of natural processes, but also over the realm that we today call "history." Even more: nature and history belong in the essential totality of beings which, in resonance with the earliest linguistic usage in Western thinking, Leibniz calls *Natura*. The word is capitalized. One of the profoundest of Leibniz's later, difficult articles thus begins: "*Ratio* est in Natura cur aliquid potius existat quam nihil." "There is a *reason* in Nature why something exists rather than nothing.[15] Here "Nature" is not one realm of beings in distinction to another realm. Nature is used in the sense we think of when we speak of the nature of things: *Natura, quam rebus tribuere solemus*: "the Nature, which we are in the habit of attributing, of adjudging to things."[16] Understood in this way, there is in the nature of things something rational why something exists rather than nothing.

The first and decisive word of the treatise, namely, *ratio*, is underlined in the manuscript. In one of the subsequent sentences Leibniz then says: *Ea ratio debet esse in aliquo Ente Reali seu causa*: "This reason (in the 'Nature' of things, according to which they have the inclination to exist rather than not to exist) must be in some sort of real being, or in its cause."[17] A first cause must exist. In the next sentence, this existing thing will be called the *ultimo ratio Rerum*, the ultimate (highest) existing reason of all things. Leibniz adds to this: *et* (namely, *illud Ens necessarium*) *uno vocabulo solet appellari DEUS*: "and (that being which necessarily exists as the highest reason) is usually named with one word: GOD."

The essential totality of beings up to the *prima causa*—to God—is held under the sway of the *principium rationis*. The jurisdiction of the principle of reason encompasses all beings up to their first existing cause, which it also includes. This reference makes clearer what is mighty about the *principium rationis*. But taken in this way, it initially only shows the scope of its jurisdiction.

However, we are raising the question about what is bepowering in the mighty Principle. We bring what bepowers into view when we hold ourselves to the formulation of the *principium rationis* Leibniz held to be the strict and only normative one, in contradistinction to the vulgar one. This strict formulation of the *principium rationis* comes to light in the correspondingly more precise title, namely the *principium reddendae rationis*: the fundamental principle of rendering reasons. This means that according to the principle of reason, reasons are not somewhere and somehow indeterminantly and indifferently present. Reason as such demands to be given back *as* reasons—namely back (*re*) in the direction of the representing, cognizing subject, *by* this subject and *for* this subject. Reason everywhere demands to come to the fore such that everything within the domain of this claim appears as a sequent, which means, such that everything has to be represented as being a consequence. Only what presents itself to our cognition, only what we en-counter such that it is posed and posited in its reasons, counts as something with secure standing, that means, as an object. Only what stands in this manner is something of which we can, with certainty, say "it *is*."

Only what is brought to a stand in a founded representation counts as a being. But a representation is a founding representation only if reasons are rendered to the cognizing, representing subject as founding reasons. To the extent that this happens—and only to that extent—cognition satisfies the demand that it be founded. This demand speaks in reason itself insofar as the demand requires that all cognition render reasons. What is bepowering about the principle of reason is the demand that reasons be rendered. This demand, the *reddendum*, pervasively bepowers all human cognition. Nevertheless, the *principium reddendae rationis* is not a mere Principle of cognition; rather, the *principium reddendae rationis* is the supreme fundamental principle of cognition, as well as of the objects of cognition because, according to the guiding thought of modern philosophy, something "is" only insofar as a founded cognition has secured it for itself as its object.

"Everything that is, *is* by virtue of . . . ," is itself a consequence of a reason, and that means it is by virtue and apropos of the demand to render reasons, a demand which speaks in the principle of reason as the *principium reddendae rationis*. What has just been said can be clarified as well as furnished with plain evidence if we follow the cited passages of Leibniz in the opposite direction back to that wherein, according to Leibniz's own statements, it is grounded.

What is to be posited as the *ultima ratio* of *Natura*, as the furthest, highest —and that means the first—existing reason for the nature of things, is what one usually calls God.

There is in the nature of things a reason why something is rather than nothing. As the first existing cause of all beings, God is called reason. But why is the principle valid that says there must be a reason why there is something rather than nothing? Leibniz begins his treatise with this principle. To repeat the wording of the principle: "*Ratio* est in Natura, cur aliquid potius existat quam nihil": "There is a *reason* in the nature of things why *something* exists rather than nothing."[18] But this sentence, which is shoved to the forefront, is itself a consequence, namely a consequence of the principle of reason. In reference to the previously mentioned sentence, Leibniz immediately continues in the text: *Id consequens est magni illius principii, quod nihil fiat sine ratione*: "This—namely what the first sentence says—is *consequens*, a consequence of that *principium magnum*, that great fundamental principle that says nothing becomes—that means nothing comes into being—without a reason."

Taken to its extreme, this means that God exists only insofar as the principle of reason holds. One immediately asks in turn: to what extent does the principle of reason hold? If the principle of reason is the mighty Principle, then its bepowering is a sort of effecting. In fact, in the treatise in question, Leibniz speaks of an efficacy, an *efficere* that accrues to the supreme principles. However, (according to the principle of reason) all effecting requires a cause. But the first cause is God. So the principle of reason holds only insofar as God exists. But God exists only insofar as the principle of reason holds. Such thinking moves in a circle. We would certainly remain far removed from Leibniz's thinking if we were to think Leibniz acquiesced to this circularity, which one can easily point out and even demonstrate is fraught with mistakes. None of us here should fancy to have already understood the cited passages of Leibniz down to their last detail. What still remains is the insight into that upon which everything depends: the principle of reason is the Principle that pervasively bepowers everything insofar as reason, according to the strict formulation of the fundamental principle, insists that each thing that is, *is* as a consequence of . . . , which is to say, by virtue of the express, complete fulfillment of the demand of reason. In the future it will serve us well to hold in view the fact that the demand-character of reason comes to the fore in the first, strict formulation of the principle of reason.

The *principium reddendae rationis* requires that all cognition of objects be a self-grounding cognition and, along with this, that the object itself always be a founded—which means, securely established—object.

Now, modern science understands itself as the exemplary mode of the founding representation of objects. Accordingly, it is based on the fundamental principle of rendering reasons. Without modern science there is no modern university. If those of us here are aware of ourselves as belonging to the university, then we move on the basis upon which the university itself rests. That is the principle of reason. However, what remains astounding is that we who are here have still never encountered the principle of reason. As such, the statement that the university rests on the principle of reason seems to be an exaggerated and weird assertion.

If the university is not built upon a principle, then perhaps it is built upon that about which the principle speaks? We heard that it speaks of a *reddendum*. The demand to render reasons for all statements—for every utterance—speaks in the principle. *From where* does this demand of reason speak to its being rendered?

Does this demand lie in the essence of reason itself? Before we inquire so far afield, let us limit ourselves to first asking whether we hear the demand to render reasons. We must answer: yes and no. Yes—for lately we have had the demand to render reasons all too oppressively in our ears. No—for we indeed hardly notice its pressing demand. Everywhere we move in the aura of the demand to render reasons and at the same time we have an uncommonly difficult time simply paying attention to this demand so as to hear that *language* in which it genuinely speaks. We indeed make use of devices to ascertain and check the radioactivity in the atmosphere. There are no devices for hearing the demand that requires the rendering of reasons. Surely the constant presence of devices and the constant presence of what the devices register bear witness to the fact that the mighty principle of reason now displays its bepowering character in a manner previously unprecedented.

Humanity now has come to the point of naming that epoch into which its historical existence enters according to the atomic energy that has become available to it. We are, one says, in the atomic age.

We don't at all need to fathom what this means. Who would presume to actually fathom this? But today we can do something else. Each person can meditate for a little while on the uncanniness that conceals itself in this apparently harmless naming of the age. Humanity defines an epoch of its historical-spiritual existence by the rapacity for, and availability of, a natural energy.

Human existence—molded by the atom.[19] Today this word [atom] names something which, perhaps for the time being, is accessible to only a limited number of "thinkers." Nevertheless, the characterization of an epoch as the atomic age probably touches on what is. For the remainder—whatever else there is and what we call culture: theater, art, film, and radio, as well as literature and philosophy, and even faith and religion—everywhere all of this hobbles around behind what the configuration of the atomic era accords to our age. One could go into all the particulars, a business the "Illustrated Newspapers" take care of these days with the greatest adroitness and courteousness. Of course, this sort of "Information" is also just a sign of the times. The word "Information"—which is [not a word of German] provenance—speaks more clearly here insofar as it means, on the one hand, the instant news and reporting that, on the other hand and at the same time, have taken over the ceaseless molding (forming) of the reader and listener. Let us no longer allow it to escape our meditative view: an epoch of human history molded by the atom.

Indeed there would be no atomic age without atomic science. That is, as we often say, a truism. Yet this would be but a half-baked truth if we let ourselves rest content with it. Hence we may and must ask: where does atomic science come from? It is governed by the discipline of nuclear physics, which today is more adequately characterized as the physics of elementary particles. Only a little while ago modern science only knew the proton and neutron as the parts of the atom. Today we know more than ten parts. And already science is swept along in the effort to push this dispersed manifold of elementary particles into a new unity that supports them. What is the significance of the sciences being swept along towards the secure establishing of an evermore adequate unity, a unity of theories and observations that offer themselves to the sciences as the resources available for cognition? We already mentioned that the questioning found in the sciences will always be goaded on to eliminate contradictions that crop up. This elimination occurs through the progress towards resolving contradictions into a unity that can bear up under—which means, give a reason for —what is apparently contradictory. The demand to render adequate reasons reigns by sweeping along cognition and questioning over and beyond contradictions.

We said the atomic age rests on atomic science, and we asked, Where does this science come from? Our question does not intend to trace the course of the history of the emergence and development of atomic science. Rather, it seeks to reflect on the innermost impulse of this science itself regardless of whether or not the investigators become aware of it. We see that the impulse and the sweep towards the constant elimination of contradictions within the many competing theories and irreconcilable facts grow out of the demand of the *principium reddendae rationis*. This demand is something other than science itself. The demand to render reasons is, for the sciences, the element within which its cognition moves, as does the fish in water and the bird in air. Science responds to the demand of *ratio reddenda* and does so unconditionally. Otherwise, it couldn't be what it is.

But while science responds to the demand of the *reddendum*—it has an ear for it—it nevertheless does not hear it in such a way that it can meditate upon it. So, if we say "atomic age" and at last say this name thoughtfully, we are then paying attention to the fact that we, who live in this age, stand under the reign of the claim of the mighty *principium reddendae rationis*. We who live today are who we are only insofar as the mighty claim of rendering reasons pervasively bepowers us. As the global epoch of humanity, the atomic age is distinguished by the fact that the power of the mighty Principle, of the *principium reddendae rationis*, displays itself (if not completely unleashed) in a strange manner in the normative domain of human existence. When I use the word "strange" here, I mean it not in a sentimental sense. One must think it in both a literal and substantive sense, namely, that the unique unleashing of the demand to render reasons threatens everything of humans' being-at-home and robs them of the roots of their subsistence, the roots from out of which every great human age, every world-opening spirit, every molding of the human form has thus far grown.

So we see the extremely odd position of modern humanity, a position the likes of which runs counter to all the popular sentiments that belong to the pedestrian notions we run around with, as though blind and deaf: the claim of the mighty Principle of rendering reasons withdraws the subsistence from contemporary humanity. We could also say that the more decisively humans try to harness the "mega-energies" that would, once and for all, satisfy all human energy needs, the more impoverished becomes the human faculty for building and dwelling in the realm of what is essential. There is an enigmatic interconnection between the demand to render reasons and the withdrawal of roots.

It is important to see the form of the movement occurring in this lofty play between rendering and withdrawal. It is important to think for a moment about the provenance of this play. It is important to ask to what extent the inconspicuous reign of the mighty Principle of reason plays along in this play. It is important to note in which province we reside when we pursue and think through the principle of reason.

Lecture Five

(handwritten marginalia)

Leibniz brought the principle of reason into view as one of the supreme Principles. Leibniz came up with the strict formulation—*principium reddendae rationis*—for the principle of reason: *Nihil sine ratione*: "Nothing is without reason." The character of reason as demanding the rendering of reasons shows itself in the *ratio reddenda*. We speak of a strict formulation of the principle of reason because this formulation takes as its measure the character of reason that showed itself for the first time to the thinking of Leibniz and his era. However, the strict formulation that has been commented upon up till now is, even in Leibniz's sense, not the complete formulation of the principle of reason.

The first public mention of the *principium rationis* is found in Leibniz's treatise *Theoria motus abstracti*. This theory considers those conditions for the possibility of movement that are independent of sensibly perceptible appearances. As a twenty-five-year-old, Leibniz sent the 1671 treatise to the Paris Academy of Sciences. In this treatise, near the end of one of the propositions set forth concerning abstractly viewed movement, he said the following: *pendet ex nobilissimo illo (proposition 24)* (where he means, *principio*) *Nihil est sine ratione*; "it (namely the proposition concerning abstract movement under consideration) depends on that most familiar and most eminent Principle: *Nothing is without reason*."[19] Leibniz here presumes that the customary formulation of the principle of reason is universally known and accepted, and yet at the same time he ascribes to the principle of reason an extraordinarily august role. The principle of reason is the *principium nobilissimum*; it is the noblest Principle. Six years later (1677), Leibniz speaks of the *principium rationis* in his comments on the writings of one of Spinoza's students. Leibniz had visited Spinoza in Amsterdam between the 18th and 28th of November 1676 on his return from London to Germany. Leibniz writes: *id, quod dicere soleo, nihil existere nisi cujus reddi potest ratio existentiae sufficiens*: "(the Principle) that I usually say (in the form): Nothing exists whose sufficient reason for existing cannot be rendered."[20]

Reason, which insists on its being rendered, at the same time requires that it, as a reason, be sufficient, which means, completely satisfactory. For what? In order to securely establish an object [*Gegenstand*] in its stance [*Stand*]. In the background of the definition of sufficing, of sufficiency (of *suffectio*), there is the guiding idea of Leibnizian thinking—the idea of *perfectio*, that is, of the completeness [*Voll-ständigkeit*] of the determinations for the standing [*Stehen*] of an object [*Gegenstand*]. Only in the completeness of the conditions for its possibility, only in the completeness of its reasons is the status [*Ständigkeit*] of an object through and through securely established, perfect.[20] Reason (*ratio*) is related to the effect (*efficere*) as cause (*causa*); reason must itself be sufficient (*sufficiens, sufficere*). This sufficiency is required and determined by the *perfectio* (*perficere*) of the object. It is certainly no accident that within the province of the principle of reason language seems to spontaneously speak of an *efficere, sufficere, perficere*, that is, of a manifold *facere*, of a making, of a producing and rendering. For Leibniz, the title of the principle of reason reads, when thought strictly and completely: *principium reddendae rationis sufficientis*, the fundamental principle of rendering sufficient reasons.[21] We could also say: the principle of adequate reasons. When, as is the case of Leibniz's discovery and defining of the principle of sufficient reason, a mighty Principle comes to light, thinking and cognition in all essential regards enters into a new sort of movement. It is the modern manner of thinking in which we daily reside without expressly perceiving or noticing the demand of reason to be rendered in all cognition. Accordingly, in a more historically concealed than historiographically visible manner, Leibniz determines not only the development of modern logic into logistics and into thinking machines, and not only the more radical interpretation of the subjectivity of the subject within the philosophy of German Idealism and its subsequent scions. The thinking of Leibniz supports and molds the chief tendency of what, thought broadly enough, we can call the metaphysics of the modern age. Therefore, for us the name of Leibniz does not stand as a tag for a bygone system of philosophy. The name names the presence of a thinking whose strength has not yet been experienced, a presence that still awaits to encounter us. Only through looking back on what Leibniz thought can we characterize the present age—an age one calls the atomic age—as an age pervasively bepowered by the power of the *principium reddendae rationis sufficientis*. The demand to render sufficient reasons for all representations speaks in what today has become the object bearing the names "atom" and "atomic energy."

Strictly speaking, we may indeed be barely able, as we will see, to speak of objects any more. If we pay attention, we see we already move in a world where there are no more ob-jects. But to be ob-jectless [*Gegen-standlose*] is not the same as to be without a stance [*Standlose*]. Rather, a different sort of status [*Ständigkeit*] emerges in what is objectless. The *principium grande*, the mighty Principle, the principle of reason in no way forfeits any of its power for a world where what is objective [*Gegenständige*] must yield to a status [*Ständigen*] of a different sort.[21] Rather the power of rendered reasons adequate [*zuständigen*] to confirm [*Beständigung*] and secure everything only now begins to display itself at its most extreme. That in such an age art becomes objectless testifies to its historical appropriateness, and this above all when nonrepresentational [*gegenstandlose*] art conceives of its own productions as no longer being able to be works, rather as being something for which the suitable word is lacking. That there are art exhibitions of modern styles has more to do with the mighty principle of reason, [with the principle] of rendering reasons, than we at first imagine. Modernity is not at an end. It only begins its completion in directing itself to the complete availability of everything that is and can be.

Our reference to the atomic age was necessary in order for us to note that —and to what extent—we are everywhere residing within the orbit of the mighty Principle of reason. The reference was meant to point us to the province from which the principle of reason addresses us, if we approach it queryingly.

If we persist on this course of thinking, then immediately we see two facets of one thing more clearly: on the one hand, we see that our commonplace scientific-technical cognition does not suffice to reach the province of the principle of reason and to get a view of what is within this province; on the other hand, we see that even the philosophical doctrine of the supreme fundamental principles as Principles that are immediately illuminating dodges the decisive questions of thinking. Inherent in the principle-character of the principle of reason is the fact that the fundamental principle admits of two formulations. Till now it seemed as though the vulgar and abbreviated formulation was not fit for initiating a fruitful discussion of the principle of reason. In contradistinction to this, the strict formulation has offered us an important insight into the demand-character of reason, into *ratio* as *ratio reddenda*. Whether this character belongs to the essence of reason *per se*, or whether it only has to do with the manner in which the essence of reason reveals itself for some specific age must remain open. For even the strict formulation of the principle of reason admits of an abbreviated form such that the vulgar and the strict formulations of the Principle suddenly appear as equally essential. The apparently clear principle of reason once more becomes opaque. To what extent it does—that still merits contemplating for a moment before we go straight on to discuss the principle of reason.

According to the strict interpretation, the principle of reason says that there is no truth, which according to Leibniz means there is no correct principle or sentence, without the reasons being rendered that are necessary for the sentence or principle. How can the strict formulation of the principle of reason, of the *principium reddendae rationis*, be restated in an abbreviated form?

Whenever our cognition feels directed to render the reasons for what it cognizes—the reason upon which and in which what is cognized firmly stands as an object—then cognition is on the lookout for reasons to render. This happens

hof. Avsgchum

inasmuch as cognition asks: Why does what is cognized exist, and why is it the way it is? In the "why?" we ask for reasons. The strict formulation of the principle of reason—"Nothing is without rendering its reasons"—can be formulated thus: Nothing is without a why.

If we contrapose the short forms of each formulation, then we gain a particular sharpness that affords us a still clearer view of the principle of reason. On the one hand it reads: nothing is without reason. On the other hand it reads: nothing is without a why. In contradiction to this we now hear the following words:

> The rose is without why: it blooms because it blooms,
> It pays no attention to itself, asks not whether it is seen.

The verses are found in the first book of the spiritual poetry of Angelus Silesius, which is entitled *The Cherubic Wanderer: Sensual Description of the Four Final Things.*[22]

The work first appeared in 1657. The verses carry the number 289 with the heading "Without Why." Angelus Silesius, whose given name was Johann Scheffler, *doctor philosophiae et medicinae*, by profession a medical doctor, lived from 1624 to 1677 in Silesia. Leibniz (1646–1716) was a younger contemporary of Angelus Silesius and was familiar with *The Cherubic Wanderer*. Leibniz often speaks in his writings and letters of Angelus Silesius. Thus, in a letter to Paccius on January 28, 1695 he once wrote: "With every mystic there are a few places that are extraordinarily clever, full of difficult metaphors and virtually inclining to Godlessness, just as I have sometimes seen in the German—otherwise beautiful—poems of a certain man who is called Johannes Angelus Silesius. . . ."[23] And in his *Lectures on Aesthetics*, Hegel says the following:

> Now the pantheistic unity, raised up in relation to *the subject* that senses *itself* in this unity with God and God as this presence in subjective consciousness, would in general yield the *mystic* as it has come to be formed in this subjective manner even within Christianity. As an example I will only cite Angelus Silesius, who with the greatest cleverness and depth of intuition and sensibility has spoken with a wonderfully mystical power of description about the substantial existence of God in things and the unification of the self with God and of God with human subjectivity.[24]

The judgments of Leibniz and Hegel about Angelus Silesius are only intended to briefly allude to the fact that the words cited from "Without Why" stem from an influential source. But one might immediately point out that this source is indeed mystical and poetic. The one as well as the other belong equally little in thinking. Certainly not *in* thinking, but perhaps *before* thinking. Leibniz and Hegel, whose thinking it is difficult to surpass in sobriety and rigor, testify to this.

Let us take a look at what is going on in the mystical words of Angelus Silesius.

> The rose is without why, it blooms because it blooms,
> It pays no attention to itself, asks not whether it is seen.

First, one should recall the short formulation of the Leibnizian *principium reddendae rationis*. It reads: Nothing is without a why. The words of Angelus Silesius speak bluntly to the contrary: "The rose is without why." Obviously the rose here stands as an example for all blooming things, for all plants and all growth. According to the words of the poet, the principle of reason does not hold in this field. On the contrary, botany will easily point out to us a chain of causes and conditions for the growth of plants. For proof of this we make use of the fact that, despite the saying of Angelus Silesius, the growth of plants has its why, that is, its necessary grounds without ever having had to bother with science. Everyday experience speaks for the necessity of the grounds of growth and blooming.

But it is superfluous to simply give an account of this necessity of grounds to the poet, for in the very same line he confirms this himself.

> The rose is without why; it blooms because it blooms.

"Because"? Does this word not name the relationship to a ground by dragging one in, so to speak? The rose—without why and yet not without a because. So the poet contradicts himself and speaks obscurely. Indeed the mystical consists in this sort of thing. But the poet speaks clearly. "Why" and "because" mean different things. "Why" is the word for the question concerning grounds. The "because" contains the answer-yielding reference to grounds. The "why" seeks grounds. The "because" conveys grounds. What is different here is the way in which the relationship to grounds is represented. In the "why" the relationship to grounds is one of seeking. In the "because" the relationship to grounds is one of conveying. But that which the different relationships concern—grounds —remains, so it seems, the same. Insofar as the first part of the first verse denies the presence of grounds and the second part of the same verse explicitly affirms the existence of grounds through the "because," there is indeed a contradiction present, that is, a simultaneous affirmation and negation of the same thing, namely of grounds. But are the grounds that the "why" seeks and the grounds that the "because" conveys equivalent? The second verse of the saying gives the answer. It contains the comment on the first verse. The entire fragment is so astoundingly clear and neatly constructed that one is inclined to get the idea that the most extreme sharpness and depth of thought belongs to the genuine and great mystics. This is also true. Meister Eckehart proves it.

The second verse in the saying of Angelus Silesius reads:

> It pays no attention to itself, asks not whether it is seen.

The first part of the second verse tells us how the "without" in the first part of the first verse is to be understood: the rose is a rose without its having to pay any attention to itself. It doesn't need to expressly take itself into consideration. Because of the way in which the rose is, it is not in need of expressly considering itself, and that means of considering all that belongs to it, inasmuch as it determines the rose, which means, founds it. It blooms because it blooms. An attention to grounds does not insert itself in between its blooming and the grounds for blooming, thanks to which grounds could first be *as* grounds. Angelus Silesius does not want to deny that the blooming of the rose has a ground. It blooms because—it blooms. Contrary to this, in order to be in the essential possibilities of their existence, humans must pay attention to what grounds are determinative for them, and how they are so. But the fragment of Angelus Silesius does not speak about this, indeed because he has something still more concealed in mind. The grounds that essentially determine humans as having a *Geschick* stem from the essence of grounds. Therefore these grounds are abysmal [22] (cf. what is said below about the other tonality of the principle of reason). But blooming happens to the rose inasmuch as it is absorbed in blooming and pays no attention to what, as some other thing—namely, as cause and condition of the blooming—could first bring about this blooming. It does not first need the ground of its blooming to be expressly rendered to it. It is another matter when it comes to humans. How humans relate to grounds comes to light in the second verse of the fragment.

Here is what is said about the rose:

> It pays no attention to itself, asks not whether it is seen.

Humans live so differently from the rose that, as they go about doing things in their world, they glance sidelong at what the world makes and requires of them. But even where such sidelong-glancing is absent, we humans cannot come to be who we are without attending to the world that determines us—an attending in which we at the same time attend to ourselves. The rose has no need of this. Thought from the point of view of Leibniz, this means that in order for the rose to bloom, it does not need reasons rendered in which its blooming is grounded. The rose is a rose without a *reddere rationem*, a rendering of reasons, having to belong to its rose-being. Nevertheless the rose is never without a ground.

The relationship of the rose to what the principle of reason says is, so it seems, two-fold.

The rose is indeed without why, yet it is not without a ground. "Without why" and "without a ground" are not equivalent. This is precisely what the cited fragment is first of all supposed to make clearer. Insofar as it is something, the rose does not fall outside of the orbit of the mighty Principle. Yet the way it belongs within this orbit is unique and thereby different from the way we humans, who also reside within the orbit of the principle of reason, belong there. Of course, if we were to jump to conclusions, we might be inclined to believe that the meaning of Angelus Silesius' fragment plays itself out in simply naming the difference between the ways according to which the rose and humans are what they are. What is unsaid in the fragment—and everything depends on this—instead says that humans, in the concealed grounds of their essential being, first truly are when in their own way they are like the rose—without why. We cannot pursue this thought any further here. For the moment we will only contemplate the words "The rose is without why"; we contemplate this in reference to the short, strict formulation of the principle of reason: Nothing is without a why.

What can we gather from this? This: the *principium reddendae rationis* does not hold for the rose and for all that is in the manner of the rose. The rose is *without* the seeking, peering-around rendering of the grounds on the basis of which it blooms. {The ground for the rose's blooming does not have, for the rose, the demand-character which requires *of* and *for* it the rendering of grounds. If it had this character, then that would mean that the rendering of the grounds of blooming *as* the grounds that rule the rose would belong to the blooming of the rose. But the rose blooms because it blooms. Its blooming is a simple arising-on-its-own} At the same time we can justifiably assert that the *principium reddendae rationis* also holds for the rose. Namely, it holds insofar as the rose becomes an object of our cognition and that we require for ourselves some information about the manner in which, that is, by which reasons and causes, under which conditions, the rose can *be* what it is.

So, what's going on here with the *principium reddendae rationis*? It holds *in the case of* the rose, but not for the rose; in the case of the rose, insofar as it is the object of our cognition; not for the rose, insofar as this rose stands alone, simply is a rose.

We see ourselves faced with a remarkable state of affairs: something, like the rose, indeed is not without grounds and yet is without why. Something falls within the jurisdiction of the vulgarly formulated principle of reason. The same something falls outside the jurisdiction of the strictly formulated principle of reason. But for Leibniz and for all modern cognition, the jurisdiction of the principle of reason as strictly conceived is, as we saw in the previous sessions, just as broad, that is, unrestricted, as is the jurisdiction of the principle of reason understood in a vulgar way. For Leibniz, the principle "nothing is without reason" is tantamount to saying "nothing is without a why." According to the fragment of Angelus Silesius this equivalence does not hold.

So by reflecting upon the fragment of Angelus Silesius, the principle of reason has not only become more opaque. The province to which it belongs lies in a fog. As is now apparent, even the attempt to keep ourselves to the strict formulation of the principle of reason does not lead to clarity. So we have dropped the question of whether Leibniz's strict formulation is, so to speak, the fundamental formulation of the fundamental principle of reason, much less whether it is the absolutely true one.

In any case, the reference to the Leibnizian form of the principle of reason has shown us that the character of the demand to render, the *reddendum*, belongs to reason. And at the same time we saw we were forced to the question: from where does this demand of reason stem? Who or what makes the demand to render reasons in and for all cognition?

Are we humans the ones who demand that our cognition in each case render reasons? Or does reason itself, from out of itself as reason, make such a demand on our cognition? But how can reason make a demand? Obviously this question can be answered only if we know sufficiently clearly wherein consists the essence of reason—only if we have first inquired into the essence of reason so as to hear on this path what it is that one calls "reason" and "*ratio*." The principle of reason should provide the most direct information to clarify all this.

How come we have not asked the principle of reason point-blank what it can tell us about reason? How come we have preferred complex detours to the straight path lying at our feet? Answer: because the detours offered us all sorts of perspectives on the principle of reason so that now, and in what follows, we can constantly glance back, as it were, to the principle of reason. For by glancing back on the principle of reason as a fundamental principle and Principle we reach a disconcerting insight. The principle *of* reason states *nothing about* reason. *The principle of reason states nothing directly about the essence of reason.* This state of affairs opened itself to us during the detours we have been traversing around the principle. Let us take good note of it: the principle of reason indeed speaks of reason and yet it is not a statement about reason *qua* reason.

What does the principle of reason say? We will get an answer only if we hear the principle of reason. For that it is necessary to pay attention to the tone in which it speaks. For the principle intones in *two different* tonalities. In each it says something different. Until now we have heard the principle of reason more in an indeterminant tonality. This allowed us to think about the principle of reason in different formulations without contemplating the source of this diversity.

The principle of reason reads: "*Nihil est sine ratione*": "Nothing is without reason." We hear this now often enough, almost to the point of tedium. We should now tune in to how, in this sentence which speaks in a hollow unison, two different tonalities vibrate. We can say: "*Nihil* est *sine* ratione." "*Nothing* is *without* reason." In the affirmative form this means: *everything has* a reason.

Yet we can also set the pitch in this way: "Nihil *est* sine *ratione*." "Nothing *is* without *reason*." In the affirmative form this means: every *being* (*as a being*) has a *reason*. What does the principle of reason speak about?

Lecture Six

The references to the principle of reason yielded by our previous course of reflection place the principle within the horizon opened up by the thinking of Leibniz, from whom it received its basic contours. Ultimately we brought the ordinary and the strict formulations of the principle to their abbreviated forms: "nothing is without reason" and "nothing is without a why." A fragment from Angelus Silesius gave us the occasion to show that the principle of reason generally does not hold in the strict formulation. For contrary to the "nothing is without a why," the fragment says:

> The rose is without why; it blooms because it blooms,
> It pays no attention to itself, asks not whether it is seen.

Roughly put, the "without why" says that the rose has no grounds. Contrary to this, the "because" in the same verse says, roughly speaking, that the rose has a ground. According to this, something such as a rose can simultaneously have a ground and be without grounds. So in the preceding session we said more precisely that the rose is indeed without why, but—in view of the "because" —nevertheless not without grounds. From this we next established what the text says about the rose when we first listened to it: a "without why" and a "because." We will next clarify, in a general way, what is meant by the "why" and by the "because" and do so without regarding the fragment of Angelus Silesius. The "why" and "because" speak of a relationship of our cognition to grounds, a relationship that at times varies. In the "why" we question, we pursue grounds. In the "because" we retrieve grounds in giving an answer. So it seems that we bring grounds into a closer relationship to us with the "because," while with the "why" we distance ourselves from grounds, so to speak. If we take a good look at it, the matter indeed is the reverse. With the "why" we pose a reason so that it stands to answer to us. On the other hand, with the "because" we turn our cognition loose in the direction of grounds and the matter that

41

is to be founded through them. With the "because" we give way to the founded matter; we relinquish the matter to itself and to the way that the grounds, in founding it, simply let the matter be what it is.

Only when taken in the rough does "the rose is without why" say the same thing as "the rose has no ground." Strictly speaking, "without why" means "without a relationship to grounds." But the "because" also names a relationship to grounds. Certainly. We must only bear in mind that what we casually call a relationship is one of the trickiest of all matters, all the more so since we are bewitched by one-sided notions about what we call a relationship. The domain in which it is in play is always normative for every relationship. For example, whoever spends time in some foreign place is denied the dwelling-relationship to a home. The relationship of dwelling in a home is lacking. But this lack of relationship is itself an essential facet of the relationship called "homesickness." [Hence a relationship can consist precisely in its lack.] We provisionally speak, with a certain uniformity, of the relationship to grounds. With the "without why" the relationship to grounds is denied; with the "because" it is affirmed. This remains correct, but also superficial. So we ask:

What does the "without" deny in comparison with the "because"? Not simply the relationship to grounds, but that the rose does without the querying, expressly representational relationship to grounds. On the other hand, the representational relationship to grounds is common to us humans. First of all, this simply shows that grounds can stand in manifold relationships to us as the cognizing creature. But are not animals and even plants also cognizing beings? Certainly. The fundamental experience[23] of Leibnizian thinking goes so far as to say that even what we are in the habit of calling lifeless material engages in representation. According to Leibniz, every being is a *living* being and as such is a representing-striving being. But humans are the only such creatures that can, in their representations, bring before themselves a ground qua ground.[25] According to a traditional definition, humans are the *animal rationale*. Therefore humans live in a representational relationship to *ratio* as the ground. Or must we say the reverse: because humans stand in a representational relationship to *ratio*, they are an *animal rationale*? Or is even this inversion insufficient? In each case, humans live with the faculty of representing grounds *qua* reasons. Other earthly creatures indeed live because of reasons and causes, but never *according to* reasons. One may therefore be tempted to dispose of the second part of the first verse—"it blooms, because it blooms"—and explain that the rose does not live according to reasons, it lives without why, but it lives because of reasons. Yet Angelus Silesius wants to say something quite different with the "it blooms, because it blooms." If he only wanted to bring the difference between the rose and humans into relief, then he could have said: "the rose blooms because the sun shines and because a lot of other things surround and determine it."

But Angelus Silesius says: "It blooms, because it blooms." This really says nothing, for the "because" is supposed to supply something else, something we can understand as the reason for whatever is to be founded. But this apparently vacuous talk—"it blooms, because it blooms"—really says everything, namely, it says everything there is to say here, doing so in its particular manner of not-speaking. The "because" seems to be a non-saying, empty, and yet it speaks plentifully of what can, at the level of this poet's thinking, be said about reason and about the "why." Nevertheless, the path we have traversed till now has not yet reached that level.

Besides this, in the mean time an obstacle pertaining to the path has presented itself upon which we will stumble even more frequently. We have set both of the abbreviated formulations of the principle of reason over against each other: "nothing is without reason"—"nothing is without why." Through a comparison of both principles we became mindful that occasionally—and then necessarily —reason is a represented reason. We are puzzled and would like to ask: can there be some sort of reason which has been dissociated from every "why" and "because" and still be a reason? A thing such as a "reason"—must it not by itself, and thereby necessarily, bear within itself its relationship to us as the thinking being? The answer to this question, as well as the preliminary considera-tion of whether we may question in this manner, depends on how we define what we constantly call "ground" or "reason" and *ratio*. Generally, how we find our way through the obscurity now gathering around the principle of reason —despite the knowledge we have gained about this principle—depends upon this definition.

This clouded perspective on the principle of reason fails to touch on something else. That "something else" is the power with which the *principium magnum, grande et nobilissimum* reigns. For, its bepowering permeates and determines what we could call the spirit of modernity, the spirit of its supposed completion, the spirit of the atomic age.

The *principium rationis* as thought by Leibniz not only determines, by the sort of demand it makes, modern cognition in general, but it permeates in a decisive manner that thinking known as the thinking of thinkers—philosophy. As far as I can see, the full import of this fact has not yet been thought through. So an aside may be slipped in with which we break off entering further into Leibnizian thinking, yet in no way concluding it: At the very least a conclusion would have to include some mention of what amounts to the most concealed, profound vision of Leibnizian thinking. Profound visions light up only in the dark. We easily let ourselves be duped about this. We often have the opinion that we too will have glimpsed what was thoughtfully glimpsed by Leibniz if we stick to the two texts in which Leibniz, as we are wont to say, summarily presented his main ideas. Leibniz composed the two texts a few years before his death, but did not publish them. One of them consists of eighteen large paragraphs; the other of ninety shorter ones. The latter is known under the title *Monadology*, a title which does not come from Leibniz. Those who retrace the thought of these paragraphs will ever anew learn a great deal. Still, the relationship of these paragraphs to the innermost movement of Leibnizian thinking that comes to light in some of the letters is like the relationship that would obtain if Hölderlin had left behind a poetic hymn by simply stringing together twenty paragraphs. And this still holds true today when we can trace the restless movement of Leibnizian thought in the manuscripts of both texts that became accessible only last year through the superb edition of André Robinet.[26] The first edition of the original French text of the *Monadology* first appeared 130 years after Leibniz's death. This thanks to a student of Hegel, Johann Erdmann.[27]

In looking back on the path traversed thus far, it is clear that if we have already given an intonation to the principle of reason, we have held more to the initial tonality, and that not accidentally. For at first we followed the commonplace ideas, interrogative orientations, and references in terms of which philosophy—even Leibniz's philosophy—treats the principle of reason. But since we are asking the principle of reason for some particulars about the essence of reason, we must now ask what the principle of reason is stating. Consequently, what we would like to know is, grammatically speaking, what is the subject and what is the predicate of the sentence. The second tonality helped us answer this question. Therefore it is also the ~~normative~~ one: "Nihil *est* sine *ratione*": "Nothing *is* without *reason.*" Every being has a reason. The subject of the principle of reason is not reason, rather: "Every being"; this is predicated as having a reason. *The principle of reason is, according to the ordinary way of understanding it, not a statement about reason, but about beings, insofar as there are beings.*

Many listeners will now quietly think, Why wasn't this obvious content of the principle of reason mentioned at the very first? Why were we instead led about for hours on detours around the principle of reason? The answer is easy: because our previous treatment of the principle of reason took and still takes it as being a principle, more precisely, as being a fundamental principle and Principle. The fundamental principle of reason indeed represents reason within a frame of reference that is essential, yet from within this frame of reference it speaks about beings and not about reason. Nevertheless, this representation of reason—as inchoately defined as it is—does make it possible for the principle of reason to have its role as the guiding principle in the derivation and founding of propositions. Seen from this point of view, this representation of reason that finds itself in the forefront has the distinction of being underivable. Even if the principle of reason posits what it posits simply on the basis of a reference to reason and is not an immediate statement about reason, the previous treatment of the *principium rationis* still remains of the greatest significance, not only in regard to its content but also as something given to us by the tradition.

If we try to discuss the principle of reason, then such an effort, like every other one, is only possible as a conversation within and with the tradition. But the tradition of previous thinking and what it has thought is not a chaotic hodge-podge of derivative philosophical views. The tradition is present, granted that we seek out the thinking given us by the tradition at that place from which, in the broadest sense, it carries us out beyond ourselves and expressly joins us to the tradition. Therefore, and only therefore, do we wander around in detours around the principle of reason.

Indeed, if we were now to directly address the principle of reason and thereby find that it doesn't at all accomplish what its title would lead us to believe, then we would have taken an important step in ascertaining this, but still this would hardly assure us that by taking this step our discussion of the principle of reason has reached a path with a panoramic perspective. Consequently our discussion of the principle of reason seeks a perspective on what is said but not articulated in the principle of reason. The perspective we now seek for our thinking is the one in which the thinking undertaken up till now already moves, a perspective which the tradition will open up to us only if we bring into view what it brings to us.

But this perspective has been blocked and distorted for a long time. The block is the principle of reason which has shoved itself into the perspective like a mountain range, a mountain range that seems to be impassable; for the principle of reason is, as the supreme fundamental principle, something underivable, the sort of thing which puts a check on thinking.

Achieving the insight that the principle *of* reason does *not* immediately speak *about* reason, rather about beings, is a dangerous step. It leads into a critical zone of thinking. We need to be helped out because our thinking often remains stranded at decisive points even when it is quite practiced. A reflection on the path offers such help. We name the zone we now have hit upon "the critical zone" because here all the steps of the discussion yet to come can still run awry despite our seeing what the principle of reason speaks about. This holds for my article "On the Essence of Reasons" which first appeared as a contribution to the Festschrift for E. Husserl in 1929.[28]

In the first paragraph of the first part of that essay one finds the following: "The principle (that is, the principle of reason) speaks *about beings*, and this on the basis of having a view of something like 'reason'. Yet what the essence of reason amounts to is not defined *in* this principle. That is presupposed *by* this principle as an obvious 'idea' [*Vorstellung*]."

These statements remain correct. Nevertheless they run awry—first, in regard to the possible paths that the principle of reason offers for the specific question concerning the essence of reasons; second, and above all, in reference to that reflection, which beckons all thinking, in whose service even the article mentioned seeks to place itself. Wherein consists the running-awry in the case before us? In general, how is it possible to run awry despite correctly ascertaining something? In a simple and thereby doubly errant manner. It befalls thinking often enough. Therefore, the errant course we have in view can instruct us as soon as we simply attend to it.

Sometimes we see and clearly have before our eyes a state of affairs. Nevertheless, we do not bring into view what is most obvious in what lies present before us. Seeing something and expressly bringing into view what is seen are not the same thing. Here, bringing into view [er-blicken] means to see into [ein-blicken] that which genuinely looks [anblickt] at us from out of what is seen—which means, what looks at us in terms of what is most proper to it. We see a great deal and bring into view very little. Even when we have brought into view what is seen, seldom are we capable of sustaining the aspect [Anblick] of what is brought into view and of holding in view what is brought into view. A constantly renewed, that is, more and more original appropriation is needed in order for mortals to have a true beholding of something. When thinking does not bring into view what is most proper to what is seen, then thinking looks past what lies present before it. The danger that thinking may overlook things is often exacerbated by thinking itself, namely by the fact that thinking too hastily presses forward to a false rationale. Such a pressing forward can be especially detrimental to a discussion of the principle of reason.

We can now apply what was briefly said about seeing, bringing into view, and overlooking to the case of the article entitled "On the Essence of Reasons." For in this article, it is plain as day that the principle "nothing is without reason" says something about beings and doesn't shed the slightest bit of light on what "reason" means. But this view of the apparent content of the principle does not attain an insight into what lies closest at hand. Instead it allows itself to be compelled to take a step that is almost unavoidable. Thus, we can portray this step as an inference:

The principle of reason is a statement about beings. Accordingly, it gives us no information about the essence of reason. So, especially in its traditional formulation, the principle of reason is not fit as a guide for a discussion of what we have in mind when we contemplate the essence of reason. We see that the principle of reason says something about beings. But what do we keep from coming into view if we acquiesce to this assessment? What is there in what we have seen that can still be brought into view? We come closer here to what can be brought into view as soon as we more clearly hear—and keep in our ear—the principle of reason in that intonation that we provisionally called the normative intonation: "Nihil est sine ratione": "Nothing is without reason." The intonation allows us to hear a unison between the "is" and "reason," est and ratio. Indeed we already heard this unison before we made the assessment that the principle of reason speaks about beings and their having a reason.

Our thinking should now bring into view what has really already been heard in the intonation. Thinking should bring into view something one can hear. In so doing it brings into view what was un-heard (of) [Un-erhört][24] before.

Thinking is a listening [*Erhören*] that brings something to view. Therefore, in thinking both ordinary hearing and seeing pass away for us, for thinking brings about in us a listening and a bringing-into-view.[25] These are strange and yet very old directives. If Plato named what constitutes the genuine element of beings ιδέα—the face of beings and that which is viewed by us; if, still earlier, Heraclitus named what constituted the genuine element in beings λόγος—the locution of beings to which we respond in hearing—then these both serve us notice that thinking is a hearing and a seeing.

Yet we are quick on the draw in explaining that thinking can be called a hearing and seeing only in a figurative sense. No doubt. What one listens to and brings into view in thinking cannot be heard with our ears nor seen with our eyes. It is not perceivable by our sense organs. If we take thinking to be a sort of hearing and seeing, then sensible hearing and seeing is taken up and over into the realm of nonsensible perception, that is, of thinking. In Greek such transposing is called μεταφέρειν. The language of scholars names such a carrying-over "metaphor." So thinking may be called a hearing and listening, a viewing and a bringing into view only in a metaphorical, figurative sense. Who says "may" here? Those who assert that hearing with the ears and seeing with the eyes is genuine hearing and seeing.

When we perceive something in hearing and seeing, the manner in which this happens is through the senses, it is sensible. This assessment is correct. Nevertheless it is still untrue, for it leaves out something essential. Of course we hear a Bach fugue with our ears, but if we leave what is heard only at this, with what strikes the tympanum as sound waves, then we can never hear a Bach fugue. *We* hear, not the ear. Of course we hear through the ear, but not with the ear if "with" here means the ear is a sense organ that conveys to us what is heard. If at some later time the human ear becomes dull, that is, deaf, then it can be, as is clear in the case of Beethoven, that a person nevertheless still hears, perhaps hears even more and something greater than before. Along with this, one should take note that "deaf" or "dumb"[26] have the sense of being dull, which is why the same word *tumb* can also be found to occur in the Greek word τυφλός, that is, dull in seeing, thus blind.

Whatever is heard by us never exhausts itself in what our ears, which from a certain point of view can be seen as separate sense organs, can pick up. More precisely, if *we* hear, something is not simply added to what the ear picks up; rather, what the ear perceives and how it perceives will already be attuned and determined by what *we* hear, be this only that we hear the titmouse and the robin and the lark. Of course our hearing organs are in a certain regard necessary, but they are never the sufficient condition for our hearing, for that hearing which accords and affords us whatever there really is to hear.

The same holds for our eyes and our vision. If human vision remained confined to what is piped in as sensations through the eye to the retina, then, for instance, the Greeks would never have been able to see Apollo in a statue of a young man or, to put this in a better way, they would never have been able to see the statue in and through Apollo. There was a thought familiar to the old Greek thinkers, a thought that one all too crudely portrays thus: like is only known through like. What is meant is that what speaks to us only becomes perceivable through our response. Our hearing is in itself a responding. In the introduction to his *Theory of Colors*,[29] Goethe refers to that Greek thought and sought to express it in German rhyme in the following manner.

> Were not the eye a thing of sun,
> How could we ever glimpse the light?
> If in us God's own power'd not run
> Could we in the divine delight?[27]

It seems that up till today we have not yet sufficiently pondered what the sunliness of the eye consists of and where in us God's own power is to be found, to what extent both belong together and give the directive to a more profoundly thought human being, to humans who are the thinking creatures.

But here the following consideration suffices. Because our hearing and seeing is never a mere sensible registering, it is therefore also off the mark to insist that thinking as listening and bringing-into-view are only meant as a transposition of meaning, namely as transposing the supposedly sensible into the nonsensible. The idea of "transposing" and of metaphor is based upon the distinguishing, if not complete separation, of the sensible and the nonsensible as two realms that subsist on their own. The setting up of this partition between the sensible and nonsensible, between the physical and nonphysical is a basic trait of what is called metaphysics and which normatively determines Western thinking. Metaphysics loses the rank of the normative mode of thinking when one gains the insight that the above-mentioned partitioning of the sensible and nonsensible is insufficient.

When one gains the insight into the limitations of metaphysics, "metaphor" as a normative conception also becomes untenable—that is to say that metaphor is the norm for our conception of the essence of language. Thus metaphor serves as a handy crutch in the interpretation of works of poetry and of artistic production in general. The metaphorical exists only within metaphysics.

What's going on with these references that look more like digressions? They are intended to make us wary so that we don't precipitously take the talk of thinking as a listening and a bringing-into-view to be mere metaphors and thus take them too lightly. If our human-mortal hearing and viewing doesn't have its genuine element in mere sense reception, then it also can't be completely unheard of that what can be heard can at the same time be brought into view, if thinking views with an ear and hears with an eye.[28] This sort of thing happens when, in hearing the unison of "is" and "reason" in the intonation of the principle of reason "Nothing *is* without *reason*," we bring something obvious into view that is present in the content of the statement of the principle of reason. What do we bring into view when we think about the principle of reason in the tonality introduced here? "Nothing *is*. . . ." What does "is" mean? From grammar we know that "is" belongs to the conjugations of the helping verb "to be". Yet it is not necessary to resort to grammar. The content of the sentence affords us plenty of information. "Nothing," that is, no being whatsoever "*is*—without *reason*." Even if it does so completely indeterminantly, the "is" always names the being of some being. So the principle of reason, which is offered as a statement about beings, says: to the being of beings there belongs something like ground/ reason. Consequently, the principle of reason proves to be not only a statement about beings; even more, what we bring into view is that the principle of reason speaks of the being of beings. What does the principle say? The principle of reason says: *to being there belongs something like ground/reason. Being is akin to grounds, it is ground-like.* The sentence "Being is ground-like" speaks quite differently than the statement "beings have a reason." "Being is ground-like" thus in no way means "being has a ground"; rather, it says: *being in itself essentially comes to be as grounding.*[29] Of course the principle of reason does not say this explicitly. The content of the principle one immediately perceives leaves unsaid what the principle of reason says. What[30] the principle of reason says does not come to language, namely, not to that language that corresponds *to that about which* the principle of reason speaks. *The principle of reason is an uttering [Sagen] of being.* It is this, but in a concealed manner. What remains concealed is not only what it says; what also remains concealed is *that* it speaks of being.

Lecture Seven

Now—that is to say, in the following sessions—everything depends on whether or not we remain gathered into what the principle of reason says implicitly. If we remain on the way to such a gathering, then we will be able to genuinely hear the principle.

The principle of reason is one of those principles that remains silent about what is most proper to it. Whatever remains silent divulges nothing. To hear what is silent requires a hearing that each of us has and no one uses correctly. This hearing [*Gehör*] has something to do not only with the ear, but also with a human's belonging [*Zugehörigkeit*] to what its essence is attuned to. Humans are at-tuned [*ge-stimmt*] to what de-termines [*be-stimmt*] their essence.[31] In this de-termining, humans are touched and called forth by a voice [*Stimme*] that peals all the more purely the more it silently reverberates through what speaks.

The principle of reason sounds like this: "*nothing* is *without* reason": "*Nihil est sine* ratione." We call this formulation of the principle the ordinary one. It implies that the principle at first and for a long time never stood out as a special principle. What it states is unremarkably common in the life of human cognition. Contrary to this, Leibniz extricated the principle of reason from its position of indifference and brought it to the level of a supreme fundamental principle. Leibniz brought the fundamental principle into the strict formulation of the *principium reddendae rationis sufficientis*. According to this formulation the principle of reason says: Nothing is without a sufficient reason, which demands to be rendered. In the affirmative form this means that every being has its sufficient reason, which must be rendered. In short: "*nothing* is *without* reason."

But finally we heard the principle of reason in a different tonality. Instead of "*Nothing* is *without* reason," it now sounds like this: "Nothing *is* without *reason*." The pitch has shifted from the "nothing" to the "is" and from the "without" to the "reason." The word "is" in one fashion or another invariably names being. This shift in pitch lets us hear an accord between being and reason. Heard in the new tonality, the principle of reason says that to being there belongs something like ground/reason. The principle now speaks of being. What the

50

principle now says, however, easily falls prey to a misinterpretation. "Ground/ reason belongs to being"—one might be inclined to understand this in the sense of "being has a reason," that is, "being is grounded." The popularly understood and presumably valid *principium rationis* never speaks of this. According to the principle of reason, only beings are ever grounded. On the contrary, "ground/ reason belongs to being" is tantamount to saying: being *qua* being grounds.[32] Consequently only beings ever have their grounds.

The new tonality reveals the principle of reason as a principle of being. Correspondingly, if we now discuss the principle in the new tonality, we move in the realm of what one can, with a general term, call the "question of being." If we understand the principle of reason as a principle of being, then we drop, or so it seems, the question of the essence of ground/reason. But the exact opposite holds true. The discussion of the essence of ground/reason first reaches its proper realm through the other intonation of the principle of reason. It may now be worthwhile to bring into view the fact that, and in which sense, something like ground/reason belongs to the essence of being. Being and ground/reason belong together. Ground/reason receives its essence from its belonging together with being qua being. Put in the reverse, being reigns qua being from out of the essence of ground/reason. Ground/reason and being ("are") the same—not equivalent—which already conveys the difference between the names "being" and "ground/reason". Being "is" in essence: ground/reason. Therefore being can never first have a ground/reason which would supposedly ground it. Accordingly, ground/reason is missing from being. Ground/reason remains at a remove from being.[33] Being "is" the abyss in the sense of such a remaining-apart of reason from being. To the extent that being as such grounds, it remains groundless. "Being" does not fall within the orbit of the principle of reason, rather only beings do.

If we painstakingly attend to the language in which we articulate what the principle of reason says as a principle of being, then it becomes clear that we speak of being in an odd manner that is, in truth, inadmissable. We say: being and ground/reason "are" the same. Being "is" the abyss. When we say something "is" and "is such and so," then that something is, in such an utterance, represented as a being. Only a being "is"; the "is" itself—being—"is" not. This wall in front of you and behind me *is*. It immediately shows itself to us as something present. But where is its "is"? Where should we seek the presencing of the wall? Probably these questions already run awry. Nevertheless the wall "is."

Hence, there is a peculiar state of affairs with the "is" and "being." In order to respond to it, we articulate what the principle of reason says as a principle of being as follows: Being and ground/reason: the same. Being: the abyss. As we remarked, to say "being" "is" ground/reason is inadmissable. This way of speaking, which is virtually unavoidable, does not apply to "being"; it does not hit upon its proper character.

On the one hand we say: being and ground/reason—the same. On the other hand we say: being—the abyss. It would be worthwhile to think the univocity of both "sentences" [*Sätze*], of phrases [*Sätze*] that are no longer "propositions" [*Sätze*].

This requires nothing less than that the manner of our thinking transform itself, transform itself such that it responds to the state of affairs that the principle of reason means when speaking as a principle of being. We arrive at this transformation of thinking neither through an exacting theory, nor through some sort of sorcery, but only by setting out on a path, by building a path that leads into the vicinity of the state of affairs we have mentioned. In so doing, it becomes clear that such paths themselves belong to the state of affairs. The nearer we come to the matter at hand, the more significant becomes the path. So if our manner of proceeding in the ensuing exposition often speaks of the path, then the matter at hand comes to language. Discussions of the path are not mere considerations of methodology; they are not merely the preparations of a drawing pencil that is never put to paper. They serve us well in reaching the realm of that state of affairs about which the principle of reason speaks as a principle of being.

This is the task of the coming sessions. We may then finally be in a position to have the opportunity to experience and appreciate for ourselves what this means: "being and ground/reason: the same" and "being: the abyss." If we discuss the principle of reason as a principle of being, we follow it off to that place to which the principle, if thought genuinely, removes us. But before we attempt a discussion of the principle of reason as a principle of being, let's think back for a moment on the beginning of the first session of the whole lecture course. It began:

> The principle of reason reads: *nihil est sine ratione*. One translates it: nothing is without a reason. What the principle states is illuminating.

On the basis of the point we have reached on our path, we can ascertain the following about these sentences: at the beginning of the lecture course the principle of reason was spoken in the commonplace tonality. Accordingly, the principle says: everything has a reason. But now, after it has been shown that the principle of reason admits of a change in tonality—perhaps even calls for one—we can no longer hold back the question: why wasn't the change in tonality immediately introduced at the beginning of the entire lecture course? How come the principle of reason wasn't immediately and exclusively thought in the new tonality? If we had, the principle of reason would have come to light as a principle of being from the very beginning. We could have dispensed with everything that has been presented in the previous sessions, provided that it is necessary to think through the principle of reason as a principle of being.

In a certain sense these points are well taken, but they do not justify our holding the path traversed till now as being unnecessary. To what extent would we have been able to bring forward immediately, at the beginning of the lecture course, the principle in the other tonality after only a short introduction of the principle of reason in the ordinary tonality? To the extent that the second tonality is not derived from the first. The second tonality rings out on its own without having any support in the first tonality. The change of tonality is sudden. Behind the change in tonality is concealed a leap of thinking. Without a bridge, that is, without the steadiness of a progression, the leap brings thinking into another realm and into another manner of speaking. Therefore, we admit that the course of the previous sessions did not chart a transition from the realm of the principle of reason into the realm of a principle of being.

As was frequently and intentionally noted, we followed detours around the principle of reason. These detours have brought us closer to the leap. Of course these detours can not replace the leap, much less execute it. But in a certain regard they have their place, namely, as a preparation for the leap. Therefore, let us now briefly recall the main points we came upon on the detour around the principle of reason. They are five in number. Recalling the five main points is intended to do more than report on what has already been said. Recalling them is intended to afford us a view into the inner connection of the five main points. This inner connection points to something unitary and unique *upon* [*an*] which we must *think* [*denken*] after the leap. In fact, we only reach such a recollective thinking-upon [*Andenken*] through the leap. With this it will then become noticeably clearer to what extent the leap from the principle of reason into the principle of being was prepared by what we have gone through up till now.

The path of the previous sessions leads us to and through a field which the leap needs for the leap-off. The leap itself hangs in the air. In what air, in what ether? We only learn this through the leap. The principle of reason is not only a principle in the sense of a supreme fundamental principle. The principle [*Satz*] of reason is a *Satz* in the eminent sense of being a leap. [The German] language knows the form of speech: With a vault, that is, with a sudden leap he was out the door. The principle of reason is a vault into the essence of being in the sense of such a leap. We really ought not any longer say the principle of reason is a principle of being; rather, we should say that the principle of reason is a leap into being qua being, that is, qua ground/reason.

The *first* of the five main points was fleetingly touched upon when we were talking about the *incubation period* of the principle of reason. What the principle of reason states in its ordinary formulation has in some fashion always resounded in Western thought. Yet measured historiographically, two thousand three hundred years were needed until the principle of reason came to light and let itself be set up as a fundamental principle. Our reference to the unusual incubation period of the principle of reason included the following question: "Where and how did the principle of reason sleep for so long and presciently dream what was unthought in it?" We let the question go without an answer.

But now we are already looking, even if still vaguely, in the direction from which an answer can come. Namely, if the principle of reason is a principle of being, then the incubation of the principle of reason is connected with what the principle in truth says, namely, that being is really still sleeping. With this we in no way mean to say that there was no being during the incubation period of the principle of reason. The history of Ancient and Medieval metaphysics testifies to the fact that being has always already come to light in the questioning of beings as such. What we said about the sleeping of being means to say that being *as such* has not yet awakened so that It looks upon us from out of its wakened essence. So long as the essence of being withdraws, we also cannot bring into view what it presciently dreamed. However, if we experience the principle of reason in the sense of a leap into being as such, then we are afforded another perspective. What we called the incubation period of the principle of reason now reveals itself as an epoch in which being *qua* being withdraws. The essence of being conceals itself in this withdrawal. This in no way means that being simply remains concealed. For the shining of being is in play in the appearing of beings as soon as beings as such appear in their being. This can be made clear through any randomly chosen everyday experience. There is no need for a hand-picked case to show this. If, for example, the meadows turn green in the spring, then in the appearing of the greening meadows, that is, in the appearing of this being, there comes to shine the prowess and rule of nature. Yet, we wander through the greening meadows without nature *qua* nature expressly bringing itself to shine forth. And even if we thereby have an inkling of the essence of nature and grasp what we have inkling of in a definitive representation or even in a concept proper, then the essence of nature still keeps itself concealed, as does being. Yet the self-concealing of the essence of being at the same time is precisely the manner that being bestows itself, proffers itself to us in beings. From this proffering comes the *Geschick*, by virtue of which there is the incubation of the principle of reason.

The *second* of the five main points was mentioned when we showed that and how Leibniz brought the principle of reason into the strict formulation of the *principium reddendae rationis sufficientis*. By being explicitly elevated to one of the supreme fundamental principles, the principle of reason first came to the fore and, so to speak, blossomed as a principle having the character of a Principle. The incubation period of the principle of reason thereby came to an end. The incubation of the principle of reason happens by virtue of the *Geschick* of being, a *Geschick* in which being as such withdraws. Now if the incubation of the principle of reason finds its end with the setting up of the principle of reason as one of the supreme fundamental principles, then this ending of the incubation must be due to the fact that, in the meantime, the *Geschick* of being has taken a turn, presumably in the sense that being as such has awakened and come to the fore. *But it is precisely at this point that the end of the incubation period of the principle of reason does not come to an end.* Indeed something in the *Geschick* of being has taken a turn, but in a totally different sense. For the principle of reason to expressly become sovereign as the supreme fundamental principle, the genuine power of the principle of reason as the *principium rationis* must first of all be set loose. The sovereignty of the principle of reason begins *only now* in the obvious sense that all cognition thoroughly responds to the demand that sufficient reasons be unconditionally rendered for every being. Because of this, the possibility of the principle of reason coming to light as a leap into being completely disappeared from view for a long time. Accordingly, we may venture to say that, in the meantime, being *qua* being still more decisively withdraws as compared to the above-mentioned incubation period of the principle of reason. But now we hear that the withdrawal of being only reigns in such a way that what withdraws simultaneously and directly abides in a shining-forth. This happens because beings as such appear in a new manner according to which they intrude and *impose* themselves on cognition. Beings appear as objects. Being comes to shine in the objectness of objects. Through a certain reciprocity, the objectness of objects, the Objectivity of Objects comes to have a bearing on the subjectivity of subjects. Being, as the objectness of objects, gets distended [*eingespannt*] into the relation between cognition and the subject. From then on this relation between subject and Object counts as the sole realm wherein a decision is made about beings regarding their being, the realm wherein a decision about being is always made solely in terms of the objectness of the object but never about being as such. Insofar as being appears in the objectness of the object, it surrenders its determinability to cognition understood in the sense of reflective representation which renders beings to cognition as objects. Thus, for the first time a realm is opened up which is expressly oriented toward the possibility of rendering the ground of beings. And with this one has, for the first time, the possibility of what we call the modern natural sciences and modern technology. The contemporary, often hackneyed battle over the sort and scope of the validity of the principle of causality has whatever footing it has only because those who participate in the battle all stand under the same demand to render sufficient reasons for cognition.

The process determining a new epoch of the withdrawal is one in which being adapts itself to the *objectness* of objects, but which, in its essence as being, thereby withdraws. This epoch characterizes the innermost essence of the age we call modernity.

So we must say that when the incubation period of the principle of reason came to an end with Leibnizian thinking, the incubation of the principle of reason as it has been known since Leibniz indeed ceases, but in no way does the incubation of the principle of reason as a principle of being cease. Rather, because the principle of reason has achieved sovereignty as a fundamental principle, as the *principium reddendae rationis sufficientis*, the incubation of the principle has been, so to speak, pushed back into a still deeper sleep, into a still more decisive withdrawal of being as such. Today it seems that the withdrawal of the essence of being is complete. We say "today" and mean the atomic age which is beginning, an age through which modernity supposedly comes to completion insofar as the initial, basic trait of this epoch unrestrictedly unfolds to its furthest extremity.

The *third* of the main points was mentioned when we discussed the *principium reddendae rationis sufficientis* as the "*principium grande, magnum et noblissimum*," as the mighty, forceful, and eminent Principle. At that point it merited demonstrating that the demand of reason to be rendered was not exhausted in counting as an abstract rule of thinking. The demand was bepowering in a strange way, namely, that the energies of nature as well as the mode of their procurement and use determine the historical existence of humanity on earth. That nature appears in these energies means that nature has become an object, and indeed one of a cognition that exhibits and secures natural processes as calculable stuff.

We add the following question concerning that which is bepowering about the principle of reason:

From where does reason's demand to be rendered speak? Does this demand lie in the essence of reason itself?

The path to the answer to even this question has been pointed out by now. Namely, if the principle of reason is in truth a principle of being, if ground/reason and being say the same thing, then the *Geschick* of being reigns, in a manner previously unprecedented, in the expressly bepowering demand of reason to be provided. Here we find some backing for the idea that in the most extreme withdrawal of being thinking first brings the essence of being into view. Presumably, this is wholly in line with human nature, provided we are indeed so fashioned that what belongs to us first comes to light in the privation of what is lost.

Bringing the essence of being into view—according to our exposition this means to think the essence of ground/reason as one with being as such. Such a project must, at the very beginning of its preparations, pay attention to the fact that what is called "ground/reason" can stand in a variety of relationships to what ground/reason grounds and how it founds it.

The *fourth* of the five main points was mentioned when we thought about a *fragment of Angelus Silesius*, who was a younger contemporary of Leibniz.

The rose is without why, but not without grounds. The "why" names the reason that always grounds in such a way that it is simultaneously represented as a ground. However, in order to be a rose, that is, in order to bloom, the rose does not need expressly to represent the ground of its blooming. Yet the rose that "blooms, because it blooms" is not without a ground. The "because" names a ground, but an odd and presumably distinguished ground. What does this mean, the rose "blooms, because it blooms"? Here the "because" does not, as is ordinary, point off toward something else which is not a blooming and which is supposed to found the blooming from somewhere else. The "because" of the fragment simply points the blooming back to itself. The blooming is grounded in itself, it has its ground with and in itself. The blooming is a pure arising on its own, a pure shining. "But what is beautiful, happily shines in itself,"[34] says Mörike in the final verse of his poem "Auf eine Lampe."[30] According to this, beauty is not a property that is added to a being as an attribute. Beauty is a lofty manner of being, which here means the pure arising-on-its-own and shining. The eldest of the Greek thinkers said Φύσις; we perversely adulterate what this word says when we translate it with "nature." The "because" names the ground, but in the fragment the ground is the simple blooming of the rose, its rose-being. The fragment "the rose is without why" does not disavow the principle of reason. Rather, the principle of reason resounds in a manner such that ground/reason can, in a certain regard, be brought into view as being and being as ground/reason. Nevertheless, this resonance does not let itself be explicitly heard much less thought about further in the realm of thinking typical of the fragment. Moreover, this resonance of ground/reason with being dies away unnoticed in favor of the demand of the *principium grande*. This dying away nevertheless is connected to what we named the *Geschick* of being, a *Geschick* which reigns in a manner such that being as such ever more decisively withdraws and indeed withdraws in favor of the priority that seems to be accorded solely to beings as that which is objective.

The *fifth* of the five main points was mentioned when we spoke the principle of reason *in a different tonality*, thereby referring to the possible diversity of pitches in the principle. Often, many sentences that we speak allow for various intonations of the individual words. In the present case the change in tonality is no random matter; rather, it is a main issue, even the main issue that determines the coming path. For through the change of tonality we hear the principle of reason become a totally different principle, different not only in reference to what the principle means as a principle of being, but also in relation to the manner in which it says what it says, the manner in which it is still a "principle." In regard to the manner of saying, we see we are faced by the question of whether the principle of being is at all still a principle or sentence in the sense of grammar and logic. Let us pay close attention to the formulation in which we articulate and write out the principle of being. The recollection of the five main points is:

1. The incubation of the principle of reason.
2. The setting up of the principle of reason as one of the supreme fundamental principles.

3. The claim of the principle of reason as the claim of the mighty Principle that determines our age.
4. Ground/reason as "why" and as "because."
5. The change of tonality in the principle of reason.

This recollection assembles our view of a simple state of affairs about whose unitariness and uniqueness we think if we think the principle [Satz] of reason as a leap [Satz] into being as such, that means if we carry out this "leap."

Lecture Eight

When heard in the other tonality as a principle of being, the principle of reason says this: being and ground/reason: the same; being: the a-byss. We seem to plunge into the fathomless via this principle. But something else happens. The principle of being shocks us, and from a direction we do not expect. In order to absorb the approaching shock, it will be necessary to bring into view all that came into view in the previous lecture, and do so with a view to its gathering unity. As a Principle, as the supreme fundamental principle, the principle of reason is a general principle. Whatever is ungraspable in general principles is normally due to the fact that we neglect to apply them.[35] An application turns to individual cases which then, as examples taken from what is clear as day, convey to us what the principle says generally and, as it were, without any real support. Now, we apply the principle of reason more often than we think. Everywhere we find things founded and such things that found, even if it is only in the prevalent mode of causation. What effects and is effected, what grounds and is grounded is, in our eyes, the whole of what is real. The principle of reason articulates what, for it, is obvious in the form *Nihil est sine causa*. Seen in this way, the principle of reason holds nothing ungraspable. This strikes us only when we contemplate the principle of reason in the opposite direction, so to speak—not in the direction of the regions and fields of its application, but rather in the direction of its own provenance, in the direction of that *from whence* the principle itself speaks. What is ungraspable about the principle now no longer lies in a neglect on our part to apply [*Anwendung*] it, but in the principle lodging [*Zu-wendung*] its claim on us. This, from whence the claim of the principle speaks, we call the site of the principle of reason. The path that is to lead to this site and is to first explore this site, we call the discussion situating the principle of reason.

Everything rests on the path. This means two different things. First, it means that it all comes down to the path, to our finding it and remaining on it—

which means to our persistence in staying "under way." The paths of thinking that belong to the situating discussion have the peculiar character that when we are under way on them we are nearer to the site than when, in order to become ensconced there, we convince ourselves that we have reached the site; for the site is of a different nature than a station or a place in space. What we call the site—here the site of the principle of reason—is what assembles what comes to be essential of a matter.

Second, that everything rests on the path suggests that everything we must bring into view shows itself only under way on the path. Whatever is to be brought into view lies on the path. Within the purview opened up by the path and through which the path leads, whatever can be brought into view at any given time is gathered from some point along the path. However, in order to reach the path of the discussion situating the principle of reason, we must leap. The leap makes itself known when we listen carefully to a change in the tonality in the principle of reason. In what follows it will become evident why no gradual transition from one tonality into the other is possible here, but that a leap is necessary. Precisely why something lies between what the principle of reason means when it is understood in the customary sense and what the principle of reason says as a principle of being remains a question—a question which at once asks what this "between" is that in some sense we leap over in the leap or, more correctly, that we leap through as through a flame.

However, there is something else we must initially bear in mind in order to keep in view the full breadth and course of the path of the situating discussion. The leap is always a leap from. . . . That from which the leap of thinking leaps is not abandoned in such a leap; rather, the realm from which one leaps first becomes surveyable when one makes the leap—surveyable in a different way than before. The leap of thinking does not leave behind it that from which it leaps; rather, it assimilates it in a more original fashion. According to this view, thinking in the leap becomes a recollective thinking, not of the bygone, but of what has-been. By this we mean the assembling of what does not pass away, but which comes to be essential, that is, lasts, inasmuch as it vouchsafes to recollective thinking new insights. In all that has-been there is harbored a vouchsafing whose treasures often remain unmined through long periods of time, treasures that nonetheless place recollective thinking again and again before an inexhaustible wellspring. Seen in terms of *Geschick*, the greatness of an era is measured not in terms of what of it has passed away and what remains, rather in terms of what of it is transitory—for instance, everything capable of being planned—and, on the contrary, what of it, even before it has come to be, belongs to what has-been insofar as it is something vouchsafed. Only what is vouchsafed holds in itself the guarantee to last.[36] But to last here means to remain as what is vouchsafed rather than simply to persevere as some transitional thing in the void of passing away. What passes and has passed away is innumerable, what has-been is rarer, rarer still is its vouchsafing.

The reference to the five main points should bring us back upon the path which leads through a realm we now know as the realm from which the leap leaps. The leap brings thinking out of the realm of the principle of reason as one of the supreme fundamental principles concerning beings into a saying that speaks of being as such.

The fifth of the main points cited names the change of tonality in the principle of reason, referring thereby to the leap. The first four main points previously mentioned characterize, on the other hand, the realm from which one leaps, and this only in a few respects, though nevertheless in a unified way. How is this so? Precisely in that the issue there was always the *Geschick* and withdrawal of being. More precisely, what we spoke of was the fact that being proffers itself to us in that it withdraws. That not only sounds strange; in fact, at first it is unintelligible because it runs counter to all that is customary to our representational thinking. Nevertheless the reference to the *Geschick* of being was intentionally brought up with the introduction of the first four main points. The term "*Geschick* of being" characterizes the history of Western thinking up till now insofar as we look back on it and into it from out of the leap. We cannot think upon what is called the *Geschick* of being so long as we have not made the leap. The leap is the vault out of the fundamental principle of reason as a principle of beings into the saying of being *qua* being.[37]

Now, even if it is possible to recollectively think upon the *Geschick* of being only from out of the leap, still the experience of the history of Western thinking in the light of the *Geschick* of being cannot be something completely strange, much less something due to an arbitrary construction of history. Therefore, the history of Western thinking must for its part give pointers that, if we follow them, allow us to bring into view—even if in a veiled way—something of what we here call the history of being. The history of being is the "*Geschick*" of being that proffers itself to us in withdrawing its essence.

The following should be noted concerning the use of the word *Geschick* when speaking of the *Geschick* of being:

We usually understand *Geschick* [destiny] as being that which has been determined and imposed through fate: a sorrowful, an evil, a fortunate *Geschick*. This meaning is a derivative one. For *schicken* ["sending"] originally denotes: "preparing," "ordering," "bringing each thing to that place where it belongs"; consequently it also means to "furnish"[38] and "admit"; "to appoint" [*beschicken*] a house, a room, means: "to keep in good order," "straightened up and tidied." Thus in "Sea Song,"[31] one of Stefan George's later and most beautiful poems, he once again heard the old resonance of the words *schicken* ["send"] and *beschicken* ["appoint"]. The poem begins:

> When on earth's rim in gentle fall
> Dips down the fiery crimson ball:

The penultimate strophe reads:

> My roof is tight, my hearth heats well
> And yet a joy does not there dwell.
> The fish nets I did fully point,
> And room and kitchen well appoint.[39]

When we use the word *Geschick* in connection with being, then we mean that being hails us and clears and lights itself, and in clearing it furnishes the temporal play-space wherein beings can appear. In light of the *Geschick* of being, the history of being is not thought of in terms of a happening characterized by a passing away and a process. Rather, the essence of history is determined on the basis of the *Geschick* of being, of being as *Geschick*, of what as such proffers itself to us in withdrawing. Both—proffering and withdrawing—are one and the same, not two different things. In both there reigns, in a different manner, what a moment ago was called vouchsafing; in both—that is, even in the withdrawal, and there even still more essentially. The term "*Geschick* of being" is not an answer but a question, among others the question of the essence of history, insofar as we think history as being and essence in terms of being. At first the *Geschick*-character of being appears quite strange to us—apart from the constantly accompanying difficulty that we may too facilely understand the discussion of being and see this discussion as trailing off into the indeterminant —but at the same time we are at a loss for what, rigorously thought, this means: being. However, if there is some truth in saying that being always proffers itself to us, as such furnishes itself to us and is an offering, then it follows that "being" means something different from "being" as it occurs in the various epochs of its *Geschick*. Yet there reigns in the whole of the *Geschick* of being something that is the same which, however, does not allow itself to be represented by means of a general concept or to be extracted as a lineament from the manifold course of history. However, what is strangest of all is that being proffers itself to us while at the same time withdrawing its essence, concealing this essence in the withdrawal.

But this most strange character of being draws attention to itself early on in the history of Western thinking. It draws attention to itself insofar as the early thinking of the Greeks must, at that point where it completes itself— with Plato and Aristotle—pay special attention to a state of affairs that subsequent thinking held in view but whose implications it did not fathom. In order to bring this state of affairs essentially and briefly into view, we may choose one of many outstanding testimonies. It is found at the beginning of the first chapter of the first book of Aristotle's *Physics*. The *Physics* is a lecture in which he seeks to determine beings that arise on their own, τὰ φύσει ὄντα, with regard to their being. Aristotelian "physics" is different from what we mean today by this word, not only to the extent that it belongs to antiquity whereas the physical sciences belong to modernity, rather above all it is different by virtue of the fact that Aristotle's "physics" is philosophy, whereas modern physics is a positive science that presupposes a philosophy. Aristotle's *Physics* remains the fundamental book of what later is called metaphysics. This book determines the warp and woof of the whole of Western thinking, even at that place where it, as modern thinking, appears to think at odds with ancient thinking. But opposition is invariably comprised of a decisive, and often even perilous, dependence. Without Aristotle's *Physics* there would have been no Galileo.

Aristotle begins his lecture by considering the path upon which thinking reaches the point of circumscribing beings that arise on their own, τὰ φύσει ὄντα, with regard to their being, as well as circumscribing this being as φύσις. "Path" in Greek is ὁδός; μετά means "after"; μεθοδος is the path upon which we pursue a matter: the method. The essential thing is to inquire into the being of beings. The being of what emerges and comes to presence on its own is called φύσις. What is going on with the path of thinking that is under way to φύσις? This path receives its particular character from the way the being of beings is overt for the discerning human. Now, it is always easy to show that particular beings, for example the earth, the sea, the mountains, the flora and fauna at all times lie overtly over against us. That is why they are familiar and immediately accessible to us. But contrary to this, that wherethrough all this—that is, all that which comes to presence on its own—emerges and comes to presence never lies over against us as do particular beings that are present here and there. Being is in no way as immediately familiar and overt to us as are particular beings. It is not as though being keeps itself completely concealed. If this happened, then even beings could never lie over against and be familiar to us. Indeed being must of itself and already beforehand shine, so that particular beings can appear. Were being not to shine, then there would be no province [*Gegend*] within which an "over against" [*ein Gegenüber*] can settle.[40] From this we come to see that, compared to beings which are immediately accessible, being manifests the character of holding itself back, of concealing itself in a certain manner. The nature of the path that is to lead to the determination of the being of beings is determined in accordance with this fundamental trait of being. With a view to the characterization of the path that leads thinking into the *province* of the being of beings, Aristotle says this at the beginning of the lecture on physics:

πέφυκε δὲ ἐκ τῶν γνωριμωτέρων ἡμῖν ἡ ὁδὸς καὶ σαφεστέρων ἐπὶ τὰ σαφέστερα τῇ φύσει καὶ γνωριμώτερα.[32]

A clarifying translation says:

"However, the path (to the being of beings) is by its essence so fashioned and directed that it leads forth from what is more familiar [*Vertrauteren*] to us, namely because for us it is what is more overt, to that which, because it emerges on its own, is in itself more overt and in this sense what is always already taken for granted [*Zugetraute*]."

We must here forego a thorough interpretation of this sentence, whose linguistic construction is equal to the composition of the most beautiful Greek vase painting. The interpretation of the sentence requires going into the first chapter of the first book of Aristotle's *Physics*. This short chapter is the classic introduction to philosophy. Even today it still makes entire libraries of philosophical literature superfluous. Whoever has understood this chapter can venture the first steps in thinking.

In the cited passage Aristotle distinguishes τὰ ἡμῖν σαφέστερα from τὰ σαφέσερα τῇ φύσει. Each is concerned with τὸ σαφές: that which is overt. More precisely, Aristotle on the one hand distinguishes what is more overt insofar as it is seen in terms of us and in regard to our perceiving; on the other hand he distinguishes the more overt which is of such a sort that it opens and manifests itself on its own. The latter is what is meant by the word φύσις: being. The "more overt" first mentioned, that is, that which is more accessible to us, is particular beings. Now, according to Aristotle's sentence the path of philosophy leads from what is more overt to us towards what emerges on its own. Consequently, we never immediately bring being into view. This is due to the fact that our eyes by themselves are not fit for directly bringing being into view, which means that in no way is it due to the fact that being withdraws. But Aristotle's sentence says exactly the opposite of that to which, through its introduction, the sentence was to bear witness for us, namely that being itself withdraws. Aristotle says: φύσις and what belongs to it is τὰ ἁπλῶς σαφέστερα. Being is what of itself is more overt. Without regard to whether or not it is expressly brought into view by us, it already shines; for it already shines even where we experience that which is only for us the more overt: particular beings. These show themselves only in the light of being.

However, if we were to be overhasty and completely ignore what is decisive, then we would concur with the assessment arrived at above that says being of itself is the more overt and is precisely what does not withdraw. If so, the question arises: has being also already cleared and lit its own essence and the provenance of this essence in the aforementioned self-nonwithdrawal? We must answer: no. In this emerging-on-its-own, in φύσις, there reigns after all a self-withdrawal, and this so decisively that without the latter the former could not reign.

Already before Plato and Aristotle, Heraclitus—one of the early Greek thinkers —had said: φύσις κρύπτεσθαι φιλεῖ:[33] being loves (a) self-concealing. But what does φιλεῖν, "to love," mean when thought in a Greek manner? It means: belonging together in the same. Heraclitus wants to say: To being there belongs a self-concealing. With this he in no way says being is nothing other than self-concealing; rather, being essentially comes to be as φύσις, as self-revealing, as what is of itself overt, but to this there belongs a self-concealing. Were concealing to fall off and away, then how could revealing still happen? Today we say: being proffers itself to us, but in such a way that at the same time it, in its essence, already withdraws. This is what the term "history of being" means. Nothing has been arbitrarily concocted under this term, but what has already been thought is thought more decisively. When one recollectively thinks upon the history of being, a history that is difficult to bring into view, this history of being first comes to light as such. When we say that being proffers itself to us while it, in its essence, also withdraws, then of course this means something still different than what Heraclitus' fragment and Aristotle's sentences designate. But first it is necessary for us to examine to what extent being can be brought into view as the *Geschick* of being by recollectively thinking upon the history of Western thought.

The talk of an incubation of being now sounds less strange. For the word "incubation" is only another name for the self-withdrawal of being into concealment, a concealment which remains the source of any revealing. Where the last trace of the concealing of being vanishes, namely in the absolute self-knowing of absolute spirit in the metaphysics of German Idealism, the revealing of beings respective of their being, that is, metaphysics, is complete and philosophy at an end.

The incubation period of the principle of reason stems from the incubation of being and the epochs of this incubation, provided that this principle is in truth a principle of being, and that the way in which this principle speaks is determined by the *Geschick* of being.

However, the end of the incubation of being as such in no way coincides with the end of the incubation period of the principle of reason. Rather, what occurs with the latter is that the principle of reason proves to be a supreme fundamental principle and thus first unfolds its claim into something all-mighty; what is uncanny here is that being as such more and more decisively withdraws. This is not contradicted when, with the mounting claim of the principle of reason as a supreme fundamental principle of thinking and knowledge, a new interpretation of the being of beings evolves. Subsequently, being reveals itself as objectness for consciousness, and this at once says: being brings itself to light as will.

It would be a delicate task, and one really quite difficult for today's representational thinking to grasp, to show the extent to which the molding of being into objectness and will say the same thing. After the preparation of Descartes, Spinoza, and Leibniz, Kant's philosophy carries out the decisive step in the fleshing out of being as objectness and will. If we hear the principle of reason in the second tonality, then the principle of reason speaks as a principle of being. The mounting claim of the principle of reason to sovereignty accordingly implies that being—namely as objectness (will)—becomes more decisively sovereign. When we have this state of affairs in view, we gain a further insight into the *Geschick* of being and indeed *from* the epoch that, according to historical periodization, one calls modernity.

A second characteristic of the history of being should be given because a great deal depends, in connection with what we have discussed up till now as well as in view of the course of what is to come, on our thinking reliably and clearly enough of what is meant by "the *Geschick* of being." Seen in the light of the history of modern thought, it concerns the relation of Kant to Leibniz. With Leibniz the principle of reason expressly attains the rank of a supreme fundamental principle. However, what is bepowering about the *principium rationis* does not consist so much in the extent of its explicit application as a rule of thinking that is adhered to; what is bepowering about the claim of the *principium rationis* rather consists in the fact that not only modern science in the form of mathematical physics, but above all that the thinking of philosophy stands under the bidding that speaks out of the demand to provide sufficient reasons.

Lecture Nine

Wolfgang Amadeus Mozart was born 200 years ago today. I am not in a position to say anything about his work, about his life, and about the influence of each on the other. Rather Mozart's own words may at this moment be able to offer us a clue on our way.

Mozart once wrote in a letter:[34]

> Sometimes during a trip in a coach, or when on a stroll after a good meal and in the night when I can't sleep, that is when thoughts come to me best and in floods. Now, those that please me are the ones I hold in mind and perhaps even hum aloud, at least so others have told me. Now, if I stick to it, soon one part after another comes to me, as though I were using crumbs in order to make a pastry according to the rules of counterpoint and the resonance of the various instruments. Now that lights up my soul, that is, if I am not disturbed. Then it becomes ever larger and I spread it out ever more fully and lucidly, and the thing truly becomes almost finished in my head, even when it is long, so that afterwards I look over it with a glance in my mind as if it were a beautiful picture or a handsome man, and hear it in the imagination not at all serially, as it must subsequently come about, but as though all at once. That is a treat. Everything —the finding and making now proceed in me in a beautiful, vivid dream. But the listening to everything all at once is indeed the best.[41]

You will realize why I introduce these words when you recall what was said earlier. Hearing is a viewing. This "looking over" the whole "with a glance," and "listening to everything at once" are one and the same.

The concealed unity of bringing-into-view and listening determines the essence of the thinking that is entrusted to us humans who are thinking beings.

We would be taking the cited letter of Mozart in a skewed and superficial manner if, interpreting it psychologically, we took it as a document describing artistic creation. The passage tells us that Mozart was one of the best listeners of all who listen, that is, he came to be this and hence still is.

Angelus Silesius, from whom we have already heard, can in his own way indicate Mozart's essence and heart through an ancient thought. Fragment 366 from "*The Cherubic Wanderer*" says:[35]

> A heart that is calm in its ground, God-still, as he will,
> Would gladly be touched by him: it is his lute-play.[42]

The saying carries the heading: "The Lute Piece of God." That is Mozart.

We can hear the principle of reason in a twofold manner: on the one hand, as a supreme fundamental principle about beings, and, on the other hand, as a principle of being. In the second case we are pointed towards thinking ground/reason as being and being as ground/reason. When this is the case, we begin trying to think being *qua* being. This means: *No longer explaining being by way of some sort of being.* Only an attempt to say being *qua* being can show how far such a beginning can go and to what limits it leads. But the path into such a thinking is nothing but the hearing of the principle of reason as a principle of being. Indeed we reach the path of such a hearing only by way of a leap. The leap leaps off of and out of a leaping-off realm. The leap relinquishes this realm and nevertheless does not leave it behind. Through this relinquishing the leap regains the leaping-off realm in a new manner, and indeed not just incidentally, but necessarily. The leap is essentially a backward-glancing leap. What we bring into view in the glance back is, according to the main points, what we are trying to grasp in a unified way when we characterize the chief trait of the realm from which one leaps.

This realm showed itself to us as the history of Western thinking. In reference to it we spoke of the *Geschick* of being. What there is to hear in the second tonality of the principle of reason as a principle of being is hardly the sort of thing about which we have no sense. Rather, its nature is such that it lays claim to us in our essence. Take notice: in our essence. This is to say that the claim of being first ushers humans into their essence. Only in the *Geschick* of being and from out of it are we *Geschick*-like, and as beings that are *Geschick*-like, we are compelled to find what is fitting—and that means at the same time to be enmeshed in missing what is fitting.

Yet in view of what there is to think, all thinking must remain acquainted with an experience that is never only an experience of particulars and thus never lets itself be briefly articulated: seldom enough do we find ourselves expressly addressed by that which lays claim to us in our essence—and that means needs us. Being proffers itself to us in this claim-laying. The way in which it lasts as this proffering is by simultaneously withdrawing into its essence. Withdrawal is a basic trait of the *Geschick* in the sense we have discussed. If we spoke of "the history of being," then this way of speaking only makes sense if we think of history in terms of *Geschick* qua withdrawal, but not if we reverse it and, as is customary, represent *Geschick* in terms of history as a happening that has the character of a constantly on-going process.

Indeed there is something else that is just as important as our first view into the history of being as *Geschick*. Namely, it is important from the very outset to note that, and to what extent, what we call the *Geschick* of being has already come to light in the history of Western thinking. In order to see this more clearly and to more compellingly appropriate this in the future we will try to glean two hints from the history of Western thinking.

We take the first from the lecture of Aristotle on "physics." The *Physics* of Aristotle intimates the essential provenance of what, thought philosophically, is metaphysics and remains throughout every transformation metaphysics. In the beginning of his lecture on physics Aristotle has sentences about the being of beings that show that being is φύσις—that which of itself is overt. This means that self-revealing is a basic trait of being. But our ordinary hearing and speaking always misunderstands this sentence when we say it in this straightforward way. Self-revealing is a basic trait of being. This sounds like the following: there is being, and one of the characteristics being has, among others, is that it reveals itself. But being is not equipped with the characteristic that it reveals itself, rather self-revealing belongs to what is apropos of being. Being has its propriety in self-revealing. Being is not beforehand something for itself that only then brings about a self-revealing. Self-revealing is not a characteristic of being, rather self-revealing belongs in the property of being. Here we use the word "property" in the singular, as for instance, the word "clientele" is used. So "property" means that wherein "being" preserves its own proper essence as its estate [*Eigentum*]. Self-revealing belongs in the property of being. Indeed even this way of speaking is still skewed. Strictly speaking, we must say that being belongs in the property of self-revealing. What is called "being" addresses us from out of this self-revealing and as this self-revealing. We cannot arbitrarily make up on our own and, by decree, establish what "being" means [*heißt*]. What "being" means is harbored in the bidding [*Geheiß*] that speaks in the basic words of Greek thinking. We can never scientifically demonstrate or hope to demonstrate what this bidding says. We either hear it or don't hear it. We can prepare for this hearing or neglect this preparation.

Aristotle says that being is that which of itself is more overt. But what of itself is more overt is at the same time for us—that means, when it comes to the type and orientation of our ordinary perception—that which is less overt. For us what counts as the more overt is individual beings. Therefore one might be inclined to think that it is because of us humans that being—that which of itself is more overt—is for us less overt, and indeed is so to the benefit of beings. That being is less overt, so one is inclined to conclude, is to the debit of us humans. But this apparently correct judgment thinks too precipitously. What does "to the debit of us humans" mean here if the essence of humans rests on the fact that it is claimed by being? That individual beings are what is more overt and being what is less overt—this can only be rooted in the essence of being, not in us—"in us" meant in such a way that we place ourselves, as it were, by ourselves in a void without relation. For, we are never the ones that we are apart from the claim of being. So it is not some characteristic of humans as conceived anthropologically that causes being to be less overt for us than individual beings. Rather, the essence of being is such that, as a self-revealing, being reveals itself in a way such that a self-concealing—that means, a withdrawal—belongs to this revealing. This is what Heraclitus' saying, commonly called Fragment 123, says: φύσις κρύπτεθαι φιλεῖ. "To self-revealing there belongs a self-concealing." As a proffering that clears and lights, being is simultaneously withdrawal. Withdrawal belongs to the *Geschick* of being.

A second reference to the history of Western thinking should give us a further insight into the extent to which the *Geschick* of being reigns as withdrawal in the history of this thinking. But what withdrawal signifies here cannot be brought often enough before our mind's eye. Self-revealing is hardly some primary characteristic accruing to "being" (as though being somehow already subsisted beforehand), and neither is withdrawal and self-withdrawal. If the latter were a characteristic of being, then this would mean that being simply remains absent in the withdrawal. According to the withdrawal understood in this way, there would then be no being. One would thus be understanding withdrawal in the sense of a process through which, for example, one withdraws acidity from wine so that it doesn't have it any more. But being is not a thing that some one of us takes away and puts to the side. Rather self-withdrawing is the manner that being essentially comes to be, that is, proffers itself as presencing. The withdrawal does not shunt being to the side; rather, self-withdrawing belongs, as self-concealing, in the property of being. Being preserves its propriety in self-revealing insofar as it simultaneously conceals itself as this self-concealing. Self-concealing, the withdrawal, is a manner in which being *qua* being lasts, proffers itself, that is, vouchsafes itself.

We will take note of the relationship between Leibniz and Kant within the history of Western thinking in order to more clearly bring the being of beings into view as *Geschick*. This reference remains compulsory within the limited perspective open to the path of this lecture.

Leibniz formulated the principle of reason and set it up as a supreme fundamental principle. Leibnizian thinking awakens and gathers the tradition of Western thinking in a new way; it gives free rein to the claim of the principle of reason as one of the supreme fundamental principles so that what concealingly bepowers in this claim could come forth.

But what is bepowering in the claim of reason, if indeed the principle of reason is a principle of being that says being and ground/reason "are" the same? Being reigns as *Geschick* in what is bepowering about the claim of reason—

and if as *Geschick*, then the manner in which it does so is as withdrawal. We should now try to take a look at the epoch of the *Geschick* of being, an epoch that determines the essence of modernity.

Though the thinking of Leibniz and Kant lies much closer to us than the thinking of the Greeks, according to the historiographical measuring of temporal distance, modern thinking is, in its basic traits, much less accessible; for the writings and works of modern thinkers are differently built, more intricate, intermingled with tradition and everywhere inserted into the dispute with Christianity. In view of this complicated situation, the following reference to Kant is but a solitary, weak beam of light. It is only supposed to help us bring into view one small thing about the reign of the *Geschick* of being within modern thinking. We thereby take the following guiding thoughts to heart:

The greater the work of a thinker—which in no way coincides with the breadth and number of writings—the richer is what is untought in this work, which means, that which emerges in and through this work as having not yet been thought. Of course this unthought has nothing to do with what a thinker has overlooked or not mastered which wiser descendants would then have to make good on.

Leibniz defined the commonplace idea about everything having a reason and about every effect having a cause as the *principium reddendae rationis sufficientis*, as the fundamental principle of rendering sufficient reasons. But in Leibniz's sense, a *ratio sufficiens*, a sufficient reason, isn't at all a ground capable of supporting a being so that it doesn't straightaway fall into nothing. A sufficient reason is one that reaches and offers to beings that which puts them in the position of fulfilling their full essence, that is, the *perfectio*. Hence with Leibniz, the *ratio sufficiens* also means the *summa ratio*, the highest reason. Here we must content ourselves with the observation that, for Leibniz, a sufficient reason is always the most far-reaching reason and thus the reason that anticipates everything. Modern thinking first found its draught with the strict formulation of the principle of reason as the *principium reddendae rationis sufficientis*. The work of *Kant* is particularly prominent in the history of modern thinking. The titles of all three of his main works begin with the word "critique": *Critique of Pure Reason, Critique of Practical Reason, Critique of Judgment.* Judgment is the faculty of judging. Pure Reason—Reason not determined by sensibility—theoretical as well as practical Reason, is a faculty of judging according to a priori Principles. That is why a critique of judgment belongs to a complete critique of pure (theoretical as well as practical) Reason. Even in the third *Critique*, Reason is the real theme. However, in Latin "Reason" is *ratio*. We will shortly hear how the Latin word *ratio*, reckoning and Reason, accrues to the meaning of "ground" (principle of reason = *principium rationis*).

Kant's thinking is a critique of pure Reason, of *ratio pura*. According to Kant, Reason is the faculty of Principles, that is, of fundamental principles, of the giving of foundations. Already in these allusions it strikes us that the principle of reason, the *principium rationis*, reigns in Kant's thinking in a remarkable way. This is precisely the reason Kant seldom speaks of the principle of reason. *Critique of Pure Reason* here never means "to criticize" in the sense of "fault finding." The *Critique* is also not a mere check and an examination. The *Critique* also doesn't simply place bounds on Reason. Rather the *Critique* brings Reason to its limit. Bounds and limits are not equivalent. Usually we mean a limit as that where something stops. But, according to the ancient Greek sense, a limit always has the character of an assembling, not of a cutting-off. A limit is that from whence and wherein something commences, emerges as that which it is. Whoever remains blind to this sense of limit will never be able to view a Greek temple, a Greek statue, a Greek vase in their presencing. The Greek sense of κρίνειν: "to distinguish" still echoes in the Kantian use of the term "critique." However, for Kant the term means a "separating out" in which something important comes into relief. A limit does not ward off something, it brings the shape of presencing to light and supports this presencing. Kant knew the lofty sense of critique. His three *Critiques* aim at what he calls the "a priori conditions for the possibility."

The phrase "a priori condition for the possibility" is the leitmotif that reverberates throughout the whole of Kant's work. The term a priori—"from earlier on" is the subsequent echo of what Aristotle calls πρότερον τῇ φύσει, that which is earlier in terms of self-revealing inasmuch as it precedes everything as that which of itself is more obvious. For Kant, the "conditions for the possibility" are a priori in this sense. "Possibility" is here tantamount to "making-possible." To what are the conditions for making-possible related a priori? Precisely to what Aristotle already knew the πρότερον τῇ φύσει relates to, namely to τὰ σαφέστερα πρὸς ἡμᾶς: that which in relation to us and for us is, in contradistinction to φύσις, to being, most immediately overt, namely beings. With the term "a priori conditions for the possibility" Kant has in mind the making-possible of that on the basis of which beings as such as a whole are determined for us. On the basis of what does this happen? Apparently on the basis of those regions of beings into which we, as humans, are placed. Humans are the *animal rationale*. As a creature of nature, they belong in the realm of nature; as rational to the kingdom of Reason, that is, of willing and therefore of freedom.

Accordingly, the *Critique of Reason* must define Reason in its relationship to nature and in its relationship to the will, and that means, to the causality of the will, to freedom. The question of the *Critique* is the question of the a priori conditions for the possibility of nature and freedom. The a priori conditions of the possibility provide whatever ground/reason there is that limits nature and freedom in their essence and hence that reaches and offers them to us in the completeness of their determinations. Concealed behind the formula "a priori conditions for the possibility" is the rendering of sufficient reasons, of *ratio sufficiens*, which as *ratio* is pure Reason. According to Kant it is only by having recourse to Reason (*ratio*) that something can be determined as to what it is and how it is a being for the Rational creature called "man." However, this now means not just that beings *are* only *qua* Objects and Objects only Objects for a subject in the sense of modern thinking; rather, it now becomes clearer that this subject, that is, Reason, *ratio*, that is, the assembling of the a priori conditions for the possibility for nature and freedom, is this assembling only in rendering sufficient reasons.

We now see what a fragment of early Greek thinking says within quite a different light:

τὸ γὰρ αὐτὸ νοεῖν ἐστίν καὶ εἶναι[36]

That, namely the same, is perceiving as well as being.

When conceived in a modern way, this means that perceiving, Reason (*ratio*), and being belong together, and indeed such that pure Reason, *ratio*, is nothing but the positing, the rendering, of sufficient reasons for whatever there is in view of how it appears as a being, which means, how it can be represented and ordered, dealt with and handled.

Nothing prevents us from being content with discussing the term "critique of pure Reason" as a historically handy label for Kant's first main work. However, we can also ponder the extent to which Kant's thinking stands thoroughly under this term as under a demand. Pure Reason, theoretical and practical Reason, will then show itself as *ratio pura* in the sense that it posits the ground/reason, that is, the ground/reason for all founding; it is what is determinative for all conditions for the possibility of beings in their unity. The *Critique of Pure Reason* brings the ground/reason for every foundation into its definitive form. Insofar as thinking becomes a critique of pure Reason through Kant, it responds to the demand of the *principium rationis sufficientis*. Through this response Kant's thinking brings the claim of the *principium rationis* to the fore in its full breadth, and indeed so much so that *ratio* is ground/reason only in the sense of *ratio* as Reason, as the faculty for fundamental principles.

This reference to what conceals itself behind the title *Critique of Pure Reason* nevertheless remains quite inadequate as long as the whole of Kant's three *Critiques* does not become present in a vividly reconstructive perusal. Seen externally, these three works lie next to each other unconnected, like three boulders. Kant himself tried over and over again to make the inner unity, which he certainly saw, visible through a rather external architectonic. Yet Kant knew more than he was capable of presenting through this architectonic of his works.

Nevertheless, what above all thwarts our insight into the essence of what proffers itself to us in the history of Western thinking under the title *Critique of Pure Reason* is the fact that we still have not satisfactorily thought through the extent to which the normative horizons of the Kantian position could only open up in the light of the principle of reason as strictly and completely formulated by Leibniz. Of course, on the other hand, the innermost trait of Leibnizian thinking is nudged into a shadow through Kant's philosophy—or more precisely, the way Kant's philosophy did what it did nudged Leibnizian thinking into a shadow in which it stands to this day. An observation must be added to this, namely, that Kant always confronted whatever writings were known at the time "of the master from Leibniz" with the greatest reverence.

Lecture Ten

"Nothing is without reason." When one paraphrases this customary formulation of the principle of reason, it reads: "Every being has a reason." With this, the reason that every being has is itself represented as some being. A reference we gave earlier to a text of Leibniz was supposed to show this. The principle of reason is a statement about beings. In the other tonality, the principle of reason sounds like this: "Nothing *is* without *reason*." When paraphrased, this means "ground/reason belongs to being." Or "being and ground/reason—the same." Heard in this way the principle speaks of being.

The passage from the first to the second tonality is a leap. However, the leap is a leap that looks back. It looks back into the leaping-off realm in order to hold it in view. The leaping-off realm is that field in which the principle of reason is not invariably called a Principle, though indeed it is often called a more or less clearly grasped guiding thought. The leaping-off realm that we have in mind here is, according to the usual way of representing it, the history of Western thinking. In this thinking, beings, as manifoldly experienced in multifariously changing concepts and names, are constantly and at every turn questioned with respect to their being. In the history of this thinking and for it, being comes to shine forth in a certain manner, namely as the being of beings. This shining forth gives a clue about being as such. The clue yields a bit of information about being, according to which being is never first posited by human cognition. Being proffers itself to humans in that it clearingly furnishes to beings as such a temporal play-space. As such a *Geschick*, being essentially comes to be as a self-revealing that at the same time lasts as self-concealing. The history of Western thinking is based in the *Geschick* of being. Of course, what this being-based means is in need of a more precise determination. What is indispensable for this is that we clearly think the unavoidably misleading term "*Geschick* of being" in the sense of: being as the responsive [*sich zusagend*], clearing-furnishing of the temporal play-space for whatever appears in whatever way —beings. The following should be noted only as a precaution:

By referring to the *Geschick* of being we are not shoving behind the history of thinking something like a deeper layer that would allow one—[as though with the flick of a switch]—to casually continue speaking of "the history of being" instead of "philosophy." In the first place, the *Geschick* of being is still so difficult for us to experience because the portrayal of the history of thinking has been passed along to us and interpreted in so many ways. Consequently, there is an almost perverse confusion of ideas and opinions about the history of philosophy. From this point of view, every exposition of a philosophy passed on by history appears one-sided. Hegel justifiably says that prosaic understanding only stumbles around in such one-sidedness and thereby skirts the issue. Conventional representational thinking is not capable of bringing into view what is simple and the same and which, in its own good time, brings itself to language and decides whether something is or is not pertinent to an exposition. This can never be judged from within the purview of ideas taken up randomly. The standard for an exposition comes from the breadth of questioning, a breadth in which the exposition takes the measure of that by which its questioning should be addressed. What we say here also holds for the two references to the history of thinking in the previous lectures that attempted to follow a clue to the *Geschick* of being by considering Aristotle and Kant.

Most essentially and radically, Kant's thinking is the critique of pure Reason, if we think this term in its full depth and breadth. Reason [*Vernunft*] means and is *ratio*, that is, the faculty of fundamental principles, that is, of ground/reason. Reason [*Vernunft*] is the ground/reason that grounds. Only when it is Rational is ground/reason pure Reason. If in harkening the leitmotif of his thinking Kant pondered the a priori conditions for the possibility of nature and freedom, then this thinking is, as a Rational cognition, the rendering of sufficient reasons for what can and cannot appear to humans as a being—it is the rendering of the sufficient conditions for the manner in which what appears can appear, as well as how it cannot appear.

To what extent did the terse reference to the inner historical connection between the *principium reddendae rationis sufficientis* and the critique of pure Reason help us gain an insight into the modern epoch of the *Geschick* of being? How does being proffer itself within the compass of Kantian thinking? This question at the same time asks how being withdraws in this proffering. In answering this question, we must restrict ourselves to a single but decisive trait of Kantian thinking. It manifests itself in the fact that Kant was the first one since the philosophy of the Greeks to again pose the question of the being of beings as a question to be developed. With this question as a question and by means of it, Kant expressly reflected upon the path that inquires into beings regarding their being—he reflects upon method. Of course all of this happens on a completely different itinerary than with the Greek thinkers because it occurs in a different dimension. The itinerary and domain of the path of Kantian questioning are characterized by *ratio*—*ratio* in the dual sense of Reason and ground.

In line with the trait of modern thinking that moves in the realm of Reason, Kant also thinks within and in terms of the dimension of Reason. As the faculty of fundamental principles, reason generally is the faculty of representing something as something. "I place something as something in front of myself"[43] is the stricter formulation of the *ego cogito* of Descartes, of the "I think." Therefore the dimension of a critique, of theoretical, practical, and technical Reason is the I-ness of the I: the subjectivity of the subject. It is in relation to the I as subject that beings, placed before the I in representation, have the character of an Object for a subject. Beings are beings as objects for a consciousness. Since consciousness allows an object to stand on *its own*, it thus represents itself along with the object—it is self-consciousness. But now, because the realm of subjectivity as the realm of *ratio* in the sense of Reason is in itself the realm of the *principium rationis*, of *ratio* in the sense of ground/reason, the critique of pure Reason investigates the sufficient reason for all objects, that is, for objects as the objects of a representing subject conscious of itself. The critical question of the sufficient reason for objects becomes the question concerning the *a priori* conditions for the possibility of the representation of objects of experience. We cannot here expound upon what these conditions consist of and the manner in which, according to Kant, they make representation possible. Something else is more important now.

The ground/reason that accords to objects their possibility as objects circumscribes what we call the objectness of objects. When being is understood in a Kantian manner, objectness is the being of experienceable beings. The objectness of objects clearly is what is most proper to objects. Nevertheless, objectness does not adhere to or in the object as some one or another of its qualities. Rather, objectness appropriates the object, but it does this not after the fact, rather before it appears as an object so that it can as such appear. The critical delimitation of the objectness of objects therefore surpasses[44] objects. But this surpassing of objects is nothing other than an entering into the realm of grounding fundamental principles, into the subjectivity of Reason. The surpassing [*Übersteig*] of objects to objectness is the passage into Reason which thereby first comes to light in its ground-positing essence. This surpassing of objects that is expressly the passage into subjectivity is, said in Latin, a *transcendere*. Therefore Kant names his critical procedure that investigates the a priori conditions for the possibility of objects the method that surpasses, the transcendental method.

Because of the confusion in which the terms "transcendence," "transcendental," and "transcendent" circulate today, it is necessary to clearly distinguish between them. Even those who believe they know the last word about what Kant understood by "transcendental method" must again freshly appropriate what was thought by Kant.

How come? Because the transcendental method is no procedure that simply moves externally around that with which it occupies itself. It is with some deliberation that Kant names the method of the *Critique*—that is, of the circumscriptive rendering of sufficient reason—"transcendental" and not "transcendent"; for Kant names "transcendent" that which lies beyond the limits of human experience, not insofar as it surpasses objects in the direction of their objectness; rather, insofar as it surpasses objects along with their objectness—and this without sufficient warrant, namely, without the possibility of being founded. According to Kant a cognition is "transcendent" that pretends to know objects inaccessible to experience. In contradistinction to this, the transcendental method has a view to the sufficient ground of the objects of experience and thereby of experience itself. The transcendental method moves within the compass of grounds that found the objects of experience in their possibility. The transcendental method circumscribes the compass of founding grounds that come into play. The transcendental method holds itself to this compass and within that which it delimits. Because it remains in the circle of the sufficient reasons for the possibility of experience, that is, within the essence of experience and is therefore in-herent, the transcendental method is immanent. But nevertheless the method is called transcendental because it pertains to the transcendent, for it critically sets the bounds of the authority of the transcendent. The transcendental method traverses the immanence of subjectivity, that is, it traverses that cognition wherein objects as the objects of representation reside as in their sufficient reason. That is their objectness, the being of beings.

We can only fathom what lives in Kant's transcendental method and what emerges as transformed in the word "transcendental" if we think the word "transcendental" in a wide arc backwards into what has-been and forwards into what, in the meantime, approaches.

We will briefly recall the following so we can have clearly before our eyes the extent to which the discussion of the transcendental lies on our path— more precisely—the extent to which it belongs to the preparation of the leap from one tonality of the principle of reason into the other. Understood in a Kantian way, the "transcendental" pertains to the surpassing of objects, that is, of experienceable beings, to objectness, that is, to being. However, the leap is the leap from out of the principle of reason as a principle about beings into the principle as an utterance of being *qua* being. The leap leaps through the realm between beings and being. The transcendental, the surpassing, and the leap indeed are not equivalent, but the same insofar as they belong together with respect to the differentiating of beings and being. If we think about the word "transcendental" and the matter named by it, and do so backwards into what has-been, then two moments result that can be briefly noted.

According to word usage, the designation "transcendental" stems from the medieval scholastics. It pertains to the *transcendens*, which designates a *modus*, a manner and a standard by which *omne ens qua ens* is measured; for example, *omnes ens est unum*, every being is *a* being and as this being it is not another being. More precisely, this *modus* of beings is defined as *modus generaliter consequens omne ens*. *Consequens* here is thought as the determination opposite of *antecedens*. It is important to take heed of this. The most general determinations of every being as such *follow* beings and are yielded from out of them. It is in this sense that they pass, they step across (*transcendere*) what belongs to every being; hence they are called "transcendentals." But for Kant, what the transcendental method investigates is not the sort of thing that is a *consequens* as are those things that stand in relation to beings in the sense of the objects of experience. Rather the objectness that affords objects the ground of their possibility is the *antecedens*, that which precedes, the a priori.

The medieval-scholastic definition of the *ens qua ens* stems from Aristotle and indeed from the beginning of Book IV of the *Metaphysics*. What we are familiar with under the title *The Metaphysics of Aristotle* is not a "work," rather a compilation, not undertaken by Aristotle, of essays whose questions at times go off into completely different regions and directions.

Seen from a literary point of view, the *Metaphysics* of Aristotle is wholly ununified; thought in terms of contents, it is made of pieces each of which has a different way of questioning.

The first sentence of the first chapter of Book 4 reads: *Εστιν ἐπιστήμη τις ἥ θεωρεῖ τὸ ὄν ἥ ὄν καὶ τὰ τούτῳ ὑπάρχοντα καθ' αὐτό.*[37] When one interpretively translates, this says: "There is something like an understanding that takes into view what is present as coming to presence and at the same time thereby (takes into view) that which is at the disposal of presencing, tendering itself from out of itself."

What is at issue here is neither the transcendental, which in Kant's sense determines beings as objects in their objectness, nor is what is at issue a *modus entis generaliter consequens omne ens*. And this for the simple reason that what is at issue is thought in a Greek way, namely *ὄv*. The *ὄv* is *φύσις τις*, the sort of thing that is an emerging-on-its-own. The *ὄv* is not *ens* in the sense of the *ens creatum* of the medieval scholastics, beings created by God. Nor is *ὄv* the object with respect to its objectness. What determines beings with respect to their being in Aristotle's sense, and how this happens, is experienced differently than in the medieval doctrine of *ens qua ens*. Yet it would be silly to say the medieval theologians misunderstood Aristotle; rather, they understood him differently, responding to the different manner in which being proffered itself to them. Then again, the *Geschick* of being is different for Kant. A different understanding becomes a misunderstanding only where it comes to a peak in a uniquely possible truth and simultaneously is subsumed under the order of what is to be understood. The method by which thinking investigates the being of beings first became the transcendental method for Kant. What is distinctive about the transcendental determination of beings as such in no way exhausts itself in the fact that beings now come to be experienced as the objects of an egological, subjective Reason. What is distinctive about the transcendental method is the fact that, as the determination of the objectness of objects, this method itself belongs to objectness. Cognition renders sufficient reasons for objects when, above all, it brings forward and securely establishes the objectness of objects and thereby itself belongs to objectness, that is, to the being of experienceable beings. The transcendental method responds to the claim of the principle of reason. The *principium rationis sufficientis* reigning in *ratio* (Reason) comes into the free openness and transparency of its bepowering through the transcendental method.

The new manner in which being proffers itself consists not only in the fact that being now comes to light as objectness. Rather, what is new is that this coming-to-light manifests a decisiveness with which being is determined within the realm of the subjectivity of Reason, and only there. The decisiveness of this *Geschick* of being means that every other grounding of the being of beings outside of the dimension of transcendental Reason is precluded; for the a priori conditions for the possibility of objects, their sufficient reason, *ratio sufficiens*, is *ratio*, Reason itself. Formally, one can even say that the objectness of objects, that is, the Objectivity of Objects is completely based in subjectivity. But this formula only speaks when we take note of the following:

Subjectivity is not something subjective in the sense of being confined to a single person, to the fortuitousness of their particularity and discretion. Subjectivity is the essential lawfulness of reasons which *pro*-vide [*zu*-reicht] the possibility of an object. Subjectivity does not mean a subjectivism, rather it refers to that lodging of the claim of the principle of reason which today has as its consequence the atomic age in which the particularity, separation, and validity of the individual disappears at breakneck speed in favor of total uniformity. Whether or not we may want to look into and attest to it today, all this is based in the *Geschick* of being as objectness for the subjectivity of Reason, for *ratio* as determined by the *principium rationis*. Its injunction unleashes the universal and total reckoning up of everything as something calculable.

Mentioning this intends neither to sketch out for you the often appealed to spiritual situation of the present day, nor to speak in favor of an unavoidable absence of alternatives. Rather, the path of this lecture leads us to mention these things, a lecture that intends to show what belongs to this path so that one can reflect on that which is. What "is" is not current events and neither is it what is present right now. What "is" is what approaches from what has-been and, as this, is what approaches. What approaches, already a long time under way, is the unconditional claim of the principle of reason in the form of complete Rationality. One needs neither the gift nor the posture of the prophets, but only the perseverance of genuinely historical thinking, in order to see this. The increasing flight from the historical tradition is for its part a sign of the claim under which the era stands. In the meantime it even seems as though this flight from history is removing the last bounds that at every turn still stand opposed to an unrestrained, complete technicizing of the world and of humans. The dwindling of the capacity for historical discernment coincides with this flight from history. An example for this should now be introduced, an example that will simultaneously show the extent to which we remain, with the previous remarks, very much on the path of a reflection on the transcendental method that distinguishes Kant's critical thinking.

We have already frequently mentioned that the era called "modernity" receives the basic trait of its history from that *Geschick* of being wherein being proffers itself as objectness and thus furnishes beings as objects. But just as frequently a consideration vis-à-vis what has been mentioned was left by the wayside. One can articulate it thus: what, after all, is so special about the fact that beings become objects? Were not beings always already objects, and this precisely where being as φύσις, as pure arising, allowed beings to come forth on their own? Didn't Greek thinking already know beings as objects and even only as objects? For example, just think of their statues.

It would serve us well to make a historical distinction in order to see clearly what is going on in this question. As we noted earlier, the word *Gegenstand* ["object"] is the translation of the Latin *objectum*. One no less than Lessing took it upon himself to resist this translation. Lessing translated *objectum* with *Gegenwurf* ["counter-throw"]. This translation is not only in fact more literal, but also more eloquent, for it speaks of the fact that something has been thrown over against, namely, over against the cognizing subject by this subject itself. *Gegenwurf* hits upon precisely that sense of *objectum* that the word even already had in the Middle Ages. An *objectum* is, for example, a golden mountain, precisely because, as we say today, objectively it does not exist, rather is only thrown to the cognizing I by an imaginative cognition. But the modern meaning of "Object" simultaneously implies the fact that what is thrown-forward—what is made available through the efforts of an investigative examination—is not merely imaginary, but is something present in its own right which is delivered to the cognizing I. However, the manner of presencing is now determined by the sufficiency of the reasons for what stands over against us, by objectness—thought in a Kantian manner: by the fundamental principles of the understanding as the Principles of Reason. Therefore, even the translation of *objectum* by *Gegenstand* [object] has its own justification, since an Object is not some mere representation of the subject—even more so, since in an Object something which is thrown over against and brought to the cognizing subject simultaneously stands on its own. Nevertheless, we should not lose track of the distinction that is now coming to light. In looking back on what was just noted, one could insist that beings already announced themselves as having the character of objects even with the Greeks. To think this would be foolish. For the Greeks, what is present indeed revealed itself as having the character of an over-against, but never as having the character of an object, if this word is taken in the sense of "Object" as conceived in a strictly modern way. "Over-against" and "object" are not equivalent. In the object [Gegenstand], the "ob" or "against" [Gegen] is determined on the basis of a representational throwing-over-against wrought by the subject. In the over-against, the "against" reveals itself in what comes over the perceiving, viewing-hearing human, over those who have never conceived of themselves as a subject for an Object. Accordingly, whatever is present is not what a subject throws forth as an Object; rather, it is what accrues to perceiving and what human viewing and hearing hold up and portray as what has come over it. A Greek statue is the aspect of something standing whose stance has nothing to do with an object in the sense of an Object. The Greek ἀντικείμενον, that which is over-against—more precisely, that which is ex-posed [das Vor-liegende] in what is over-against—is something completely different than an object in the sense of an Object. In the presencing of the Gods, in their espying of us, the Greeks experienced the most uncanny and most enchanting over-against: τὸ δεινόν. But they did not know objects in the sense of Objects. The counter [Gegen] and the en-counter [Be-gegnen] here have a different sense.

Thus if, as happens now more frequently, one meditates on the phenomenon of an encounter, then one must have made good on a presupposition underlying the neatness of this undertaking. There must already be great clarity about whether the phenomenon of an encounter is to be dealt with in the domain of the subject-object relation and represented in a modern way in terms of the subject as a person, or whether it is to be sought in the realm of the over-against. To thoughtfully traverse the warp and woof of this realm is far more difficult and has hardly begun.

Goethe, who in 1792 wrote an essay with the title "The Essay as Mediator of Object [Objekt] and Subject,"38 often and liberally used the word Gegenstand [object]; he was also still aware of the old form of the "over-against" that speaks more clearly, for example, in the phrase: "we sat across from" or "over-against one another."

Two senses emerge in the Goethean use of the word "object": object as Object for a subject and object as an "over against one." What is difficult to grasp here is the sense of the "over," which means many things: "over" as "out over," as "above" and as "beyond". The "over" becomes clear in the verb "to sur-prise": to swiftly, unexpectedly, suddenly come over one. Indeed the "over" and "surprise" nowhere speak more richly and perhaps even in a more Greek manner than in the last strophe of Hölderlin's hymn "Die Wanderung" from 1801.39 It begins "Happy Suevien, my mother . . ."

If more mildly breathe the airs,
And loving arrows of the morning
Pierce us who are all too patient,
And downy clouds bloom
Over us and our timid eyes,
Then we'll say, how do you
Come, Charitinnen, to the wilds?
The handmaidens of the heavens
Are oh so wonderful,
As everything divinely borne.
If by stealth one tries to overcome it,
It becomes for him a dream,
If he uses force to make himself
Its peer it punishes him.
Often it surprises one
Who hardly ever thought it.[45]

Instead of
"thought"
Hölderlin first
wrote "hoped."

Lecture Eleven

Rest of motion

We are trying to get a view into an epoch of the history of being, an epoch which, when measured historiographically, is called "modernity." This serves our intention of clarifying that and how a withdrawal of being simultaneously reigns in the *Geschick* of being. Seen in terms of being, this means that being lasts as the withdrawing proffering of the temporal play-space for the appearing of what, in response to the *Geschick* and its bidding, is called "beings." What in Greek is called τὰ ὄντα, in Latin *ens*, in French *l'être*, in German *das Seiende* [beings] has in every case already been decided by the epochal clearing and lighting of being. Incidentally, it is no accident that the Greek language speaks most clearly and distinctly when it names what we call *Seiende* [beings] in the neutral plural. For beings are always individually occurring beings and thus multifarious; contrary to this, being is unique, the absolute singular in unconditioned singularity.

In the course of perusing the various eras of the history of Western thinking we seek a view into the *Geschick* of being. Such a course has assumed in advance that the history of Western thinking rests in the *Geschick* of being. But that wherein something else rests must itself be at rest. Ordinarily we conceive of rest as the cessation of movement. Represented in a mathematical-physical way, rest is only a limiting case of movement, which, for its part, is predetermined as a change of position measurable according to spatio-temporal coordinates. If rest is represented in advance as a cessation or limiting case of movement, then the concept of rest is reached by way of a negation.

But when one really thinks about it, rest is not an omission; rather, it is the assembling of motion, that assembling which first emits motion from itself. In the emission it does not merely discharge motion and send it off, but it actually retains it. Accordingly, motion is based in rest. So if we assume that the history of Western thinking is based in the *Geschick* of being, then in thinking what we call "the *Geschick* of being" we think a rest or repose, an assembling

84

into which all movements of thinking also are gathered, regardless of whether or not thinking is immediately aware of this.

We assume such a relationship between the *Geschick* of being and the history of thinking. In speaking here of "as-suming" we mean "to receive" what comes over thinking: to "as-sume" in the sense, as we say, of "taking on" an opponent in a fight; only here the assuming or taking-on is not hostile and the fight is not one of hate. Assuming and taking here have the sense of a responding that listens and brings something into view.

If we assume that the history of Western thinking rests in the withdrawing *Geschick* of being, then this is not simply some personal assumption we advance in the sense of an opinion that randomly befalls some matter and is enmeshed in a preconceived view.

The above-mentioned assumption that the history of thinking rests in the *Geschick* of being is not a personal opinion, but a reception of being. That this is so shows itself with a certain transparency if we briefly reflect on something that we indeed have already intimated, even mentioned, yet till now have not explicitly discussed. Of all the difficult things to grasp in this world it is the most difficult to grasp because it lies closest to us, insofar as it is ourselves.

Near the beginning of the lecture course, and then more frequently, we spoke of the exacting claim of the principle of reason and of the fact that we follow the claim without further ado; for we are those who are claimed. It is only as the ones so claimed that we are capable of assuming, that is, of receiving what proffers itself to us. We are the ones bestowed by and with the clearing and lighting of being in the *Geschick* of being. However, apropos of being such beings we are also the same ones that being touches in and by its withdrawal, the same ones to whom being, as such a *Geschick*, refuses the clearing and lighting of its essential provenance.

The words Hegel spoke on October 22, 1818 at the opening of his lecture course at the University of Berlin seem to stand in opposition to this:

> The courage of truth, faith in the power of the spirit, is the first condition of philosophical studies; one should honor oneself and deign to esteem the highest things. One cannot think highly enough of the greatness and power of the spirit; the sequestered nature of the universe harbors no power which can oppose the courage of cognition; it is necessary that it open itself before one and lay its riches and its profundities before one's eyes and bring joy to them.[40]

We would be thinking neither highly nor concretely enough if we were to understand these words as a pretension of the thinking person vis-à-vis the absolute. It is precisely the opposite: the preparedness to respond to the claim as that which being qua the absolute concept proffers to thinking and which in a decisive way molds in advance the epoch of the completion of Western metaphysics. Since the being of beings makes itself absolutely known to metaphysical-ontological thinking in the shape of the absolute concept, the most radical withdrawal conceals itself in this proffering of being. It will become clear how this is pertinent when, in what follows, we make a concluding characterization of an epoch of the history of being, the epoch of Kantian philosophy.

The sentence before the parenthetical remark about Hegel should be repeated: we are the ones bestowed by and with the clearing and lighting of being in the *Geschick* of being, and accordingly the same ones that being touches in and by its withdrawal, the same ones to whom being, as such a *Geschick*, refuses the clearing and lighting of its essential provenance. As the ones bestowed by being in the *Geschick* of being we stand—and indeed do so in accordance with our essential nature—in a clearing and lighting of being. But we do not just stand around in this clearing and lighting without being addressed [*unangesprochen*]; rather we stand in it as those who are claimed [*Anspruch*] by the being of beings. As the ones standing in the clearing and lighting of being we are the ones bestowed, the ones ushered into the time play-space. This means we are the ones engaged in and for this play-space, engaged in building on and giving shape to the clearing and lighting of being—in the broadest and multiple sense, in preserving it.

In the still cruder and more awkward language of the treatise *Being and Time* (1927) this means that the basic trait of Dasein, which is human being, is determined by the understanding of being. Here understanding of being never means that humans as subjects possess a subjective representation of being and that being is a mere representation. Nicolai Hartmann and many contemporaries understood, in their own way, the point of departure of *Being and Time* in this sense.

Understanding of being means that according to their essential nature humans stand [*steht*] in the openness of the projection of being and suffer [*aussteht*] this understanding [*Verstehen*] so understood. When understanding of being is experienced and thought of in this way, the representation of humans as subjects is, to speak in line with Hegel, put aside. According to their essential nature, humans are thinking beings only insofar as they stand in a clearing and lighting of being. For, in our history of thinking this has meant to respond to the bidding of being, and on the basis of this response to have a dialogue about beings in their being. In the history of Western thinking this "having a dialogue" (διαλέγεσθαι) develops into dialectics.

What is the purpose of these remarks which at first seem thoroughly marginal? They serve the purpose of opening up our eyes to the fact that and how the history of thinking stays in relation to the *Geschick* of being. The history of thinking is something different than the mere chronicle of changing opinions and doctrines of philosophers. The history of thinking is the bestowing of the essence of humans by the *Geschick* of being. The essence of humans is bestowed with the wherewithal to bring to language beings in their being. Basically, what has just been said is nothing other than an interpretation, thought through from the point of view of the question of being, of the old definition of human nature: *homo est animal rationale*; humans are the creatures endowed with Reason.

Only insofar as humans are en-dowed by the *Geschick* with the wherewithal to think beings as such can one say that whatever is proffered in the *Geschick* is the history of *thinking*. Within this history, being proffers itself to the thinking of Kant as the objectness of the objects of experience. Intrinsic to this objectness is the fact that a cognition replies to it, a reply in which objectness first gains its full determination. This reply is the sort of cognition that Kant calls the transcendental method.

In the introduction to the second edition of the *Critique of Pure Reason* Kant says the following, which is a clearer formulation of the same sentence from the first edition:

> I call all knowledge transcendental that in general occupies itself not with objects, but with the mode of our knowledge of objects insofar as this can possibly be *a priori*.[41]

The transcendental method is intrinsic to the manner in which objects can be objects for us. Cast as objectness, being clears and lights itself in a novel manner. For the Greek thinkers beings were never objects; rather, they were that which continues on towards us from what lies over against us.[46] Beings were more [*war seiender*] than our objects. Indeed, we may be of the opinion that beings appear most purely as what is present in its own right when they show themselves as objects, which means, objectively. This opinion is errant, granting that we think the concept of an object in a manner that does it justice.

In terms of the history of being, it is important to sharply distinguish between what comes to presence in what is over-against us and what comes to presence in objectness. The status of an object is determined by cognition on the basis of the a priori conditions for the possibility of cognition. It is by referring back to a subject that cognition, so determined, goes about rendering the sufficient reasons for the presencing of what comes to presence as Objects. By rendering sufficient reasons this cognition receives the unique character that determines the modern relationship of humans to the world, and that means, makes modern technology possible.

The rendering of sufficient reasons resounds more clearly in Lessing's translation of *objectum* by *Gegenwurf* ["counter-throw"] as a throwing-forth which is thrown forth by a subject. Lessing's word *Vorwurf* [motif] still retains, in the language of art and the artist, the sense of the subject of a work. *Vorwurf* is actually the literal translation of the Greek word πρόβλημα.[47] Incidentally, in order to mention it as food for thought, today everyone uses, in our much misused language, the word "problem" when, for example, the auto mechanic, an honorable man, cleans the dirty spark plugs and remarks: "That's no problem." It certainly isn't.

When the being of beings proffered itself as the objectness of objects, the *Geschick* achieved a previously unprecedented decisiveness and exclusiveness. But the decisiveness with which the essential provenance of being withdraws also corresponds to this proffering. Namely, if *ratio* as Reason, that is, as subjectivity is the wellspring of *ratio* in the sense of ground/reason and its demand to be rendered, then the question of the essential provenance of being as objectness cannot find a site within the domain of *ratio*. Why not? Because through *ratio* as subjectivity we see the fact that and how Reason implies the fullness of every possible *rationes*, of every possible reason, and thus Reason harbors in itself the ground/reason for every foundation. What is transcendental about Kant's transcendental method is the cognition that responds to the rendering of sufficient reasons, and that means the cognition that is based upon the demand to render these reasons. The transcendental is in no way a procedure invented by human thinking. Just as what is transcendental about this method peeps back into the φύσις of the Greeks, so it points forward into the newest epoch of the *Geschick* of being. For the dialectic which one finds in the metaphysics of German Idealism is grounded in the transcendental method implied by the objectness of objects —that is, by the being of *experienceable* beings. When one thinks this dialectic in a being-historical manner as transformed into historical-dialectical material- ism, one sees that it determines the contemporary history of humanity in a manifold manner. In our age the world-historical conflict has come closer than the short-sighted, political and economic power struggles would like us to think.

The most radical withdrawal of being begins with the proffering of being as objectness insofar as the essential provenance of being can never come into view as a question and as worth questioning. Why not? Because the complete founding of beings as such is also contained and concluded in the domain of *ratio* as Reason and subjectivity, a domain which is the be and end all.

{When speaking of the *Geschick* of being, "being" means nothing other than the proffering of the lighting and clearing that furnishes a domain for the appear- ing of beings in some configuration, along with the contemporaneous withdrawal of the essential provenance of being as such. The age in which Western thinking was setting up the principle of reason as the supreme fundamental principle was an age at play in an epoch of the *Geschick* of being that even now orients our contemporary historical existence, orienting it even if, for our part, we only know the names of the thinkers of this epoch—Leibniz, Kant, Fichte, Hegel, Schelling—and no longer experience their inner affinity and common destiny.}

Nevertheless the history of Western thinking shows itself as the *Geschick* of being when and only when we glance back upon the whole of Western thinking *from the point of view of the leap* and when we recollectively preserve it as the

Geschick of being that has-been. At the same time we can prepare for the leap only by speaking in terms of the history of being, a history that has been experienced in terms of *Geschick*. The leap leaves the realm from which one leaps while at the same time recollectively regaining anew what has been left such that what has-been becomes, for the first time, something we cannot lose. That into which the leap anticipatorily leaps is not some region of things present at hand into which one can simply step. Rather, it is the realm of what first approaches as worthy of thought. But this approach is also shaped by the traits of what has-been, and only because of this is it discernible. We must take all that is ranged under the first four of the five main points mentioned earlier and think it back into the history of being. The fifth main point regarded the change in the tonality of the principle of reason. A leap from out of the principle of reason as a fundamental principle about beings into the principle of reason as an utterance of being concealed itself behind the change of tonality of one and the same principle. As a recollective anticipatory principle, the principle [*Satz*] is thus a "vault" [*Satz*] in the sense of a leap [*Sprung*]. If we fully think through the polysemic word *Satz* not only as "statement," not only as "utterance," not only as "leap," but at the same time also in the musical sense of a "movement," then we gain for the first time the complete connection to the principle of reason.[48] If we understand the word *Satz* in the musical sense, then what Bettina von Arnim wrote in her book *Goethe's Correspondence with a Child* also holds for our path through the principle of reason:

> If one speaks of a movement [*Satz*] in music and how it is performed, or of the accompaniment of an instrument and of the understanding with which it is treated, then I mean precisely the opposite, namely that the movement leads the musician, that the movement occurs, develops and is concentrated often enough till the spirit has completely joined itself to it.[42]

Said in the second, unusual tonality, the principle of reason sounds like this: "Nothing *is* without *reason*." The emphasized words "is" and "reason" now allow a unison between being and reason to resound. The principle now says what it says through this unison. What does the principle say? It says: being and ground/reason belong together. This means that being and ground/reason "are" in essence the same. When we think the same—more precisely, sameness— as a belonging together in essence, then we keep in mind one of the earliest thoughts of Western thinking. Accordingly, "the same" does not mean the empty oneness of the one and the other, nor does it mean the oneness of something with itself. "The same" in the sense of this oneness is the indifference of an empty, endlessly repeatable identity: A as A, B as B. Thought in the sense of what in essence belongs together, the same indeed bursts the indifference of what belongs together, even more it holds them apart in the most radical dissimilarity; it holds them apart and yet does not allow them to fall away from each other and hence disintegrate. This holding-together in keeping-apart is a trait of what we call the same and its sameness. This holding [*Halten*] pertains to a "relation" [*Verhältnis*] that still stands before thinking as what is to be thought. But through metaphysical thinking it does come to light in a particular shape; it does so most purely in Hegel's *Logic*.

When we say: being and ground/reason: the same, then being and ground/reason are not clumped into the greyness of an empty oneness such that one may then say "ground/reason" instead of "being" and instead of "being" say "ground/reason" according to one's inclination. Rather, each of the words give us something different to think, something which nevertheless we do not immediately appreciate even if the principle of reason is read in the second tonality: "nothing *is* without *reason*." This means that ground/reason reigns in the "is." But ground/reason grounds such that what it grounds *is*, that means, is a being.

The more sharply we distinguish "being" and "ground/reason," the more decisively are we compelled to ask: how do being and ground/reason come and belong together? To what extent does the principle of reason in the second tonality speak a truth, a truth whose import we can hardly imagine?

In the mean time we have spoken for a number of class periods about "being" and "reason" without our having fulfilled the most pressing requirement, which is to grasp that about which we have continually spoken—namely, "being" as well as "reason"—with rigorous concepts and thus to secure in advance the necessary reliability for the course of the discussion. Why this neglect? The neglect comes from what we were speaking about when we were recalling the history of being and the principle of reason as one of the supreme fundamental principles. In recalling these things, being was spoken of in the sense of φύσις, of what emerges-on-its-own; being was spoken of in the sense of the objectness of the objects of experience. We talked about reason as *ratio* and as *causa*, as conditions for the possibility. Of course what we haven't taken as our immediate topic of conversation, but which nevertheless could and should have shown a little bit of itself in a mediate fashion on the path up to this point, is the following: what we in different ways named "being" and "reason" and which was brought into a certain light in such a naming cannot, for its part, be put in a definition in the academic sense of traditional concept formation. If henceforward we neglect something that remains inadmissable to the matter at hand, then strictly speaking it is a matter of a neglect that in fact isn't one at all. But does this then mean the names that in various ways bring "being" and "reason" to language—does this mean that the thought we think in the historically diverse names for being and reason is fragmented into a chaotic dissemination? Not at all; for, in what looks like a chaotic manifold of representations when plucked out of history and shoved together historiographically, there is a sameness and simplicity of the *Geschick* of being that comes to light and, in accord with this, a solid constancy in the history of thinking and its thoughts.

We only seldom and with difficulty bring into view the fullness and proper character of this "same" [in the history of thinking]. Being proffered itself to early Greek thinking as, among others, φύσις. For Kant, being means the objectness of objects. Now, even if for Kant this object is principally nature and the Greek word for being, φύσις, is translated by *natura* and nature; and even if φύσις on the one hand and objectness on the other hand give the appearance of meaning the being of nature, we nevertheless cannot then conclude that what proffered itself in the early and in the modern *Geschick* of being—in φύσις and in objectness—is the same. In any event it is not what one calls "nature." Yet traits of the *Geschick* of being can be introduced in which we can discern the extent to which basic words as disparate as φύσις and "objectness" indeed speak the same.

Initially, as well as later on, being cleared and lit itself, though in different ways, as having the character of a shining forth, of a shining that lingers, of a presencing, of the over-against and countering. The citation of these moments is still merely a listing of references, far removed from an insight into the particular epochs of the full *Geschick* of being and into the way in which the epochs suddenly spring up like sprouts. The epochs can never be derived from one another much less be placed on the track of an ongoing process. Nevertheless, there is a legacy[49] from epoch to epoch. But it does not run between the epochs like a band linking them; rather, the legacy always comes from what is concealed in the *Geschick*, just as if from one source various streamlets arise that feed a stream that is everywhere and nowhere.

This remark has a fundamental significance for every discourse about being, whether it occurs in this lecture or elsewhere in thinking and pondering what has been thought. When we say "being," when we say "is," it is no hollow sound. We understand what we say, that is, what we articulate. At the same time we are at a loss when we have to say—here that means, when we have to bring into view—*what* we think. And we remain perplexed when we assent to the fact that we think what is historically the same, despite the various manners of representation, experiencing, and expression. We gladly avoid being perplexed and take refuge in common opinions. Associated with being perplexed is the absence of any inkling about the fact that what is most worthy of thought is what we thoughtlessly think in the word "being." Yet the usual and customary manner in which we understand and speak of "being" resists letting one fault it as being careless and doing away with it. This customary sort of relation to "being" necessarily belongs to the way that humans, residing among beings, first and foremost respond to the *Geschick* of being. Therefore, even the thoughtful question of being always remains alien and disturbing, most of all for those who attempt to ask it. This points up a difference between the sciences and philosophy. In the former, one has the excitement and stimulation of the ever-novel and successful; with the latter, one has the consternation of what is simply the same, of what does not admit of success since nothing can follow from it—this because thinking, insofar as it ponders being, thinks back into ground/ reason, that is, its essence as the truth of being.[50]

Yet what the word *Grund* and the corresponding names name can be exhibited only with even greater difficulty, especially when we seek to bring into view what is the same that is touched upon in previously used names like *Grund* [reason], *ratio, causa, Ursache* [cause], "condition for the possibility."

In order to blaze a path here we must make the best of the fact that our exposition has come to a standstill in a crude form. What was noted concerning the understanding and saying of the word "being" holds equally in regard to what is to be thought via the word *Grund* [ground/reason]. In the previous sessions, all of us have understood the often mentioned word *Grund* in some manner. Hence we were able to set aside what we are now no longer able to pass over: the discussion of the word *Grund* and the names in the history of thinking that name what is generally characterized by the German word *Grund*.

So that we do not stray from the path with these discussions, we should recall what it is we want to achieve. It is an insight into the fact that and how "being" and "ground/reason" "are" the same. In other words, we want to hear what the principle of reason says in the second tonality as an utterance of being. Such a hearing does not simply bear something in mind. Rather, if it occurs correctly, a hearing [*Hören*] that thinks experiences that to which we always already, that is genuinely, belong [*ge-hören*].

When we ask what is called *Grund*, then we at first mean what the word signifies; the word signifies something; it gives us something to understand and does so because it speaks to us of something.

Seen wholly apart from the historical character of the polysemy of a word, language nevertheless has an essentially historical character such that it appears to us to be a complex of words whose words, as one says, are the bearers of meaning and thereby have a meaning. That such is the case with words—that there are word-meanings—we hold as being as obvious as the fact that beings appear to us as Objects. Hence both of these representations are also related in a way. Apropos of this ordinary representation of words, namely that they have a meaning, we find various meanings of the word *Grund*. When we ask after the fundamental meaning [*Grundbedeutung*] of the word *Grund*, we have, with this very question, already answered, that means introduced, what we mean by *Grund*, namely the basis, the fundus upon which something rests, stands, and lies. We speak of foundation walls [*Grundmauern*], of a fundamental rule [*Grundregel*], of a fundamental principle [*Grundsatz*].

Lecture Twelve

We have reached a point in the course of this lecture course where a leap out of the principle of reason as the supreme fundamental principle about beings into the principle of reason as an utterance of being occurs. The passage from the ordinary tonality of the principle into the unusual one stands, as a leap, under no compulsion. The leap remains a free and open possibility of thinking; this so decisively so that in fact the essential province of freedom and openness first opens up with the realm of the leap. Precisely because of this, we are obliged to prepare the leap. To do so it was necessary for us to make the realm from which one leaps visible and make the relationship one sustains with this realm clear. The realm from which one leaps is the history of Western thinking experienced as the *Geschick* of being. Insofar as the *Geschick* of being makes its *Geschick*-like claim on the thinking essence of historical humanity, the history of thinking is based in the *Geschick* of being. The history of being is therefore not some on-rolling series of transformations of a detached, self-subsistent being. The history of being is not an objectively representable process about which one could tell "histories of being." The *Geschick* of being intrinsically remains the history of the essence of Western humanity insofar as historical humanity is engaged in constructively inhabiting the lighting and clearing of being. As the withdrawal apropos of *Geschick*, being is already intrinsically in a relationship to the essence of humanity. Yet being is not anthropomorphized through this relationship; rather, through this relationship the essence of humanity remains domiciled in the locale of being.

(On the occasion of an exchange with Ernst Jünger I have clarified the determination of being discussed here in reference to modern nihilism. The essay has in the meantime 'appeared as a separate piece with the title "The Question of Being.")

What the phrase "*Geschick* of being" means is difficult to approach for a thinking such as ours that has been almost completely relegated to objective cognition.

93

But the difficulty does not lie in the matter at hand; rather, it has to do with us—which is to say that the *Geschick* of being is not only not a self-contained ongoing process, but it also is not something lying over against us. Rather, it is more likely that the *Geschick* itself is *as* the conjunction of being and human nature.[51] We deliberately say "more likely" because even put in this way the suspicion is not put to rest that being essentially comes to be as something separate from humans.

The *Geschick* of being is, as an appeal and claim, the verdict on the basis of which all human speaking speaks.[52] The Latin for *Spruch* [verdict] is *fatum*. But as the verdict of being in the sense of the self-withdrawing *Geschick*, fate [*Fatum*] is not something fatalistic for the simple reason that it can never be any such thing. Why not? Because being, in proffering itself, brings about the free openness of the temporal play-space and, in so doing, first frees humans unto the openness of whatever fitting essential possibilities they happen to have.

In the leap-off, the leap does not shove the leaping-off realm away from itself, rather in leaping the leap becomes a recollective appropriation of the *Geschick* of being. For the leap itself, this means that it leaps neither away from the leaping-off realm, nor forward into a different, sequestered domain. The leap only remains the leap as a leap that recollectively thinks upon [the *Geschick*]. However, recollectively thinking-upon [*An-denken*] the *Geschick* that has-been means to bear in mind [*bedenken*], and indeed to bear in mind that which, in what has-been, is still unthought as that which is to be thought. Only a thinking that is a fore-thinking [*vor-denkendes*] responds to this. To recollectively think-upon what has-been is to fore-think into the unthought that is to be thought. To think is to recollectively fore-think. It neither dwells on what has-been as a past represented by historiography, nor is it a representational thinking that stares with prophetical pretenses into a supposedly known future. Thinking as a recollective fore-thinking is the leaping of the leap. This leap [*Sprung*] is a movement [*Satz*] to which thinking submits.

Implied in this is that thinking must ever anew and more originally [*ursprünglich*] make the leap [*Sprung*]. There is no repetition and no recurrence when it comes to this ever more inaugural leaping. The leap is necessary until the recollective fore-thinking to being *qua* being has been transformed by the truth of being into a different saying.

In the course of pointing to the history of thinking as the *Geschick* of being, we constantly spoke of "being" and "ground/reason" because it was unavoidable. What these words say can never be drawn together and packaged in a definition. To intend to do such a thing would be to pretend to be able to smoothly and nonchalantly grasp all the essential determinations of "being" and "ground/reason," and of being able to do this in a representation that would hover above time. But so conceived, the temporal would be the particular, limited actualization of the supratemporal contents of the definition. Of course one is in the habit of offering up such actualizations, even those of values and ideas, as the characteristic mark of the historical. The representation of history as the actualization of ideas has its own long-standing history. This representation of history is almost ineradicable. If we think about it, then of course what the unbiased eye sees is that the representation of history as the temporal actualization of supratemporal ideas and values does not stem from the experience of history. Without deliberation and consideration, this commonplace representation of history takes the Platonistic—not the Platonic—splitting up of the world into changing sensible and unchanging supersensible domains and transposes it into what initially appears as the course of human actions and passions, and as such a course of events it is called history.

While this commonplace representation of history does not let itself be disposed of by any decree, it also does not let itself be disposed of by other standards of measure that would attempt to directly modify this representation. It would be fatuous to want to do such a thing. For, this representation of history and its stubborn claim is itself determined by the *Geschick* of being, and that means by the dominance of metaphysical thinking. Of course, the handy representation of history as the temporal actualization of what is supratemporal makes more difficult any effort to bring into view that which is unique, the unique concealed in the enigmatic constancy which at times erupts and is assembled into the suddenness of what is genuinely *Geschick*-like. The sudden is the abrupt that only apparently contradicts that which is constant, which means, that which endures. What is endured is what already lasts.[53] But what already lasts and until now was concealed is first vouchsafed and becomes visible in what is abrupt. We must calmly confess that we never reach the vicinity of the historicity that is to be thought with a view to the *Geschick* of being so long as we remain ensnared in the web of representations which, all in all, blindly take refuge in the distinction between the absolute and the relative without ever going on to sufficiently determine that solely upon which this distinction can be determined, limited. What place or site is this? It is the site to which we are under way with the question concerning the principle of reason insofar as we discuss what the principle says in the second tonality. This being-under-way gives us an opportunity, at least now and then, to bring into view the sense in which "being" and "ground/reason" name what "is" the same. For this "same" is simultaneously what is constant and what at times lights up in the suddenness of a *Geschick* of being.

We now ask: What is called "ground/reason"? What is it that calls us to think the word "ground/reason"? One often says that a word means something, that a word relates to a matter through its meaning. This is a commonplace representation of what a word is. But it remains questionable whether it could withstand a more rigorous reflection on the essence of language. Even when we take language to be nothing but an instrument for information, the speaking of language never becomes a mechanism that functions uniformly everywhere.

If we restrict ourselves to Western languages and acknowledge this restriction as a limit from the very beginning, we may say that our languages speak historically. Given that there must be some truth in saying that language is the house of being, then the historical speaking of language is oriented and ordained by a particular *Geschick* of being. In terms of the essence of language, this means that language speaks, not humans. Humans only speak inasmuch as they respond to language on the basis of the *Geschick*. But this responding is the genuine manner in which humans belong in the lighting and clearing of being. Therefore the polysemy of a word does not primarily stem from the fact that when we humans talk and write we at times mean different things with one word. Polysemy is always an historical polysemy. It springs from the fact that in the speaking of language we ourselves are at times, according to the *Geschick* of being, struck, that means addressed, differently by the being of beings.

We speak of a foundation wall [*Grundmauer*], of a basic rule [*Grundregel*], of a fundamental principle [*Grundsatz*]. But we are going to notice shortly that while this meaning of *Grund* is indeed quite commonplace, it is at the same time quite abstract; that is, it is taken out of and cut loose from the realm from which the word, in a more inaugural manner, speaks the meaning we mentioned previously. On the one hand *Grund* indicates the depth, for example, of the bottom of the sea [*Meeresgrund*], of the valley floor [*Talgrund*], of the meadowland [*Wiesengrund*], of a crevasse, of low-lying land and terrain; in a broader sense it means the earth, the surface of the earth. And even today in the Allemanic-Swabian dialect *Grund* has the even more original meaning of "humus," which is loam, the heavy, fertile soil. For instance, a flower bed that has too little soil must be given more of it in order for there to be satisfactory growth. On the whole, *Grund* means the more deeply lying and, at the same time, supportive realm. Thus we speak "from the bottom of the heart" [*Herzgrund*]. Already in the sixteenth century, "to get to the bottom" [*auf dem Grund kommen*] meant "to ascertain the truth," "ascertain what actually is." *Grund* is the sort of thing from which we arise and that back to which we return insofar as the *Grund* is that upon which something is based, that on which something depends, that from which something follows. The language of thinking speaks of an essential ground [*Grund*] in this regard, of the grounds for the emergence [*Enstehungsgrund*], of the motive [*Beweggrund*], of the premise of an argument [*Beweisgrund*]. The relationship of *Grund* to essence, emergence, movement, and proof [*Beweis*] already comes to light early on in the history of thinking, even if in a rather hodge-podge way. Yet when one talks of essential grounds, grounds for the emergence, motive, and argument, it remains a question whether these stem from a regard for *Grund* or from a regard for being. But how can this question remain if being and *Grund* "are" the same? In accordance with these references, but pursuing them more radically, Hegel, in his uncommonly keen ability to hear the innermost thinking of language, often used the phrase "to go to ruins" [*zum Grunde gehen*]. What in Hegel's sense—and here that means in the literal sense—hits bottom [*zum Grunde geht*] does not thereby disappear; rather what "hits bottom" first of all finds the ground and with this discovery it enters into a movement of origination. "To hit bottom"—for Hegel that means that the determinations of a matter converge on the unity that hold sway over all the determinations.

With such remarks that can easily be proliferated we can indeed get wound up in a discussion of the single word *Grund*. We have not yet brought into view anything of the site from which the principle of reason speaks insofar as we hear it according to the second tonality that allows the belonging-together of *Grund* and being to resound. We hear this resonance when we contemplate the fact that the principle of reason—more precisely its being set up as one of the supreme fundamental principles by Leibniz—prepares that epoch of the history of being in which being comes to light as transcendentally molded object-ness. If we contemplate this, then we take heed of the following:

What [in German] is called the *Grundsatz vom Grund* [fundamental principle of reason] is the abbreviated translation of the title *principium reddendae rationis sufficientis*. *Grund* is the translation of *ratio*. It may have become superfluous in the meantime to state this. What is more, this statement is a platitude so long as we don't give a second thought to what is going on in this and similar translations. Translating and translating are not equivalents if in one instance what one is concerned with is a business letter and in another instance a poem. The former is translatable, the latter is not. In the meantime, modern technology —more precisely, the modern, logistical interpretation of thinking and speaking congenial to it—has already put in gear translation machines. But in translating it is not only a matter of what one is translating at the moment; rather, it is a matter of which language is being translated into which language. What we have said just now concerns relationships pertinent to translating which can easily be seen if one has limited knowledge and a little bit of circumspection. Nevertheless, even here we can miss a decisive trait that runs through all essential translations. By this we mean those translations, in those epochs which are ready for them, that convey a work of poetry or thinking. The trait we have in mind consists in the fact that in such cases, the translation [*Übersetzung*] is not only an interpretation, but it is also a legacy [*Überlieferung*]. As a legacy, it belongs to the innermost movement of history. In terms of what was remarked upon earlier, this means that in any given epoch of the *Geschick* of being, an essential translation responds to the manner in which a language speaks in that *Geschick* of being. Of course we pointed out only in an allusive manner how Kant's *Critique of Pure Reason* responds to the exacting claim of the principle of sufficient reason and brings this response to language. But *Vernunft* [Reason], just as much as *Grund* [grounds] speak as translations of the one word, *ratio*. In historical terms this means that the critique of pure Reason is the thinking that thinks in the light of the principle of sufficient reason, a thinking from out of which the word *ratio* speaks with its dually singular utterance that, in a single stroke, names both "Reason" and "grounds." *Ratio* and that which is thought in it is passed along in such a speaking. The passing-along meant here is what moves genuine history. Under hazard of appearing to exaggerate, we may even say that if *ratio* did not speak in modern thinking with the double sense of "Reason" and "grounds," then there would not be Kant's critique of pure Reason as the circumscription of the conditions for the possibility of the object of experience.

So it may be that our assessment that the word *Grund* is the translation of *ratio* has lost its character as a platitude. It should be suggested only in passing that the classical sources for the insight into the passing along, as a legacy of the *Geschick*, of *ratio* as "grounds" and "Reason" to modern thinking are Paragraphs 29 to 32 of Leibniz's *Monadology*. The *Monadology* is said to be one of the last writings of Leibniz. It deals with the Principles of philosophy. The ninety paragraphs of this text allow the scaffolding of Western—especially modern—metaphysics to be more clearly discerned than almost any other work of thinking in the age before Kant. This text of Leibniz, originating in the year 1714, was first published in 1840 in the original French text from the Hannover Library by a student of Hegel, Johann Ed. Erdmann.[43]

Grund is the translation of *ratio*. What *Grund* names and what the principle of reason speaks about passes along what is experienced and thought in the dually singular utterance of *ratio*. We must inquire into this. We can only do so here in a sketchy way. We will hold our itinerary in view so that it doesn't come down to a random word-clarification; for it merits bringing into view that and how being and ground/reason "are" the same. This means that it merits taking up and recalling the extent to which the sameness of being and ground/reason announces itself at the commencement of the history of being, and indeed announces this only then to remain, as this sameness, unthought and unheard over a long period of time. Yet at the same time, what is unheard [*Ungehörte*] is what is unprecedented [*Unerhörte*]—what is unique in the history of being and its commencement.

Ratio speaks in the word *Grund* and indeed does so with the dual sense of Reason and grounds. Being a ground/reason also characterizes what we call a cause, in Latin *causa*; this is why the principle of reason, as we have frequently mentioned, also reads: *Nihil est sine causa*. In step with a long tradition and habit of thinking and speaking, we no longer find anything exciting about the fact that *ratio* simultaneously names "Reason" and "grounds." Thinking carefully, we nevertheless must agree that what *Grund* means—namely, depth and earth and footing—simply has nothing immediately to do with Reason and perception. Yet no one contests that *ratio* simultaneously signifies "Reason" and "grounds." Where does this double sense of *ratio* come from?

The Latin word *ratio* originally and genuinely meant neither "Reason" nor "grounds," rather it meant something else. This something else is nevertheless not so completely different as to be able to keep the word *ratio* from speaking later on in the dual sense of "Reason" and "grounds." A passage from Cicero can be cited so that we can directly seek out the classical realm of the saying of the Latin word *ratio*. At the same time it throws a light on the context of the issue that we would like to think about. Cicero says:

Causam appello rationem efficiendi, eventum id quod est effectum.[44] (

Translated in the usual manner this says: "When I speak of a cause, I mean the ground/reason of an effecting; by effect, I mean what comes about as a result."

What is going on in this statement of Cicero? It seems as though it brings more shadows and darkness over the matter than light into it. But so it is and fortunately so, as soon as we free ourselves of the blind haste with which we translate the Latin words with ones common to us: *causa* with *Ursache* [cause], *efficere* with *bewirken* [to effect], *effectus* with *Wirkung* [effect]. These translations are thoroughly correct. But their correctness is also what is insidious, for through their correctness we become ensnared in historically later, modern and—today —normative representations. So ensnared we no longer hear anything of what is said in the Roman word and how it is said. So if we take heed of this, it always remains questionable whether our hearing goes back far enough.

Causam appello rationem, eventum id quod est effectum: Here we find *ratio* and *causa* spoken in conjunction with *efficere* and *eventus*. The word *eventus* is perhaps the key to Cicero's statement, which almost sounds like the pronouncement of a schoolmaster without any trace of world-historical significance. Nevertheless, such a trace lies in the words we have cited. *Eventus* is what comes about; *efficere* is a bringing-forth and a producing. One speaks of *ratio* in the realm of producing and coming about, a word which we may no longer translate with "grounds" and "Reason," for if we did, we would block the path whose line of sight we should hold to at this point. But then how are we supposed to translate *ratio efficiendi*? *Ratio* is the *ratio* for what is to be produced, its cause, *causa*. Having a relation to *efficere* is what characterizes *ratio* as *causa*. This *causa* belongs to the realm of producing, whereby something comes about. To what extent does *causa* belong to this realm? To the extent that it has the character of *ratio*. What does *ratio* mean here? Is *ratio* aligned with the realm of *efficere* or even bounded by it? Not at all. The reverse is true. The realm of *efficere* and *eventus* belong to that of *ratio*. We do not experience what this word names |

by citing this passage precisely because everything that Cicero says here leads back to *ratio*. Nevertheless, Cicero's statement is still informative.

Ratio belongs to the verb *reor*, whose guiding sense is "to take something for something"; that for which something is taken is placed under, sup-posed. In such a placing-under, that under which something is placed is readied for what will be placed under it. "Putting something in order for something," "to take one's bearings from something" is the sense of our verb *rechnen* [reckon]. To reckon with something, to take something into account means to keep one's eye on it and to act accordingly. To reckon or count on something means to expect it and thereby to figure it as something upon which to build. The genuine sense of "reckon" is not necessarily connected to numbering. This also holds for what one calls calculus. "Calculus" is the playing piece used in draughts, and hence the reckoning stone. "Calculation" is reckoning as deliberating: one thing is placed over against another so as to be compared and appraised. Hence, reckoning in the sense of an operation with numbers is a special kind of reckoning distinguished by the essence of quantity. In reckoning with and on something, that which is thus reckoned is produced for cognition, brought into the open. Through such reckoning something comes about; thus *eventus* and *efficere* belong in the realm of *ratio*. The briefly discussed, genuine, and therefore broad sense of the verb "to reckon" is named by the Latin verb *reor*.

"*Ratio*" is called "reckoning." When we reckon, we represent what must be held in view, namely, that with which and in terms of which we reckon with some matter. What is thus reckoned and computed affords us an account of what is going on with something, what is in it that determines it. What comes to light in an account is that upon which something depends for being the way that it is. *Ratio* is called "reckoning," but reckoning has a dual sense. On the one hand "reckoning" means reckoning as a deed; on the other hand it means what is yielded in such a deed, what is reckoned, the presented calculation, the account.

We say "to render an account." The language of the ancient Romans says: *rationem reddere*. *Reddere* necessarily belongs to *ratio* insofar as the means and ends with which some matter or action is reckoned are presented in the reckoning and the account. The fact that the *principium rationis* is a *principium reddendae rationis* lies in the essence of *ratio* itself. As an account it is in itself a *reddendum*. This is not projected and forced upon *ratio* from out of the blue. The *reddere* is prefigured in and called for by the essence of *ratio* as reckoning. Reckoning on . . . and reckoning with . . . is a deliberate tendering [of something].

Let us think for a moment about an important transitional thought. Heard in the second tonality, the principle of reason says: being and ground/reason —the same. In the meantime we heard that being lights and clears itself as a *Geschick* of being. Hence in a particular *Geschick*, a particular configuration of ground/reason, namely *ratio*, converges with reckoning, with accounting, as being the same. But if the *reddendum* belongs to the essence of *ratio*, the sort and sense of the *rationem reddere* also changes along with it. The literal phrase is indeed the same as used by the ancient Romans and by Leibniz, but in terms of the *Geschick* of being it is exactly this "same" that changed such that it introduced the configuration of the modern epoch and prepared what was raised by Kant's thinking into the light of day under the title of the "transcendental." With Leibniz the *reddere* is connected to and accomplished by a representing I that is defined as the subject certain of itself. Such an interpretation of the essence of humans and thereby of that which receives what is offered in the *reddendum* would have been alien to the Romans, although no more decisively foreign than it would be for Greek thinking. Leibnizian thinking hears in the *reddendum* a demand whose character is from a different *Geschick*. For with him *ratio* is the *principium*, the prevailing demand that is normative for all beings with regard to their being. It requires the rendering of the account of the very possibility for a full accounting which computes everything that is a being. The *ratio sufficiens*, the genuinely and uniquely sufficient reason, the *summa ratio*, the final account of exhaustive calculability, of the calculus of the universe, is *Deus*, God. What does Leibniz say about God in regard to the universe? In 1677 (at the age of thirty-one) Leibniz wrote a dialogue on the *Lingua rationalis*,[45] that is, on calculus, which is the sort of reckoning that is in the position of giving a full accounting of the relations between word, sign, and thing—and thus for everything that is. In this dialogue and in other essays, Leibniz had anticipated the fundamentals not only for what today are used as thinking machines, but even more, of what determines their manner of thinking. In a handwritten marginal note to this dialogue Leibniz remarks: *Cum Deus calculat fit mundus.* When God reckons, a world comes to be.

All that is needed is a ready and willing glance into our atomic age in order to see that if God is dead, as Nietzsche says, the calculated world still remains and everywhere includes humans in its reckoning inasmuch as it reckons up everything to the *principium rationis*.

Lecture Thirteen

The principle of reason reads: Nothing is without reason. *Nihil est sine ratione.* "Reason" [*Grund*] is the translation of *ratio*. A translation becomes a legacy when the speaking of basic words translates one historical language into another one. If it rigidifies, a legacy can degenerate into a burden and a handicap. It can become this because a legacy [*Überlieferung*] is genuinely, as its name says, a delivering [*Liefern*] in the sense of *liberare*, of liberating. As a liberating, a legacy raises concealed riches of what has-been into the light of day, even if this light is at first only that of a hesitant dawn. That *Grund* is the translation of *ratio* means to say that *ratio* has passed over into *Grund*, a legacy which already early on speaks with a double sense. Of course, the passing over of the two senses of *ratio* into "grounds" and "Reason" first reaches its decisive configuration where the *Geschick* of being determines that epoch which, according to historiographical periodization, is called "modernity." Provided being and ground/reason "are" the same, then the modern *Geschick* of being must also transform the ancient Roman double sense of *ratio*.

As separate as the two senses in the double sense of *ratio* may be—namely "ground" as footing and earth and "Reason" as perception and hearing[54]—both meanings are allied already early on, even if one did not expressly think about their belonging-together. We must say in a more appropriate manner that both tendencies of this double sense—Reason and grounds—are traced out in what *ratio* names. Then what does *ratio* mean? We answered with the translation of the word *ratio;* "reckoning." But here "reckoning" is to be thought in the sense of the verb *reor,* which is related to the noun *ratio.* "Reckoning" means "to orient something in terms of something," "to represent something as something." That *as which* some particular thing is represented [*vorgestellt*] as being, is what it is imputed [*das Unterstellte*] as being. Broadly conceived, this reckoning also determines the sense of the word "calculus." One speaks of mathematical calculus. But there is also another kind. Even Hölderlin used the word "calculus" in a deeper sense in the "Remarks" to his translations of Sophocles' *Oedipus Rex* and *Antigone*. In the "Remarks to *Oedipus*" one reads:

> Other artworks lack, compared with the Greek, reliability; at least they have been, in every way, judged more according to the impressions that they make than according to their lawful calculus and the other ways of proceeding whereby beauty is produced.[46]

And further:

> In the tragic, the law, the calculus, the way that a system of perceptions—the entire human as one under the influence of the elements—develops, the way that representation and perception and reasoning proceed one after the other in different successions but always according to a certain rule, is more a matter of balance than of a pure series.

And the "Remarks to *Antigone*" begin:

> "The rule, the calculable law of Antigone is related to that of Oedipus as ∕ is to ∖, so that the balance is more in the beginning toward the end than the end toward the beginning."[47]

Insofar as both remarks speak of "balance," the calculus spoken of here also seems to be represented in a quantitative-mechanical, mathematical way. Indeed the balance of which Hölderlin speaks belongs to scales and the balancing out of the artwork, that is, it belongs to tragic presentation in tragedy.

Ratio is calculus, reckoning in the broad, high, and usual sense. Reckoning, as orienting something in terms of something, always presents something and thus is in itself a yielding, a *reddere*. The *reddendum* belongs to *ratio*. But as is always the case when it comes to the context of the history of being from out of which *ratio* speaks, when it later speaks as "Reason" and "ground," the *reddendum* has a different sense. Implied here is that one finds in modernity the moment of the unconditional and thoroughgoing demand to render mathematically-technically computable grounds—total "Rationalizing."

In talking of the *principium reddendae rationis*, Leibniz indeed speaks in Latin, but he does not thereby speak the language of the ancient Romans. Nevertheless, what the Romans called *ratio* has passed over into the representation of what "Reason" and "grounds" say in modernity.

But how is it that *ratio* in the ancient sense could bifurcate in a manner such that it speaks with the double sense of "grounds" as well as of "Reason"? How this could happen must have become clear to those who really have an ear out. A few references to this "how" are still needed, for we are speaking of a bifurcation of *ratio* into *ratio* as "Reason" and *ratio* as "grounds." To talk of this bifurcation should make it understandable that both words, "Reason" and "grounds"—and all that they say—are divergent, but nevertheless are held in one and the same root and stalk, which is why even in their divergence —and precisely in this divergence—they converge. The Old High German word for a bifurcated bough, a bifurcated tree trunk and the entire tree that has grown in this shape is *Zwiesel*. We often find such forked growths under the old, towering pines of the upper Black Forest. How is *ratio* a forked growth? *Ratio* means "reckoning" in the broadest sense, and accordingly we say "one reckons on something with something for something"; we also say: "counts," without numbers coming into the picture. In reckoning, something is imputed, not arbitrarily and not in the sense of a suspicion; what is imputed is that due to which a matter is the way it is. What is thus imputed, computed, is that upon which something rests, namely what lies present before us, supportive, what is reckoned in a reckoning; *ratio* is therefore the basis, the footing, that is, the ground. In imputing, reckoning represents something as something. This representing of something as something is a bringing-before-oneself that deals with some particular thing that lies present, and in such a dealing-with perceives the condition it is in vis-à-vis that in terms of which and by which it is reckoned. Reckoning, *ratio* as such a perceiving, is Reason. *Ratio* is, as reckoning: grounds and Reason.

We are trying to think the principle of reason as an utterance of being. The principle says: being and *Grund*: the same. In order to think about what has been said, we ask: What does *Grund* mean? The answer is: in passing itself along, the word *ratio*—which also means "Reason"—speaks in the word *Grund*. The extent to which *ratio* is a bifurcation, a forked growth, has been commented upon. The question that thinks back to what the principle of reason says as an utterance of being has thereby changed and now goes: to what extent "are" *ratio* and being the same? Does the forked-word *ratio*, which now speaks vicariously and in a double sense for the word *Grund*, point at all to a belonging-together, that is, to a sameness with being? One can immediately bring into view nothing of this in the forked word *ratio*. Neither the one tine nor the other of the bifurcated word "reckoning," "account," that is, neither *Grund* ["grounds"] nor "Reason" immediately name being.

The question we are faced with by the principle of reason is this: to what extent "are" being and *ratio* the same? To what extent do grounds and Reason (*ratio*) on the one side, and being on the other belong together?

{If we were capable of seeing this question through in its full import, then for the first time a glimmer could strike us of what, as the *Geschick* of being, illuminates and at the same time casts a shadow over the history of the West, and today in a modified way that means, over planetary world history.}

If we ask to what extent being and bifurcated *ratio* "might be" the same, that is belong together, then it seems the only thing worth asking about has to do with the accommodation of being on the one side and, on the other side in the averred belonging-together, bifurcated *ratio*. If one has something like this in mind, then the belonging-together in question appears as though it were some third thing, like a roof, a vault that stands ready, as it were, to accommodate. To think this would be cockeyed. Rather, the belonging-together must already light up from what has its abode in it and therefore what also already speaks for itself: being speaks to us, even if in various manners, as φύσις—emerging-on-its-own—as οὐσία—presencing—as objectness. Likewise, *ratio* speaks as "grounds" as well as "Reason." Belonging-together is precisely what remains genuinely opaque and questionable. This belonging-together must come to light from out of what belongs to the "together," granted that here the "together" means something else and something different than the welding together of two otherwise separate pieces. Accordingly, being *qua* being must belong to *ratio*, as well as the reverse: bifurcated *ratio* itself speaks of its affiliation with being, if we pay careful enough attention to what it is saying. But, if we ponder what *ratio* says, namely "reckoning," then we find nothing in it that would speak for an affiliation with being. How come the word *ratio* does not answer us when we ask about the extent to which an affiliation with being is contained in what is named by *ratio*? On the one hand, this comes from the fact that we now run the risk of taking the word *ratio* by itself and, as it were, detached from what it says, which is always a historical saying. On the other hand, in regard to the affiliation of *ratio* with being, we fumble around in the dark because it all too easily slips our mind that the word "being" also always only speaks historically. From this there comes an important directive. The question of the extent to which being and *ratio* belong together can only be asked in terms of the *Geschick* of being and answered by thinking back into the *Geschick* of being. But we only experience the *Geschick* of being in traversing the history of Western thinking. This starts with the thinking of the Greeks. The commencement of the *Geschick* of being finds its fitting response and preserve in the thinking of Greek culture from Anaximander to Aristotle. We ask the question of the belonging-together of being and *ratio* in an inaugural and being-historical way only when we think the question and what it asks in a *Greek* way.

The path of our question is sketched out by listening to the principle of reason. Therefore we went from *Grund* back to *ratio*. But *ratio* speaks in a Latin-Roman way and not a Greek way, which means, not such that in the hearing of this word we would already be in the position to ask our question in an inaugural and being-historical way. Or might the Roman word *ratio* also simultaneously speak in a Greek manner? So it does in fact. For within the history of thinking, *ratio* is, for its part, a word that translates, that means, a word that passes something along. Just as the bifurcated word *ratio* passes over into the basic words of modern thinking—"Reason" and "grounds"—so a Greek word speaks in the Roman word *ratio*: it is called λόγος. Accordingly, we only hear the principle of reason in the second tonality—that is, in a being-historical manner and hence in an inaugural manner—when we say the theme of the principle in Greek: τὸ αὐτό (ἐστιν) εἶναί τε καὶ λόγος—εἶναι and λόγος (are) the same. In fact one nowhere finds among the Greek thinkers a principle worded in this way. Nevertheless, it names the trait of the *Geschick* of being of Greek thinking, and this in a manner such that it points forward into the later epochs of the history of being.

In looking back on the question which we circumscribed more precisely above, we must now consider: to what extent does an affiliation with being, that means with εἶναι, speak in all that is said in the Greek word λόγος? In terms of the Latin *esse* and the German auxiliary verb *sein* [to be], this Greek word means "coming to be present." Explained in terms of its Greek sense, "being" means "to shine with and down here into that which is unconcealed, and thus, while shining, to last and abide."

To what extent does being, thought in this way, belong together with *Grund* and *ratio*? As long as we leave the question in this form, it remains confused and deprives us of every clue to the answer. The confusion resolves itself if we ask to what extent does "to be," thought in a Greek manner as "coming to be present," belong together with λόγος? Put another way, to what extent does a belonging-together with being, thought in a Greek manner, speak in what the word λόγος names. To what extent "are" λόγος and "coming to be present" the same? What does λόγος mean?

Much will have been gained for the exacting treatment of this decisive and wide-ranging question if we no longer let what has come up on the path of this lecture slip from sight. What is this? A truly simple insight that we are wont to take too lightly because it is simple. What does this insight show us? It acquaints us with the following: "grounds" and "Reason" are the translations, which now means, the historical legacy of bifurcated *ratio. Ratio* is the translation, that now means, the historical legacy of λόγος. Because this is the case, we therefore may think λόγος neither in terms of our more recent representations of "grounds" and "Reason," nor even in the sense of the Roman *ratio.* How else are we to think it? Answer: in a Greek manner, in the sense of Greek thinking and speaking. This seems to be a plausible piece of advice, namely the sort of advice that is none, for what does it mean: "thinking and speaking in a Greek manner"? It means that what is Greek about the thinking and speaking we now undertake is determined precisely by λόγος and as λόγος. Therefore, we ought not convince ourselves that it is easy to think about the Greek word λόγος and what it says in a Greek manner, and that means, to think about it regardless of the representational thinking that is commonplace with us.

Difficult as the task seems to be, we must rise to the occasion, assuming that in the meantime we have found it necessary to listen to what the principle of reason genuinely says, that means, says in the other tonality, which means that in the meantime we have experienced the principle of reason addressing us with the exacting claim under which our era stands world-historically. What does λόγος mean, when thought in a Greek manner? The answer here inevitably turns out to be crude. It restricts itself to the sort of references that help us think, in a manner apropos of the history of being, what the principle of reason says in the second tonality: being and ground/reason. The Greek noun λόγος belongs to the verb λέγειν. It means "to gather, to lay one beside the other." In this case it can happen that the one is laid beside the other such that the one is oriented towards the other, conforming to it. The Latin *reor* and *ratio* represent the sort of orienting and conforming that is a reckoning, which is why the Roman word *ratio* is suited to translate the Greek word λόγος into Roman thinking. Even in Greek, λόγος can have the sense of "reckoning," "orienting one thing towards another," an orienting that we still more generally call "the relating of something to something." Λόγος can mean the equivalent of the Latin *relatio*: relation. But how is it that λόγος can mean this? Because λόγος and λέγειν name something more essential than the gathering and reckoning we had in mind just a moment ago; the verb λέγειν is a word for "to say" and λόγος means "a statement" and "legend." Every dictionary gives this information. One accepts it as obvious that where we say *sagen* ["to say"] the Greeks say λέγειν. In the end, what the two, literally different, words mean passes as obvious. Yet it may be time to ask: in what is the essence of saying based for the Greeks?

"Saying" means, when thought in a Greek manner, "to bring to light," "to let something appear in its look," "to show the way in which it regards us," which is why a saying clarifies things for us. But then how come a saying for the Greeks is a λέγειν, λόγος? Because λέγειν means "to gather," "to lay-next-to-each-other." But such a laying is, as a laying that gathers, raises up, keeps and preserves, an allowing-to-lie-present that brings something to shine forth, namely that which lies present. However, that which lies present is what comes-to-presence-on-its-own; λέγειν and λόγος allow what comes to presence to lie present in its presencing. Λόγος as λεγόμενον simultaneously means that-which-has-been-said, which means, what-has-been-shown, which means, what-lies-present as such—what comes to presence in its presencing. We say: beings in their being. Λόγος names being. But as that which lies present, as what presents itself, λόγος is simultaneously that upon which something else lies and is based. We say: the footing, the ground. Λόγος names the ground. Λόγος is at once presencing and ground. Being and ground belong together in λόγος. Λόγος names this belonging-together of being and ground. It names them insofar as it, in one breath, says: "allowing to lie present as allowing to arise," "emerging-on-its-own": φύσις, "being"; *and*: "allowing to lie present as presenting," laying a bed of soil, "grounds": "ground/reason." Λόγος names in one breath being and ground/reason.

But with this naming, the differentiation into being and into ground/reason remains concealed, and with this differentiation the belonging-together of the two conceals itself.

In terms of the history of being, it is only at a particularly high—perhaps highest—moment that the belonging-together of being and ground/reason accrues to the word λόγος. In the history of early Greek thinking, Heraclitus used the word λόγος in this sense. But the word λόγος is at the same time a word that conceals. It doesn't allow the belonging-together of being and ground/reason *as such* to come to the fore. Now one would like to expect that the belonging-together of being and ground/reason gradually comes to light in the train of the history of thinking. This is exactly what doesn't happen, rather the opposite does. The difference between being and ground/reason is what first becomes overt, but not in the sense of a distinction which, implying a connection between being and ground/reason, refers both to a belonging-together. Being and ground/reason show themselves as different in the sense of what is separated and divided. However, because the belonging-together of being and ground/reason reigns in what is concealed, what is separated does not fall asunder into unconnectedness. Rather, ground/reason comes to be represented as something else, not as being, but as connected to what being, for its part, determines, namely beings. It is in this way that the belonging-together of being and ground/reason reigns in what is concealed. This belonging-together never came to light— much less was it taken up by conceptual thinking—neither in terms of its *Geschick*-configuration, nor in terms of ground/reason and its forms. Instead, something obvious monopolizes things in the history of thinking, namely what was mentioned at the beginning of the first lecture: every being has a ground/reason. This is run of the mill for representational thinking. To what extent? To the extent that the representation of beings with respect to the fact that they are, and are in this and that way, is a representation that has being in sight and hence, although without knowing it, has something like ground/reason in sight. Therefore, it is natural for representational thinking to ask for ground/reasons and to revert to Principles.

If later on the principle of reason is formulated, it at first articulates nothing but the obvious [that every being has a reason]. But the principle itself, which, as it were, sanctions this obviousness, for its part claims this obviousness as its own. So the principle of reason counts as an immediately intuitive law of thinking. How come? It comes from the fact that being and ground/reason "are" the same, yet their belonging-together is forgotten, which means, if understood in a Greek way: concealed. But this can't be thought as long as we understand λόγος in terms of *ratio* and "Reason." In this case we also do not become aware of the extent to which the Roman *rationem reddere* is not the equivalent of the Greek λόγον διδόναι. One can correctly translate this Greek phrase with "giving an account," "to specify the reason," but one does not thereby think in a genuinely Greek manner. Thought in a Greek manner, λόγον διδόναι means "to tender something present in whatever way it is presencing and lying present," namely, to tender it to an assembling perception. Insofar as every being continues to be determined by being, that means, by grounding, beings themselves are always founded and grounded beings—and this in the various manners whose plurality and provenance cannot be discussed here.

{Only two references should be briefly made as to how, from early on in the history of thinking, being and ground/reason converge, so much so that their belonging-together and provenance remain concealed. But this convergence is now a falling-asunder. Of course, as soon as we have for once brought this curious belonging-together into view, it is, as always in such cases, easy to find and point it out everywhere.

Though it had other names in early Western thinking, "being" means λόγος. Heraclitus, who is the same thinker who spoke this word [λόγος], also called being φύσις.

As an allowing to arise that also assembles and harbors, being is that First from which those that arise first arise as the enduring particulars of what it has assembled—being is the First from which all this proceeds into the unconcealed that has opened up. As λόγος, being is the First from which whatever is present presences—in Greek: τὸ πρῶτον ὅθεν. "The first from which" is that from out of which commences every particular being that is, and that by which it continues to be held in the sway as something that has commenced; in Greek "to commence" is called ἄρχειν. Λόγος thus develops into the πρῶτον ὅθεν, that is, into the ἀρχή—said in the Latin of the Romans, into the "*principium*." The fact that all thinking and acting, every modus vivendi seeks Principles in a representational way and holds itself to them stems from the essence of being as λόγος and φύσις. Here the belonging-together of being and Principle and *ratio*, of being and reason as Rational ground is instituted. But all of this is in no way obvious; rather, it is a single mystery of a unique *Geschick*.

Being, in the sense of λόγος, is what assembles and allows something to lie present. In λόγος, what lies present comes into the light of day, and indeed as being the sort of thing due to which particular beings stand one way rather than some other way vis-à-vis each other. That due to which something is and is the way it is rather than some other way shows itself as the sort of thing that is indebted to what we just named [namely, being in the sense of λόγος]. As something already lying present, that to which something is due—that to which something is indebted—is called αἴτιον in Greek. The Romans translate it with the word *causa*; [in German] one says: *Ursache* [cause]. Both—*Ursachen* [causes] and Principles—have the character of being grounds; because they stem from the essence of ground/reason, they belong, along with this essence, with being. Therefore, Principles and causes determine beings on into the future and link all representations of beings. The sovereignty and claim of principles and causes so quickly becomes so natural and full-blown that it looks as though they and they alone—for what rhyme or reason one doesn't know—determine beings in their being.

If in modernity being is transcendentally determined as objectness and this as the condition for the possibility of objects, then being disappears, as it were, in favor of what is called "the condition for the possibility" and is a kind of Rational ground and grounding.}

When we were led to say more clearly what the talk of the history of being as the *Geschick* of being is supposed to mean, we referred to the fact that being, in that it proffers, clears and lights itself, at the same time withdraws. The talk of the withdrawal remained obscure and to many ears had the ring of a mystical assertion nowhere anchored in the matter at hand. Now we can more clearly hear the words about the withdrawal of being. The words say that being conceals itself as being; namely, in its inaugural *Geschick* as λόγος being conceals its belonging-together with ground/reason. But the withdrawing does not exhaust itself in this concealment. Rather, inasmuch as it conceals its essence, being allows something else to come to the fore, namely ground/reason in the shape of ἀρχαί, αἰτίαι, of *rationes*, of *causae*, of Principles, *Ursachen* [causes] and Rational grounds. In withdrawing being leaves behind these shapes of ground/reason whose provenance goes unrecognized. Yet this lack of recognition is not experienced as such, for it is recognized by everyone that all beings have a ground/reason. One finds nothing unusual in this.

So it is in withdrawing that being proffers itself to humans in a manner that conceals its essential provenance behind the thick veil of Rationally understood grounds, causes, and their shapes.

Heard in the second tonality, the principle of reason says: being and ground/reason: the same. What is said here will speak more clearly as soon as we think back and listen in a manner apropos of the *Geschick* of being to how λόγος speaks as the basic word of Heraclitus. In the second tonality, the principle of reason is not a metaphysical principle, rather a phrase thought in terms of the *Geschick* of being. Its more precise formulation therefore must run: as the *Geschick* commences, being hails as λόγος and that means, hails in the essence of ground/reason. Seen in terms of the commencement of the *Geschick* of being, being and ground/reason "are" the same, and they remain the same, but in a belonging-together that diverges into a difference that varies historically.

Inasmuch as we follow the second tonality, we no longer think being in terms of beings; rather we think it qua being, namely as ground/reason, that means, not as *ratio*, not as *Ursache* [cause], not as Rational ground and Reason, rather as a letting-lie-present that assembles. But being and ground/reason are not an empty oneness; rather, it is the concealed fullness of what first comes to light in the *Geschick* of being as the history of Western thinking.

During our first discussion of the second tonality of the principle of reason this meant: being and ground/reason: the same. Simultaneously this meant: being: the a-byss.

In terms of the *Geschick*, being "is" the same as ground/reason, as being's more original name, λόγος, says. Insofar as being essentially comes to be as ground/reason, it has no ground/reason. However this is not because it founds itself, but because every foundation—even and especially self-founded ones—remain inappropriate to being as ground/reason. Every founding and even every appearance of foundability has inevitably degraded being to some sort of a being. Being *qua* being remains ground-less. Ground/reason stays from being, namely, as a ground/reason that would first found being, it stays off and away. Being: the *a*-byss.

Now, does all we have just said simply stand next to all we said earlier: being and ground/reason: the same? Or does one even exclude the other? In fact, it seems so if we think according to the rules of ordinary logic. According to these "being and ground/reason: the same" amounts to saying: being = ground/reason. Then how could the other one hold: being: the a-byss? This is what shows itself as what is to be thought now, namely, being "is" the a-byss insofar as being and ground/reason: the same. Insofar as being "is" what grounds, and only insofar as it is so, it has no ground/reason.

If we think about this, and if we persist in such thinking, then we notice that we have leaped off from the realm of previous thinking and are in the leap. But do we not fall into the fathomless with this leap? Yes and no. Yes —insofar as now being can no longer be given a basis in the sense of beings and explained in terms of beings. No—insofar as being is now finally to be thought *qua* being. As what is to be thought, it becomes, from out of its truth, what gives a measure. The manner in which thinking thinks must conform to this measure. But it is not possible for us to seize upon this measure and what it offers through a computing and gauging. For us it remains that which is im-measurable. However, so little does the leap allow thinking to fall into the fathomless in the sense of the complete void that in fact it first allows thinking to respond to being *qua* being, that is, to the truth of being.

If we hear the principle of reason in the other tonality and think about all we hear, then this thinking-about is a leap, indeed a far-reaching leap that brings thinking into a play with that wherein being *qua* being finds its repose; that wherein being finds its repose is not the sort of thing upon which it depends for its ground/reason. Through this leap, thinking enters into the breadth and depth of that play upon which our human nature is staked. Humans are truly capable of playing and of remaining in play only insofar as they are engaged in this play and thereby at stake in the play. In which play?

So far we have barely experienced this play and have not yet considered its nature, which means, what the play plays and who plays it, and how the playing is to be thought here. If we aver that this play wherein being *qua* being finds its repose is an elevated and even the most elevated play, and is free from everything arbitrary, then very little has been said as long as this elevation and that which is most elevated about it is not thought in terms of the mystery of the play. Indeed the manner of our thinking until now does not suffice to think this, for as soon as we attempt to think the play, which means to think it according to its mode of representation, we take this play as something that is. So just as a ground/reason belongs to the being of a being, so it belongs to the play. Thus the nature of the play is determined as it is everywhere determined, namely as the dialectic of freedom and necessity within the horizon of ground/reason, of *ratio*, of rules, of rules of play, of calculus. Perhaps one might have more appropriately translated the Leibnizian sentence *Cum Deus calculat fit mundus* with: When God plays, a world comes to be.

The leap into the other tonality of the principle of reason directs a question to us which reads: does the nature of the play let itself be suitably determined in terms of being *qua* ground/reason, or must we think being and ground/reason, being *qua* abyss in terms of the nature of play and indeed of the play which engages us mortals who are who we are only insofar as we live in proximity to death, which as the most radical possibility of existence is capable of bringing what is most elevated to the clearing and lighting of being and its truth. Death is the as yet unthought standard of measure of the unfathomable, which means, of the most elevated play in which humans are engaged in on earth, a play in which they are at stake.

Is it not merely a playful act if now, at the close of the lecture course on the principle of reason, we almost violently haul in thoughts about play and about the belonging-together of being and ground/reason with play? It may seem so as long as we keep on neglecting to think in terms of the *Geschick* of being, and that means neglecting to entrust ourselves to the liberating engagement in the legacy of thinking and to do so in a way that recollectively thinks upon it.

The path of thinking traversed in this lecture course leads us towards hearing the principle of reason in another tonality. That required us to ask: to what extent "are" being and ground/reason the same? The answer offered itself up to us on the path returning to the commencement of the *Geschick* of being. The path led through the tradition according to which *ratio* in the double sense of reckoning speaks in the words "ground" and "Reason." But λόγος, when thought in a Greek way, speaks in *ratio*. Only when we contemplated what λόγος meant for Heraclitus in early Greek thinking did it become clear that this word simultaneously names being and ground/reason, naming both in terms of their belonging-together. Heraclitus uses different names to name what he names λόγος, names which are the basic words of his thinking: φύσις, the emerging-on-its-own, which at the same time essentially comes to be as a self-concealing; κόσμος, which for the Greeks simultaneously meant order, disposition,[55] and finery which, as flash and luster, brings about a shining; finally, that which hails him as λόγος, as the sameness of being and ground/reason, Heraclitus names αἰών. The word is difficult to translate. One says: "world-time." It is the world that worlds and temporalizes in that, as κόσμος,[48] it brings the jointure of being to a glowing sparkle. According to all that is said in the names λόγος, φύσις, κόσμος, and αἰών we may hear that Unsaid we name "the *Geschick* of being."

What does Heraclitus say about αἰών? Fragment 52 runs: αἰών παῖς ἐστι παίζων, πεσσεύων παιδὸς ἡ βασιληίη. The *Geschick* of being, a child that plays, shifting the pawns: the royalty of a child—that means, the ἀρχή, that which governs by instituting grounds, the being of beings. The *Geschick* of being: a child that plays.

In addition, there are also great children. By the gentleness of its play, the greatest royal child is that mystery of the play in which humans are engaged throughout their life, that play in which their essence is at stake.

Why does it play, the great child of the world-play Heraclitus brought into view in the αἰών? It plays, because it plays.

The "because" withers away in the play. The play is without "why." It plays since it plays. It simply remains a play: the most elevated and the most profound.

But this "simply" is everything, the one, the only.

Nothing *is* without *ground/reason*. Being and ground/reason: the same. Being, as what grounds, has no ground; as the abyss it plays the play that, as *Geschick*, passes being and ground/reason to us.

The question remains whether and how we, hearing the movements of this play, play along and accommodate ourselves to the play.

mitspielen und uns in das Spiel fügen.

ADDRESS

The Principle of Reason

The principle of reason reads: *nihil est sine ratione*. One translates this with: *nothing* is *without* reason. What the principle states can be paraphrased as follows: everything has a reason, which means each and every thing that *is* in any manner. *Omnes ens habet rationem*. Whatever happens to be actual has a reason for its actuality. Whatever happens to be possible has a reason for its possibility. Whatever happens to be necessary has a reason for its necessity. *Nothing* is *without* reason. ₍ₛₒₕₐₙ ₙᵢ₎

We have an eye out for grounds in all that surrounds, concerns, and meets us. We require a specification of reasons for our statements. We insist upon a foundation for every attitude. Often we content ourselves with the most immediate reasons; after a while we investigate the more remote reasons; finally we try to get at the first reasons and ask about the ultimate reason. In all founding and getting to the bottom we are already on the path to a reason. Therefore, we find that what the principle of reason states is commonplace, and because it is commonplace, it is immediately illuminating. So it happens that what the principle of reason says isn't even immediately expressly posited as a principle, much less proposed as a law.

Frequently the content of the principle—which in abridged form reads: nothing without reason—is only recognized when formulated as follows: *nihil fit sine causa*, nothing happens without a cause. Now, it is certain that every cause is a kind of reason. But not every reason brings something about in the sense of causation. Thus, for example, the universally valid statement "All men are mortal" indeed contains the reason for our seeing that Socrates is mortal. But that universal statement does not bring about—is not the cause for—the fact that Socrates dies.

Nihil sine ratione, nothing without reason—thus reads the formula (which is hardly ever articulated) of a notion that is normative everywhere, a notion to which we have entrusted our cognition. Yet two thousand three hundred years

117

were needed in the history of Western thinking, which began in the sixth century BC, before the familiar idea "Nothing without reason" was expressly posited as a principle and came to be known as a law, recognized in its full import, and deliberately made unquestionably valid. During this period the principle of reason slept, so to speak. Even up to the present hour we have scarcely thought at all about this curious fact, nor even asked why it may be that this little principle needed such an extraordinarily long incubation period. For it was only in the seventeenth century that Leibniz recognized the long-since commonplace idea "nothing is without reason" was a normative principle and described it as the principle of reason. But was something unique and grand supposed to come to light through this general and little principle of reason? Is the unusually long incubation period a preparation for an unusual awakening, a quickening to a wakefulness that no longer admits of sleep, least of all, an incubation, an oracular slumber? [56]

But the Latin title Leibniz gave to the principle betrays the kind of principles to which he figured the principle of reason belonged. Nothing without reason, *nihil sine ratione*, is called the *principium rationis*. The principle is now a Principle. The principle of reason becomes a fundamental principle. But it is not just one fundamental principle among others. For Leibniz it is one of the supreme fundamental principles, if not the most supreme one. Therefore Leibniz highlights the fundamental principle of reason with adjectives. Leibniz calls it the *principium magnum, grande et nobilissimum*: the grand, the powerful, the most eminent Principle. To what extent does the principle of reason deserve this distinction? The content of the fundamental principle can teach us something about this.

In showing the extent to which the principle of reason founds all principles —that means, first of all, founding every principle as a principle—Leibniz raised the *nihil sine ratione*, nothing without reason, to a supreme fundamental principle. This character of the principle of reason becomes clear in the complete Latin title Leibniz gave the Principle. Leibniz characterizes the principle of reason as the *principium reddendae rationis sufficientis*. We will translate this title while discussing its individual determinations. The *principium rationis* is the "principium reddendae rationis." *Rationem reddere* means: to render the reason. We have a threefold question.

1. How come a reason is always a rendered reason?
2. How come a reason must be rendered, that is, explicitly brought forward?
3. To whom or to what is a reason rendered?

Leibniz answered the first question with a short but significant observation. A reason is a rendered reason, *quod omnis veritatis reddi ratio potest*, "because a truth is only the truth if a reason can be rendered for it."[49] For Leibniz, truth is always—and this remains decisive—*propositio vera*, a true proposition, that is, a correct judgment. Judgment is *connexio praedicati cum subjecto*, the connection of what is stated with that about which a statement is made. That which, as the unifying unity of subject and predicate, supports their being connected is the basis, the ground of judgment—it gives the justification for the connection. Reason renders an account of the truth of judgment. "Account" in Latin is called *ratio*. The ground of the truth of judgment is represented as *ratio*.

Accordingly, in a letter to Arnauld, Leibniz writes: "Hanovre le 14 juillet 1686: *il faut tousjours qu'il y ait quelque fondement de la connexion des termes d'une proposition, qui se doit trouver dans leur notions. C'est là mon grande principe, dont je croy que tous les philosophes doivent demeurer d'accord, et dont un des corollaires est cet axiome vulgaire que rien n'arrive sans raison, qu'ont peut tousjours rendre pourquoy la chose est plustost allé ainsi qu'autrement. . . ."* In translation: "*it is always necessary that there be a foundation for the connecting of the parts of a judgment, in whose concepts these connections must be found.* Precisely this is my grand Principle about which, I believe, all philosophers must concur —and this common axiom remains one of its corollaries—that nothing happens without a reason that one can always render as to why the matter has run its course this way rather than that."[50]

The grand Principle is the *principium reddendae rationis*, the fundamental principle of rendering reasons.

We ask the second question: how come reasons must be expressly brought forward qua reasons? Because reason is *ratio*, that is, an account. If it is not given, judgment remains without justification. It lacks evident correctness. Judgment itself is not truth. Judgment is only true when the reason for the connection is specified, when the *ratio*, that is, an account, is given. Such a giving is in need of a site where the account is delivered and rendered.

We ask the third question regarding the *ratio reddendae*: to whom or what must reasons be rendered? Answer: to humans who determine objects as objects by way of a representation that judges. But representation is *representare*—to present something, to make something present to humans. After Descartes, followed by Leibniz and all of modern thinking, humans are experienced as an I that relates to the world such that it renders this world to itself in the form of connections correctly established between its representations—that means judgments—and thus sets itself over against this world as to an object. Judgments and statements are correct, that means true, only if the reason for the connection of subject and predicate is rendered, given back to the representing I. A reason is this sort of reason only if it is a *ratio*, that means, an account that is given about something that is in front of a person as the judging I, and is given to this I. An account is an account only if it is handed over. Therefore, *ratio* is in itself *ratio reddendae*; a reason is, as such, a reason that is to be rendered. When the reason for the connection of representations has been directed back —and expressly rendered—to the I, what is represented first comes to a stand [*Stehen*] such that it is securely established as an object [*Gegenstand*], that means, as an Object for a representing subject.

But a rendered reason only effects such a bringing-to-a-stand of objects when it gives, in a sufficient way, an account adequate for the secure establishing of objects. The reason to be rendered must be a *ratio sufficiens*.

Leibniz once wrote the following about the principle of reason: (*principium rationis*) *quod dicere soleo nihil existere nisi cuius reddi potest ratio existentiae sufficiens*. The principle of reason "that I usually say (in *the form*): nothing exists for which the sufficient reason for its existence cannot be rendered." The reason that incessantly lays claim to its being rendered in every judgment about an object at the same time demands that, as a reason, it suffices—which means, that it be completely satisfactory as an account. For what? So that it can in every regard and for everyone—that means fully—bring an object to stand in the entirety of its stance. The completeness of the reasons to be rendered—*perfectio* —is what originally guarantees that something is, in the literal sense, firmly established—secured in its stance—as an object for human cognition. Only the completeness of the account, perfection, vouches for the fact that every cognition everywhere and at all times can include and count on the object and reckon with it.

Nothing is without reason. The principle now says that every thing counts as existing when and only when it has been securely established as a calculable object for cognition.

So wherein consists the grandness of the principle of reason as the *principium magnum, grande et nobilissimum*, the grand, powerful, and eminent Principle? Answer: in the fact that this Principle decrees what may count as an object of cognition, or more generally, as a being. This claim to decree what is called the being of beings speaks in the principle of reason. When Leibniz first expressly and completely formulated the principle of reason as such a Principle, what he thereby articulated is the fact that human cognition, in a decisive and unavoidable manner, had come to be taken up into the claim of the *principium rationis* and held in the sway of its power. The *principium rationis*, the principle of reason, becomes the fundamental principle of all cognition. This means: dominated by the *principium rationis* cognition becomes unmistakably Rational, and governed by Reason. For from time immemorial *ratio* has meant not only "account" in the sense of that which stands to account for something else, that is, founds it. *Ratio* also means "account for" in the sense of "vindicating," of confirming something as being in the right, of correctly figuring something out and securing something through such a reckoning. Reckoning in this broad sense is the way humans take up something [*aufnehmen*], deal with it [*vornehmen*], and take it on [*annehmen*], which means, in general perceive [*ver-nehmen*] something. *Ratio* is a manner of perceiving, which means, it is Reason.[57] Rational [*vernünftige, rationale*] cognition follows the *principium rationis*. The principle of reason is the supreme fundamental principle of Reason insofar as Reason first fully develops its essence as Reason through the principle of reason. The principle of reason is the fundamental principle of Rational cognition in the sense of a reckoning that securely establishes something. One speaks of Rational grounds. By virtue of Leibniz's giving the little, barely thought principle *nihil sine ratione*—nothing without reason—the complete and strict formulation of the powerful fundamental principle, the incubation period of the principle of reason [in one respect] ended. Since then, the exacting claim reigning in the fundamental principle has displayed an authority of which no one before ever had an inkling. This brings to fruition nothing less than the innermost, and at the same time most concealed, molding of the age of Western history we call "modernity." In the history of humanity, the authority of the powerful fundamental principle becomes more powerful the more pervasively, the more obviously, and accordingly the more inconspicuously the principle of reason determines all cognition and behavior. And that's the way things stand today.

Therefore, those of us here today must ask whether and how we hear the exacting claim that speaks from out of the grand fundamental principle of all cognition. Are we then on the track of the power of this claim? Yes. Surely modern humanity hears this claim. It hears [*hören*] it in an oddly decisive manner, namely, such that it evermore exclusively and quickly becomes slavish [*hörig*] to the power of the fundamental principle. Even more: today humanity runs the risk of measuring the greatness of everything grand only according to the reach of the authority of the *principium rationis*. Without really understanding it, we know today that modern technology intractably presses toward bringing its contrivances and products to an all-embracing, greatest-possible perfection. This perfection consists in the completeness of the calculably secure establishing of objects, in the completeness of reckoning with them and with the securing of the calculability of possibilities for reckoning.

The perfection of technology is only the echo of the demand for *perfectio*, which means, the completeness of a foundation. This demand speaks from out of the *principium reddendae rationis sufficientis*, from the fundamental principle of rendering sufficient reasons. The step we have just taken in our thinking should be briefly repeated as a transition to the following:

Modern technology pushes toward the greatest possible perfection. Perfection is based on the thoroughgoing calculability of objects. The calculability of objects presupposes the unqualified validity of the *principium rationis*. It is in this way that the authority characteristic of the principle of reason determines the essence of the modern, technological age.

And today humanity has gone a long way in following the surge toward something that never before in its history could have happened. Humanity enters the age to which it has given the name "the atomic age." A book that just appeared and that figured on having a broad readership, bears the title: *We Will Live*

Through Atoms. The book is equipped with a blurb by the Nobel Prize winner Otto Hahn and with a preface by the current Minister of Defense, Franz Joseph Strauβ. At the close of the Introduction, the author of the work writes:

> The atomic age can become a prosperous, happy age full of hope, an age in which we live through atoms. It all depends on us![51]

Certainly—it all depends on us; it depends on us and a few other things, namely whether we still reflect, or whether in general we still can and want to reflect. If we still want to enter on a path of reflection, then above all we must come to terms with the distinction that holds before our eyes the difference between mere calculative thinking and reflective thinking. We will now try to reflect on the principle of reason so that we can see this difference.

We begin our reflection such that for once we attend to what conceals itself in the apparently harmless naming of an age "the atomic age." What is so special about this? For the first time in its history, humanity interprets an epoch of its historical existence on the basis of the rapacity for, and the procuring of, a natural energy. And it already looks as if the criteria and power of contemplation are lacking by which we might experience what is alienating and uncanny in such an interpretation of the present age, and to experience it openly enough such that we would be constantly and ever more decisively struck by it.

The existence of humanity molded by atomic energy!

Whether atomic energy is used peacefully or is mobilized for war, whether the one supports and provokes the other—these remain questions of a second order. For above all else we must question further ahead and still further back. *What, after all, does it mean that an age of world history has been molded by atomic energy and its unleashing?* Perhaps some already have the answer inasmuch as they judge that the atomic age means the dominance of materialism, which is why it is important to rescue the old spiritual values over against rapacity for the material. Yet this answer would be altogether too superficial, for materialism is not at all something material. It is itself a mind-set. It blows in here no less strongly from the West than from the East. One can read in the American periodical *Perspectives*, whose German edition is handled by S. Fischer Verlag, the following:[52]

> Over a long period of time, the loss of a few of the old values may influence the stability of culture, but its coherence in the coming generations depends on the fact that people have—or believe to have—what are held up to them as values.
>
> The values of income, consumption, social status and mass culture distinguish themselves from those values that are circumscribed by land ownership, crafts, and ownership of smaller factories, and in this sense the tenor of American culture has completely changed under the influence of technology. For machines themselves

have taken the American worker, employee, and entrepreneur away from machines and have displaced their interests and energies from the production of goods to the earning of money in order to be able to purchase and enjoy goods.

From these few passages it becomes clear that materialism is the most menacing mind-set because we most easily and for the longest time mistake the insidious nature of its violence.

Therefore we ask anew: what, after all, does it mean that an age of world history is molded by atomic energy and its unleashing? It means, precisely, that the atomic age is dominated by the force of the demand that threatens to overpower us through the principle of rendering sufficient reasons.

How are we to understand this? Atomic energy is unleashed by splitting the nucleus of atoms in huge numbers. The unleashing of this natural energy occurs through the work of the most modern natural sciences that ever more unequivocally prove to have the normative function and form of the essence of modern technology. Not long ago the only parts of the atom that the sciences knew of were the proton and neutron. Today they already know of more than ten. By virtue of these facts, research sees itself driven on to reassemble the dispersed manifold of elementary particles into a new unity. It is important to avoid contradictions that crop up in observed facts and in the theories that are set up in order to explain these facts. This occurs by bringing contradictory judgments into an agreement. (For this a unity is necessary that links what is contradictory.) However, what supports and determines the linking of representations in judgment is always a sufficient, rendered reason. From this it becomes clear that the quest for a contradiction-free unity of judgments, and the progress towards the corresponding securing of this unity, comes from the force of the demand to render sufficient reasons for all cognition. The authority of the powerful fundamental principle of reason is the element in which the sciences move just as fish do in water and birds do in air.

Goethe says all of this to us most beautifully in the two last verses of a late poem:[53]

> But research strives and rings, never tiring,
> After the law, the reason *why* and *how*.[58]

Goethe had an inkling of how the tirelessness of research, if it pursues its advance blindly, exhausts humanity and earth in their innermost essence. Yet Goethe could not have anticipated where the tirelessness of modern research would lead when it hands itself over to the authority of the powerful fundamental principle of rendering sufficient reasons as the sole, unconditional standard of measure. To what has this led? To a change in scientific cognition, a change through which the essence of modern science completes itself.

By unleashing vast amounts of atomic energy, science, steered by modern technology, is now free from having to search further for new sources of energy. But at the same time, this freedom is converted into a still more forceful bondage to the demand of the fundamental principle of reason. So now, research must in a new way direct all its prospects to taming the unleashed energies of nature. What does this mean?

It means: to securely establish the utility of atomic energy and, even before this, to securely establish its calculability such that, for its part, this making-secure constantly prompts the engaging of new safety mechanisms. The force of the demand to render sufficient reasons thereby mushrooms into something immeasurable. The fundamental character of contemporary human existence that everywhere works for certainty is consolidated under the force of this demand. (Parenthetically, Leibniz, the discoverer of the fundamental principle of sufficient reason, was also the inventor of "life insurance.") Yet, the work of safeguarding life must itself constantly be secured anew. The basic word for this fundamental demeanor of contemporary existence is: "information." We must hear this word with an American–English pronunciation.[59]

"Information" at one and the same time means the appraisal that as quickly, comprehensively, unequivocally, and profitably as possible acquaints contemporary humanity with the securing of its necessities, its requirements, and their satisfaction. Accordingly, the representation of human language as an instrument of information increasingly gains the upper hand. For the determination of language as information first of all creates the sufficient grounds [zureichenden Grund] for the construction of thinking machines and for the building of frameworks for large calculations. Yet while information in-forms, that is, apprises, it at the same time forms, that means, arranges and sets straight. As an appraisal, information is also the arrangement that places all objects and stuffs in a form for humans that suffices to securely establish human domination over the whole earth and even over what lies beyond this planet.

In the form of information, the powerful Principle of providing sufficient reasons holds sway over all cognition and thus determines the present world-epoch as one for which everything depends on the provision of atomic energy.

In order to introduce reflective thinking, we asked whether modern and contemporary humans hear the demand that speaks from out of the powerful fundamental principle of all cognition. We answered yes and showed how. Contemporary humanity constantly hears the fundamental principle of reason inasmuch as it becomes increasingly slavish to the principle.

But supposing that this slavishness is not the only or the genuine manner of hearing, then we must yet once more ask the question: do we hear the demand of the principle of reason? We now pay attention to the fact that we only truly hear a demand when we respond to that which genuinely appeals to us. But does an appeal speak in the demand of the principle of reason? And do we listen in the direction from whence the powerful fundamental principle speaks. We must confess: no! To what extent not? To the extent that we do not clearly and decisively enough hear and think about what the principle of reason really says.

As generally promulgated, the principle of reason reads: "*nihil* est *sine* ratione," *nothing* is *without* reason.

Ordinarily we pay no attention to the fact that the tiny word "is" passes by as something obvious when we listen to the usual way of stating the principle. But how come we should listen to the "is"? The fundamental principle of reason says: every being has a reason. The principle is a statement about beings. But we experience a being as a being only when we attend to the fact that and how it *is*. Hence, in order to really hear the principle about beings we must become aware that the "is" in the principle "nothing is without reason" sets the pitch that tunes everything. When we listen to it, that is, when we open ourselves to what really speaks in the principle, the principle suddenly intones differently. No longer "*nothing* is *without* reason," rather, "nothing *is* without *rea*son." Whenever it speaks of beings, the tiny word "is" names the *being* of beings. When the "is" means "being" and sets the pitch in the principle, "reason" is also taken up along with it in the intonation: nothing *is* without *reason*. Being and reason now ring in unison. In this ring[60] being and reason ring out as belonging together in one. The principle of reason now has a different ring and says: ground/reason belongs to being. The principle of reason no longer speaks as a supreme fundamental principle of all cognition of beings, which says every being has a reason. The principle of reason now speaks as a word of being. The word is an answer to the question: what, after all, does "being" mean? Answer: "being" means "ground/reason." Nevertheless, as a word of being the principle of reason can no longer mean to say: being has a ground/reason. If we were to understand the word of being in this sense, then we would represent being as a being. Only beings have—and indeed necessarily—a ground/reason. A being *is* a being only when grounded. However, being, since it is itself ground/reason, remains without a ground/reason. Insofar as being—which itself is ground/reason—grounds, it allows beings to be beings.

{However, because Leibniz and all metaphysics come to a halt with the principle of reason as a fundamental principle about beings, metaphysical thinking requires, according to the fundamental principle, a first reason for being: in a being, and indeed the being that is most of all;}[54]

Because beings are brought into being by being *qua* ground/reason, every being inevitably is allotted a ground/reason. For otherwise it would not be. Understood as the fundamental principle of rendering sufficient reasons, the principle of reason is thereby true only because a word of being speaks in it that says: being and ground/reason: the same.

According to the assertion just made, this word of being is supposed to answer the question: what after all does "being" mean? But is this an answer when we are told: "being" means "ground/reason"? Instead of getting an answer, we once again run into a question. For we immediately ask: what, after all, does "ground/reason" mean? Now, the only answer to this is: "ground/reason" means "being". "Being" means "ground/reason"—"ground/reason" means "being": here everything goes around in a circle. We become dizzy. Thinking stumbles into perplexity. For we don't quite know what "being" or "ground/reason" mean. But if the word of being as ground/reason does answer the question of the meaning of being, this answer initially remains impenetrable to us. We are missing the key that would open it up so that we could have an insight into what the word of being says. It is already difficult and complicated enough just to seek out the missing key. Therefore, in this lecture we have chosen another path in order to at least open an outer gate. An entree to this path may possibly be given to us by the poet whose verse circumscribes that cognition which stands under the sway of the fundamental principle of rendering sufficient reason.

Goethe says of modern science:

> But research strives and rings, never tiring,
> After the law, the reason, *why* and *how*.

The "but" at the beginning of the first line sets research over against another attitude and demeanor that no longer tirelessly strive after the ground/reason for beings. Whenever we pursue the ground/reason of a being, we ask: why? Cognition stalks this interrogative word from one reason to another. The "why" allows no rest, offers no stop, gives no support. The "why" is the word for the tireless advance into an and-so-forth that research, in the event that it simply and blindly belabors itself, can take so far that it perforce can go too far with it.

The word of being says: being—itself ground/reason—remains without a ground/reason, which now means, without why. If we attempt to think being as ground/reason, then we must take the step back, back from the question: "why?".

But then what are we supposed to stick to?

In the "Collected Sayings" from 1815 Goethe says:[55]

> How? When? and Where?—The gods remain mute!
> You stick to the *because* and ask not *why*?[61]

The "why" unfolds itself in the questions: How? When? Where? It asks about the law, the time, the site of what happens. Questioning the space-time-law-regulated course of movement is how research pursues the "why" of beings. But Goethe says:

You stick to the *because* and ask not *why*?

What does "because" mean? It guards against investigating the "why," therefore, against investigating foundations. It balks at founding and getting to the bottom of something. For the "because" is without "why," it has no ground, it is ground itself.

The word "ground" [*Grund*] means that which lies deeper, for example, the bottom of the sea [*Meeresgrund*], the valley floor [*Talsgrund*], the bottom of one's heart [*Herzensgrund*]. Compare this to Goethe's sonnet "Powerful Surprise":[56]

> What also may be mirrored from ground to grounds
> He changes it ceaselessly to a dale.[62]

Ground is that upon which everything rests, that which is already present as what supports all beings. The "because" names this supportive presence before which we simply pause. The "because" points to the essence of grounds. If the word of being as the word of grounds is a true word, then the "because" also points to the essence of being.

Yet what does the "because" [*weil*] really mean? It is the shortened word for *dieweilen* [whereas]. An older manner of speaking goes:

> One must strike the iron while [*weil*] it is hot.

Here the "while" in no way means: "since—because," rather "while" denotes *dieweilen* [whereas], which means, as long as—the iron is hot—during. "To while" [*Weilen*] means: "to tarry," "to remain still," "to pause and keep to oneself," namely in rest.[63] In a beautiful verse Goethe says:[57]

> The fiddle stops and the dancer whiles.[64]

"Whiling", "tarrying," "perpetuating" is indeed the old sense of the word "being" [*sein*]. The while that every founding and every "why" guards against names the simple, plain presence that is without why—the presence upon which everything depends, upon which everything rests. "The while" names the ground. But *qua* the Whereas, "whiling" also names "the abiding": being. "Whiling" names both: being and ground; it names the abiding, being as the ground/reason. Being and ground/reason—in whiling—the same. Both belong together.

The little principle of reason—"*Nothing* is *without* reason"—at first speaks as the grand fundamental principle, the *principium grande*. The principle is grand by virtue of the force of its demands on all cognition. The little principle of reason—"Nothing *is* without *reason*"—both speaks as a word of being and names this as the ground/reason.

Indeed it is only because the word of being is true that the fundamental principle of cognition is valid. It is as a word of being that the principle of reason first gives a ground/reason to the fundamental principle of cognition.

The word of being as ground/reason is capable of such grounding.[65] By virtue of this capacity it is a mighty word. It is grand, but in a completely different sense than the grandness of the force of the fundamental principle. As a word of being, the principle of reason is grand in the sense of great capability, great felicity, all-powerful. It does not speak by the force of a demand for a why. The mighty word is a word without force, it speaks to us only of the meaning of "being."

Nevertheless, we must ask: why? For we cannot leap out of the present age that is held in the sway of the fundamental principle of rendering sufficient reasons. But at the same time we may not desist from holding to the "because" when we listen to the word of being as the word of ground/reason. We must do one thing: follow the force of the fundamental principle for all cognition; we may not abandon something else: pondering what is all-powerful in the word of being.

The principle of reason says: nothing is without reason. But now every word of the principle speaks in its own manner.

The claim of the fundamental principle speaks in the principle of reason. The appeal of the word of being speaks in the principle of reason. However, the appeal is much older than the claim. For during the uncommonly long incubation period of the principle of reason, the word of being always already appealed to Western humanity as the word of ground/reason. Without this appeal there would be no thinking in the form of philosophy. But also, without philosophy there would be no Western European science, no unleashing of atomic energy. But the appeal in the word of being as the word of ground/reason remains mute in comparison to the proclamations of the fundamental principle in the evermore noisy and generally alarming force of its claim.

Whereas this is the case, one misses hearing in the noise the appeal that speaks through the principle of reason, and still does so most frequently and stubbornly even today.

It depends on us, so it is said. But not on whether we live from atoms, rather whether we can be the mortals that we are, namely, those to whom being appeals. Only such beings are capable of dying, that means, to take on death as death.

It depends on whether we are patient and watchful, awake enough for the stillness of the appeal in the word of being to prevail over the clamor of the claim of the *principium rationis* as the fundamental principle for all cognition. It depends on whether the force of the claim of the "why" submits to the enabling appeal of the "because."

You stick to the *because* and ask not *why*?[66]

Goethe's words are a hint. Hints only remain hints when thinking does not twist them into definitive statements and thereby come to a standstill with them. Hints are hints only as long as thinking follows their allusions while meditating on them. Thus, thinking reaches a path that leads to what has from time immemorial shown itself in the tradition of our thinking as worthy of thought, and simultaneously veils itself.

Perhaps something simple belonging to what is worthy of thought has drawn a bit closer. We name it when we say: being is experienced as ground/reason. Ground/reason is interpreted as *ratio*, as an account.

Accordingly humans are the *animal rationale*, the creature that requires accounts and gives accounts. According to this determination, humans are the reckoning creature, reckoning understood in the broad sense of the word *ratio*— originally a word in Roman commercial language—as already taken over by Cicero at the time that Greek thinking was converted into Roman cognition.

Being comes to be experienced as ground/reason. Ground/reason is interpreted as *ratio*, as account. Humans are the reckoning creature. This holds in the various transformations, and indeed unequivocally, throughout the entire history of Western thought. As modern European thinking, this thinking brought the world into the contemporary era, the atomic age. In view of this simple, and for Europe, uncanny state of affairs, we ask:

Does the above mentioned determination that humans are the *animal rationale* exhaust the essence of humanity? Does the last word that can be said about being run thus: being means ground/reason? Or isn't human nature, isn't its affiliation to being, isn't the essence of being what still remains, and even more disturbingly, worthy of thought? If this is the way it's going to be, may we give up what is worthy of thought in favor of the recklessness of exclusively calculative thinking and its immense achievements? Or are we obliged to find paths upon which thinking is capable of responding to what is worthy of thought instead of, enchanted by calculative thinking, mindlessly passing over what is worthy of thought?

That is the question. It is the world-question of thinking. Answering this question decides what will become of the earth and of human existence on this earth.

F IDEAS

ideas ...

_urnal of the history of ideas inc.,
_ew York, 1940-

46   433-452

- you can't present a Satz as a proof.

- Satz says X, it can't say it's a demand

- it's in poetic text that manner of saying
  is said

- Grundsatz — or post. of can't be und. in
  terms of either. sentences must already
  tell you of manner of their presentation.
  they say their Vorläufigkeit

- sentence that expresses int. int. can't say what
  it is

BIBLIOGRAPHICAL NOTES

Heidegger's bibliographical references have been filled out whenever possible. Supplementary information, including English translations, has been given in brackets. Though in most cases existing translations have been consulted, I have translated all German and French sources from the original, including Heidegger's translations of Greek and Latin texts.

1. *Opuscules et fragments inédits de Leibniz,* ed. Louis Couturat (Paris, 1903; reprint, Hildesheim: Georg Olms Verlagsbuchhandlung, 1966), p. 515 [Leibniz, "An Introduction to a Secret Encyclopedia," in *Leibniz: Philosophical Writings,* ed. G. H. R. Parkinson, trans. Mary Morris & G. H. R. Parkinson (London: J. M. Dent & Sons, 1973), p. 9].
2. C. W. Ceram, *Gods, Graves, and Scholars: The Story of Archaeology* (New York: Alfred A. Knopf, 1956).
3. Johann Wolfgang Goethe, *Sprüche und Prosa,* ed. Rudolf Steiner (Stuttgart: Freies Geistesleben Verlag, 1967), p. 34 [*Maximen und Reflexionen,* in *Goethes Werke,* Hamburger Ausgabe, ed. Erich Trunz and Hans Joachim Schrimpf (Munich: Verlag C. H. Beck, 1978) no. 351, 12:412].
4. Gottfried Wilhelm von Leibniz, "Brief an Joh. Bernoulli," in *Mathematische Schriften,* ed. C. I. Gerhardt (Hildesheim: Georg Olms Verlag, 1971), 3/1:321.
5. Aristotle, *Metaphysics,* Γ (Book IV) 1006[a] 6–8.
6. Novalis, Minor III, p. 171; Wasmuth III, n. 381 ["Logische Fragmente" (no. 9), in *Schriften: Die Werke Friedrich von Hardenbergs* (Berlin: Verlag W. Kohlhammer, 1981), 2:523–24].
7. Christian Wolff, *Philosophia Prima Sive Ontologia,* in *Gesammelte Werke,* ed. Jean Ecole (Hildesheim: Georg Olms Verlag, 1962), Sect. II, Vol. 3, §866, p. 645. Cf. Wolff, *Institutiones Metaphysicae, Gesammelte Werke,* Sect. III, Vol. 25, §339, p. 230.
8. Leibniz, "Consilium de Encyclopaedia nova conscribenda methodo inventoria" in *Opuscules,* ed. Couturat, p. 32.
9. Aristotle, *Metaphysics,* Γ (Book 4), chap. 3 ff.
10. Heidegger, "Der Ursprung des Kunstwerkes" in *Holzwege,* (Frankfurt a.M.: Vittorio Klostermann, 1950), p. 49 ["The Origin of the Work of Art" in *Poetry, Language, Thought,* trans. Albert Hofstadter (New York: Harper and Row, 1971, p. 61]; "Die Frage nach der Technik," in *Vorträge und Aufsätze* (Pfullingen: Neske Verlag, 1954), p. 28 ["The Question of Technology," in *Basic Writings,* ed. David F. Krell (New York: Harper and Row, 1978), p. 302]; and "Wissenschaft und Besinnung," ibid., p. 49 ["Science and Reflection," in *The Question Concerning Technology and Other Essays,*" trans. William Lovitt (New York: Harper and Row, 1977, p. 159].
11. Leibniz, "Specimen inventorum de admirandis naturae Generalis arcanus," in *Philosophische Schriften,* ed. C. I. Gerhardt (1875; reprint, Hildesheim: Georg Olms

Verlag, 1965), 7:309 ["A Specimen of Discoveries about Marvellous Secrets of a General Nature" in *Philosophical Writings*, ed. Parkinson, p. 75].

12. Leibniz, *Philosophische Schriften*, ed. Gerhardt, 7:309 [*Philosophical Writings*, ed. Parkinson, p. 75].

13. Leibniz, *Philosophische Schriften*, ed. Gerhardt, 7:309 [*Philosophical Writings*, ed. Parkinson, p. 75].

14. Leibniz, *Philosophische Schriften*, ed. Gerhardt, 7:199 ["On the Universal Science: Characteristic" in *Monadology and Other Philosophical Essays*, trans. Paul Schrecker and Anne Martin Schrecker (New York: Bobbs-Merrill, 1965), p. 13].

15. Leibniz, *Philosophische Schriften*, ed. Gerhardt, 7:289 ["A Resumé of Metaphysics," in *Philosophical Writings*, ed. Parkinson, p. 145].

16. Leibniz, "De ipsa natura sive de vi insista actionibus creaturarum, pro Dynamicis suis conformandis illustrandisque," in *Philosophische Schriften*, ed. Gerhardt, 4:504 ["On Nature itself, or on the inherent Force and Actions of Created Things" in G. W. Leibniz, *Philosophical Papers and Letters: A Selection*, trans. Leroy E. Loemker, 2d ed. (Dordrecht: D. Reidel, 1969), p. 498].

17. Leibniz, *Philosophische Schriften*, ed. Gerhardt, 7:289 [*Philosophical Writings*, ed. Parkinson, p. 145].

18. Leibniz, *Philosophische Schriften*, ed. Gerhardt, 7:289 [*Philosophical Writings*, ed. Parkinson, p. 145].

19. Leibniz, *Philosophische Schriften*, ed. Gerhardt, 4:232 [Leibniz, *Philosophical Papers and Letters*, ed. Loemker, p. 142].

20. Leibniz, *Philosophische Schriften*, ed. Gerhardt, 1:138, n. 23.

21. Leibniz, *Monadologie*, §32, in *Philosophische Schriften*, ed. Gerhardt, 6:612 [*Philosophical Writings*, ed. Parkinson, p. 184].

22. Angelus Silesius, *Der cherubische Wandersmann*, ed. Will-Erick Peudert (Leipzig: Dieterich'sche Verlagsbuchhandlung, Sammlung Dieterich), Vol. 64, p. 37, no. 289 [*The Cherubinic Wanderer*, trans. Maria Shrady (New York: Paulist Press, 1986), p. 54].

23. Leibniz, *Leibnitii opera*, ed. L. Dutens (Geneva: 1768), 6:56.

24. G. F. W. Hegel, *Vorlesungen über die Aesthetik*; ed. Glockner (Stuttgart: Friedrich Frommann Verlag, 71)[5th ed.], 12:493 [*Aesthetics: Lectures on Fine Art*, trans. T. M. Knox (Oxford: Clarendon Press, 1975), 1:371].

25. Leibniz, *Monadologie*, §29, in *Philosophische Schriften*, ed. Gerhardt, 6:611 [*Philosophical Writings*, ed. Parkinson, p. 183].

26. André Robinet, *Principes de la nature et de la grâce fondés en raison/Principes de la philosophie ou Monadologie* (Paris: Presses Universitaires de France, 1954).

27. Joannes Eduardus Erdmann ed, *Pera Philosophia* (Berlin: Berolini, 1840), pp. 705–712.

28. Heidegger, "Vom Wesen des Grundes," in *Holzwege: Gesamtausgabe* (Frankfurt a.M.: Vittorio Klostermann, 1976), 9:123–175 [*The Essence of Reasons*, bilingual edition, trans. Terrence Malick (Evanston, Ill.: Northwestern University Press, 1972)].

29. Goethe, *Zur Farbenlehre: Didaktischer Teil*, in *Goethes Werke*, ed. Erich Trunz, Hamburger Ausgabe (Munich: Verlag C. H. Beck, 1975), 13:324.

30. Eduard Mörike, "Auf eine Lampe," in *Sämtliche Werke*, ed. Herbert G. Göpfert (Munich: Verlag C. H. Beck, 1958), p. 85 ["On a Lamp," in *Friedrich Hölderlin and Eduard Mörike: Selected Poems*, trans. Christopher Middleton (Chicago: University of Chicago Press, 1972), p. 205].

31. Stefan George, "Seelied," in *Gesamtausgabe: Das Neue Reich* (Berlin: George Bondi, 1927), 9:130–131 ["Sea Song," in *Poems*, trans. Carol North Valhope and Ernst Morwitz (New York: Pantheon, 1943), pp. 234–235].

32. [112] Aristotle, *Physics*, 184a 16 ff.

33. Heraclitus, Fragment 123.

34. "Auszüge aus Mozartsbriefen," *Das Musikleben*, I. Jahrgang, 1. Heft, Mainz, 1948.

35. Angelus Silesius, *Der cherubische Wandersmann*, ed. Will-Erick Peudert, fifth book, no. 366 [*The Cherubinic Wanderer*, trans. Maria Shrady].

36. Parmenides, Fragment 3.

37. Aristotle, *Metaphysics*, Γ (Book IV) 1003a 20–23.

38. Goethe, "Der Versuch als Vermittler von Objekt und Subjekt" in *Goethes Werke*, ed. Dorothea Kuhn and Rike Wankmüller, Hamburger Ausgabe (Munich: Verlag C. H. Beck, 1975), 12:10–20 ["The Experiment as Mediator between Subject and Object," in *Scientific Studies*, trans. Douglas Miller (Boston: Suhrkamp Verlag, 1983), 12:11–17].

39. Friedrich Hölderlin, "Die Wanderung" (1801), in *Sämliche Werke*, ed. Friedrich Beissner (Stuttgart: Verlag Kohlhammer, 1951) 2/1:141 ["The Journey," in *Friedrich Hölderlin: Poems and Fragments*, trans. Michael Hamburger (New York: Cambridge University Press, 1980), p. 399].

40. Hegel, "Rede zum Antritt des philosophischen Lehramtes an der Universität Berlin," in *Berliner Schriften 1818–1831*, ed. Johannes Hoffmeister (Hamburg: Verlag Felix Meiner, 1956) pp. 8–9.

41. Immanuel Kant, *Kritik der reinen Vernunft*, B 25 [*The Critique of Pure Reason*, B 25].

42. Betinna von Arnim, "Goethes Briefwechsel mit einem Kind," letter dated November 11, 1807, in *Sämtliche Werke* ed. Waldemar Oehlke (Berlin: Propyläen, 1920) 3:168 [*Goethe's Correspondence with a Child*, trans. unknown, (Boston: Ticknor and Fields, 1861), pp. 101–2].

43. Erdmann, ed., *Pera Philosophia* (Berlin: Berolini, 1840), pp. 705–712.

44. Cicero, *De Partitione Oratoria*, §110; bilingual edition, trans. H. Rockham (Cambridge: Harvard University Press, Loeb Classical Library, 1968), pp. 394, 395.

45. Leibniz, "Dialogus," in *Philosophische Schriften*, ed. Gerhardt, 7:191 [*Philosophical Papers*, ed. Loemker, p. 185, n. 4].

46. Hölderlin, "Anmerkungen zum Oedipus," in *Sämtliche Werke*, 5:195–96 ["Remarks on Oedipus," in *Friedrich Hölderlin: Essays and Letters on Theory*, trans. Thomas Pfau (New York: SUNY Press, 1988), p. 101].

47. Hölderlin, "Anmerkungen zum Antigonä," in *Sämtliche Werke*, 5:265; ["Remarks on Antigone," in *Friedrich Hölderlin: Essays and Letters on Theory*, trans. Thomas Pfau, p. 109].

48. Heraclitus, Fragment 30. [This is rendered by Kirk and Raven *The Presocratic Philosophers* (Cambridge: Cambridge University Press, 1969), p. 199: "This world order [the same of all] did none of gods or men make, but it always was and is and shall be: an ever-living fire, kindling in measures and going out in measures."]

49. Leibniz, *Philosophische Schriften*, ed. Gerhardt, 7:309 [*Philosophical Writings*, ed. Parkinson, p. 75].

50. *Briefwechsel Leibniz, Arnauld, und dem Langrafen Ernst v. Hessen-Rheinfels*, ed. C. L. Grotefend, (Hannover: Verlag Hahnschen Hof-Buchhandlung, 1846), p. 49. Cf. Leibniz, *Philosophische Schriften*, ed. Gerhardt 2:56, 62. [*Discourse on Method, Correspondence with Arnauld, and Monadology*, trans. George R. Montgomery (LaSalle, Ill.: Open Court, 1973), p. 132].

51. Otto Hahn, and Franz Josef Strauss, et al., *Wir werden durch Atome leben*, (Berlin: Blanvalet, 1956).

52. Max Lerner, "Universale Technologie und neutrale Techniker," *Perspectiven* 14 (1956):145ff. ["Big Technology and Neutral Technicians," *Perspectives* 14 (1956):123ff. There are apparent minor discrepancies between the German trans-

lation Heidegger is quoting (which we have not been able to locate) and the original English version (which we have located).]

53. Goethe, "Chinesisch-Deutsche Jahres- und Tageszeiten," in *Werke*, Hamburger Ausgabe, ed. Trunz, 1:389.

54. Leibniz, *Philosophische Schriften*, ed. Gerhardt, 7:289ff. [*Philosophical Writings*, ed. Parkinson, p. 145ff.].

55. Goethe, "Gott, Gemüt, und Welt," in *Werke*, Hamburger Ausgabe, ed. Trunz, 1:304 ["God, Soul and World," in *The Works of Goethe*, ed. Hjalmar H. Boyesen (New York: George Barrie, 1885), 1:186].

56. Goethe, "Mächtiges Überraschen," in *Werke*, Hamburger Ausgabe, ed. Trunz, 1:294 ["Sonnet I: Immense Astonishment," in *Selected Poems*, trans. Christopher Middleton (Boston: Surkamp Verlag, 1983), 1:177].

57. Goethe, *Faust: Erster Teil*, in *Werke*, Hamburger Ausgabe, ed. Trunz, 3:38 [*Faust*, trans. Walter Kaufmann, bilingual edition (Garden City, N.Y.: Doubleday, 1963), p. 139].

NOTES ON THE TRANSLATION

[1.] "Resound" translates *anklingen*, whose root, *klingen*, means "to sound" or "ring." Other than the substantive *Anklang*, which is a technical musical term, *anklingen* is no longer used in a sonic sense in German and instead is used exclusively in the figurative sense of "to be reminiscent of" or "to remind one of" or "to call to mind." Heidegger means both the sonic and the figurative senses; "to sound" and "to call to mind" are central to the development of Heidegger's exposition. Also, see Note 25 p. 136.

[2.] "Every being has a reason" could also be translated "Every being has a cause" or "a ground." See Translator's Introduction.

[3.] There is a play on words here between *eingehen* ("to occur to us") and *einleuchten* ("to enlighten us"). *Eingehen* means, most literally, "to go into." Here it has another common sense: "to realize" or "come to see," as "to get into one's head" (without the English connotation of "stubbornness").

[4.] See Translator's Introduction on *Grund*.

[5.] The usual rendering of *Erörterung* is "discussion." However, since the root word *Ort* ("site") is an important element in what Heidegger means with this term, one should understand "discussion" as a discourse that situates something. See below, p. 59f.

[6.] See Translator's Introduction for the difference between Principle and principle.

[7.] *Wie sich der Satz vom Grund im Feld des abendländischen Denkens ausnimmt* could also be translated as: "how the principle of reason constitutes an exception in the field of Western thinking" or "how the principle of reason operates in the field. . . ."

[8.] *Ginge das Denken diesen Weg zum Grunde, dann. . . . Diesen Weg zum Grunde gehen* means "to take this path to reason," but *zugrunde gehen* means "to be ruined," as a ship "runs aground." The allusion is that "the (this) path to reason" is the same as "to be ruined." See below, pp. 96f.

[9.] *Der Satz des Grundes ist der Grund der Sätze. Der Satz des Grundes ist der Grund des Satzes.* The switch from the dative *vom* to the genitive *des* emphasizes the ambiguous relation between *Satz* and *Grund*, the two primary terms in "the principle of reason."

[10.] This sentence could also read: "Nothing takes root in us any more."

[11.] *Das im höchsten Ansehen Stehende bringt diese Ansicht aus ihm selber mit. Dieses Ansehen beruht in seinem Aussehen. Das von sich her im höchsten Ansehen Stehende öffnet die Aussicht in jene Höhe, von deren Aussehen her alles andere jeweils sein Aussehen empfängt und sein Ansehen besitzt.* This is one of the most difficult passages to translate in the entire text; for instance: *Aussehen* means both "the visible look, appearance of something," as well as "the outlook one has (on life)." The German more clearly conveys the point here that, for the Greeks, seeing and being seen simultaneously occurs within and as a field of relations in which prestige is essential in constituting this field of relations.

[12.] For a discussion of the word *Geschick* see Translator's Introduction.

[13.] In this passage Heidegger has used several words of Latin origin rather than German equivalents.

[14.] See Translator's Introduction on "Capitalization."

135

[14a.] There appears to be a mistake in Heidegger's text: where he refers to the "or" in Leibniz's sentence, the text reads *sine* (without) rather than *seu* (or).

[15.] Heidegger's word *machten* is translated as "bepowers."

[16.] . . . *um das Vorstellen der Gegenstände handelt, . . .*" The sense of complementary movements—a "back and forth"—is more immediately apparent in the German *Vorstellen* and *Gegenstand*.

[17.] I render *Anspruch* here as "claim," and elsewhere as "exacting claim" or "demand," depending on the context. All these senses are in play in each instance.

[18.] Heidegger's example (*die Zustellung des Posts*: the delivery of the mail) has been changed to an example more suitable to the term "render," which like "deliver" translates *zustellen*.

[19.] "Molded" translates *geprägt*, a word that means: "to *stamp* the hallmark in silver," "to *coin* a new word," "to *mint* a coin," and "to have experiences that *mold* one's life." Heidegger means to invoke several of these senses with *prägen* and its cognates.

[20.] Heidegger's discussion here revolves around cognates of the verb *stehen*, "to stand."

[21.] A paraphrase of what Heidegger means by *das Gegenständige* might be "whatever is defined in its essence by standing in relation to other things in the way that an object stands, namely, oppositionally." The subtle shift from *Ständigkeit* in the previous sentence to *das Ständige* in this sentence emphasizes the stance of what stands.

[22.] *Deshalb sind diese Gründe ab-gründig.* This could also be translated as "Therefore, these grounds come from" or "are separate from reason."

[23.] *Die Grund-erfahrung. . . .* can also mean "the experience of reason."

[24.] *Unerhört*, which is translated "un-heard (of)," "unprecedented." Both of these senses are in play here.

[25.] *Das Erhörte* means "that which is brought forth in such a way that it is heard"; *erblicken* means "to bring something into view." However, *erhören* also means "to grant," as we might say "that to hear someone's request is to grant it."

[26.] Heidegger uses *tumb* here, which is an Old High German form of *dumm*.

[27.]

> *Wär nicht das Auge sonnenhaft,*
> *Wie könnten wir das Licht erblicken?*
> *Lebt nicht in uns des Gottes eigne Kraft,*
> *Wie könnt uns Göttliches entzücken?*

[28.] . . . *dann ist es auch nicht völlig unerhört, daß Hörbares zugleich erblickt werden kann, wenn das Denken hörend blickt und blickend hört.*

[29.] *Sein west in sich als gründendes.*

[30.] In these final sentences, there is an ambiguity in the German *wovon*, which can mean "from where" or "whence" and "about which."

[31.] The hyphenation of *be-stimmen* and *ge-stimmen* emphasizes the root *stimmen*. One of the many ways this sentence could be read is: "Man is disposed towards that which gives voice to his essence."

[32.] *Sein ist als Sein gründend.*

[33.] *Demgemäß bleibt der Grund vom Sein weg. Der Grund bleibt ab vom Sein.*

[34.] *Was aber schön ist, selig scheint es in ihm selbst.*

[35.] Here and in the following discussion of "the ungraspable," there is an ambiguity in the German concerning what "ungraspable" predicates. The "in" in "What is ungraspable in general principles . . . ," translates *von*, and can also be rendered as "What is ungraspable by . . ." as well as "What is ungraspable about. . . ." In the first of these alternative renderings "ungraspable" predicates that to which the principle is applied. The second predicates the principle itself. Below one finds this ambiguity between the predication of the contents grasped *by* the principle and the principle itself. There "holds" translates *hat* to preserve some of this ambiguity.

[36.] *Nur das Gewährte hat in sich die Gewähr zu währen.* The German *wahr*, or "true," is an important root in the principal words of this sentence. In addition, the German prefix *Ge-* indicates both a past participle and a collective.

[37.] *Der Sprung ist der Satz aus dem Grundsatz vom Grund als einem Satz. . . .*

[38.] "Furnish" translates *einräumen*, which literally means "in-clearing," and includes the senses of "to grant or allow," "to provide," and "to make a place for."

[39.] *Wenn an der kimm in sachtem fall*
    Eintaucht der feurig rote ball:
    . . . .
    Mein herd ist gut, mein dach is dicht,
    Doch eine freude wohnt dort nicht.
    Die netze hab ich all geflickt
    Und küch und kammer sind beschickt.

[40.] The German reader immediately recognizes the allusion to the term *Gegenstand*, translated as "object." Viewed etymologically, *Gegenstand* means "that which stands over against."

[41.] Musicologists have since reached the consensus that this letter is incorrectly attributed to Mozart.

[42.] *Ein Herze, das zu Grund Gott still ist, wie er will Wird gern von ihm berührt: es ist sein Lautenspiel.*

[43.] *Das ich stelle etwas als etwas vor mich . . .*

[44.] The word used here, *hinausgehen*, can mean "to result in."

[45.]

    Wenn milder athmen die Lüfte,
    Und liebende Pfeile der Morgen
    Uns Allzugedultigen schikt,
    Und leichte Gewölke blühn
    Uns über den schüchternen Augen,
    Dann werden wir sagen, wie kommt
    Ihr, Charitinnen, zu Wilden?
    Die Dienerinnen des Himmels
    Sind aber wunderbar,
    Wie alles Göttlichgeborne.
    Zum Traume wirds ihm, will es Einer
    Beschleichen und straft den, der
    Ihm gleichen will mit Gewalt;
    Oft überraschet es einen,
    Der eben kaum es gedacht hat.

[46.] *Sondern das aus dem Gegenüber her An-währende.*

[47.] *Vorwurf* in German also means "reproach," especially in the sense of something that is "thrown up in someone's face." *Problema* in Greek is built on the root verb βάλλειν, which means "to throw," and the suffix πρό, or "forward."

[48.] The primary musical sense meant here is "movement," as when one speaks of a string quartet comprising three movements.

[49.] See the Translator's Introduction on *Überlieferung*.

[50.] . . . *weil das Denken, insofern es dem Sein nachdenkt, in den Grund zurück, d.h. dessen Wesen als die Wahrheit des Seins denkt.*

[51.] "Conjunction" translates *Gegeneinanderüber*. As Heidegger makes clear, he uses *Gegeneinanderüber* to supplement the sense of *gegenüberliegen*, which means "to lie over against" and can imply a certain indifference of what lies over against and that over against which it lies. Contrary to such indifference Heidegger here describes the relation of humans and being as a *Gegeneinanderüber*, which implies a state of affairs in which these two "terms" face and oppose each other, mutually determining each other even to the extent of being nothing outside this mutually determining relation. If it were not for the Hegelian overtones, *Gegeneinanderüber* could be rendered as "dialectical relation."

[52.] *Das Geschick des Seins ist als Zuspruch und Anspruch der Spruch, aus dem alles menschliche Sprechen spricht.*

[53.] *Augesdauert wird das je schon Währende.*

[54.] Heidegger here is drawing upon the original sense of *Vernunft*, whose Old High German root, *firnunft*, means comprehension, sense perception, insight.

[55.] *Fügung*: This word, not unlike *Geschick*, has meanings that range from "jointure," to "coincidence," "submission," "ordainment," "fate" and "providence."

[56.] "Oracular slumber" refers to a rite practiced by the pre-Hippocratic devotees of Asclepius, the healer. When ill, the follower would sleep in or near the temples (Asculapiadae) presided over by his priestly successors. Their dreams were to suggest a cure.

[57.] See Note [54.].

[58.] "Doch Forschung strebt und ringt, ermüdend nie, / Nach dem Gesetz, dem Grund *Warum* und *Wie*."

[59.] Heidegger uses several words in this passage which are Latinate rather than Germanic.

[60.] The German word here is *Klang*, a technical musical term.

[61.] "Wie? Wann? und Wo?—Die Götter bleiben stumm! / Du halte dich ans *Weil* und frage nicht *Warum*?"

[62.] "Was auch sich spiegeln mag von Grund zu Gründen, / Er wandelt unaufhaltsam fort zu Tale."

[63.] Here Heidegger moves from *weil* [because] to *weilen* [to while, or abide].

[64.] *Die Fiedel stockt, der Tänzer weilt.*

[65.] *Das Wort von Sein als Grund vermag solches Gründen.*

[66.] Here Goethe's phrase could also be given the paraphrasing translation: "You hold the *while* and refrain from asking *why*?"

GLOSSARIES

The two following glossaries represent a selection of the most important German terms and their English translations. They are not, however, comprehensive: the German-English glossary does not always provide all the English renderings of a given German word, and the English-German glossary likewise does not always list every German word that an English word renders. An effort has been made to coordinate the entries of the two glossaries so as to facilitate their use. The glossary of cognate words is comprehensive in that it includes all the words related to the root word that occur in Heidegger's text.

GERMAN–ENGLISH

Abgrund: abyss
abspringen: to leap from
Absprung: leap-off
Absprungsbereich: the realm/region from which one leaps
Anblick: aspect
anblicken: to regard; look upon; look at
andenken: to think upon; recollectively think(-)upon
andenkend-vordenkender Satz: recollectively anticipatory leap
Aneignung: appropriation
anfangen: to commence
anfänglich: inaugural
anklingen: to resound
anschicken: to set about
Ansehen: countenance
Ansicht: regard
ansprechen: to address
Anspruch: claim; demand; exacting claim; address
das An-während e: what continues on toward us
Anwesen: presencing
anwesen: to come to be present; to presence
Anwesende: what is present; what comes to presence

das von sich her Anwesende: what is present in its own right
das von-sich-her-Anwesende: what comes to presence on its own
Aufgehen: arising
das von-sich-her-Aufgehende: what emerges on its own
das von-sich-her-Aufgehen: emerging-on-its-own
aus ihm selbst Aufgehen: arising on its own
aus-sich-Aufgehen: arising-on-its-own
aufgehen: to emerge; to arise
aufstellen: to formulate; set up
Ausblick: perspective
Ausschau: lookout
Aussehen: look
Aussicht: lookout; perspective
beanspruchen: to (lay) claim; insist
Bedeutung: meaning
befreien: to free
Befreien: liberating
Befreiung: liberation
begegnen: to encounter
begreifen: to conceive
Begriff: concept
begründen: to found
Begründung: foundation
beibringen: to convey

139

das Beigestellte: what is made available
beistellen: to provide
Beistellung: availability
berechenbar: calculable
die Berechenbarkeit: calculability
Berechnen: calculation
berechnen: to figure on
das Berechnete: what is reckoned
Berechnung: calculation
Bereitstellung: making available; procuring
bergen: to harbor; conceal
beschicken: to appoint; bestow; orient
die Beschickten: the bestowed ones
Beschickung: bestowing
Bestand: stuff; constant presence; stability
Beständigung: confirming
Bestehen: existence
bestellen: to order
Betonung: intonation
bewahren: to preserve; keep
bisweilen: sometimes
Blick: view; glance
blicken: to glimpse; view
Boden: basis; terrain; footing; roots
Bodenlose: fathomless
Bodenständigkeit: subsistence
darstellen: to portray; plot; describe
Darstellung: portrayal; exposition
Dasein: existence; Dasein
dieweilen: whereas
durchmachten: to bepower pervasively
durchwalten: to hold in the sway; held under the sway
(sein) Eigenart: what is peculiar (to it)
das Eigene: what is apropos; propriety; proper character
eigene: specific; proper
Eigenschaft: property
das Eigenste: what is most proper
das Eigentliche: genuine element
Eigentum: estate
eigentümlich: peculiar; particular
Eigentümliche: peculiar character
einräumen: to furnish; straighten up; usher
die Eingeräumte: the ushered ones
einzig: uniquely; singular; only
das Einzigartige: what is unique
Einzigartigkeit: unique character
Einzigkeit: uniqueness

entbergen: to reveal
Entgegen: countering
entgegenwarten: to (await to) encounter
Entgegenwerfen: throwing-over-against
entgegnen: to point out; reply
Entgegnung: reply
entsprechen: to respond; correspond
Entsprechung: response
entziehen: to withdraw
Entzug: withdrawal
das Erblickbare: what can be brought into view
erblicken: to bring into view; glimpse
ergründen: get to the bottom
erhören: to listen
Erkennen: cognition; knowledge
erkennen: to know; discern
Erkenntnis: knowledge
erklingen: to ring out
errechnen: to compute; figure out
feststellen: to establish; ascertain; firmly establish; make an assertion
Feststellung: assessment; pronouncement
frei: free and open
Freiheit: freedom and openness; freedom
die Gebrauchten: the ones engaged
das Geeignete: appropriate
Gefüge: warp and woof
Gegen: counter; against
Gegend: province
Gegeneinanderüber: conjunction
Gegenstand: object
Gegenständige: what is objective
Gegenständigkeit: objectness
gegenständlich: objective
gegenstandlos: objectless
Gegenstehen: obstancy
das Gegenstehende: what stands over against us
das Gegenüber: over-against
gegenüberliegen: to lie over against
Gegenwart: present
Gegenwurf: counter-throw
Gegner: opponent
Gegnerschaft: opposition
Geheimnis: mystery
gehören: to belong to; to be intrinsic; pertinent
Geist: spirit
Gepräge: configuration

geprägte: configured; molded
das Gerechnete: what is reckoned
geschichtlich: historical
Geschichlichkeit: historicity
Geschichte: history
Geschick: destiny
geschicklich: having a *Geschick*
das Geschickliche: what is proffered in the *Geschick*
Gewähr: guarantee
gewähren: to vouchsafe
gewährleisten: to guarantee
das Gewährte: what is vouchsafed
Gewesen: what has-been
großmächtig: mighty
das Großmächtige: something all-powerful; what is mighty
Grund: ground; reason(s); soil; ground/reason; basis; fundamental reason
zum Grunde gehen: to go to ruins; hit bottom
Grund und Boden: footing
grundartig: akin to grounds
gründen: to ground
grundhaft: ground-like
Grund-Satz: principle-reason
Grundsatz: fundamental principle
grundsätzlich: fundamental
herausstellen: to produce; to bring forward
sich herausstellen: to prove to be; come to light
Herkunft: provenance
Herrschaft: authority; sovereignty; dominance
hindurchklingen: to reverberate
hinstellen: to hold up
hören: to hear; listen
hörig: slavish
Incubation: incubation
Incubationszeit: incubation period
das Jähe: what is sudden
jeweilig (Seiende): particular; individual
jeweils: whatever happens to be; in each case; during a given time
Klang: ring; resonance
klingen: to ring; sound
sich lichten: to clear and light
lichtend: clearingly
Lichtung: clearing and lighting
Macht: power

Machtanspruch: injunction
das Machten: bepowering; bepowering character
machten: to bepower
das Machtende: what is bepowering
Machtbereich: orbit
Machtbezirk: dominion
Machtspruch: decree
mächtig: mighty
Metapher: metaphor
Metaphysik: metaphysics
nachstellen: to pursue
Nächstliegendes: (what is) obvious; what lies closest at hand; what lies under our nose
Nähe: vicinity
Objekt: Object
das Offenkundige: the overt
Ort: site
Ortschaft: locale
das Plötzliche: what is abrupt
prägen: to cast; mold
Prägung: shaping; form; configuration; molding
Prinzip: Principle
Rechenschaft: account
rechnen: to reckon; count on; figure
rechnendes Denken: calculative thinking
Rechnung: account; reckoning
rechtfertigen: to account for
richten: to orient; conform
Rückblick: look back; glance back
Rücksicht: regard
Sage: legend
Sagen: saying; speaking; utterance
sammeln: to gather
Sammlung: gathering
Satz: principle; sentence; leap; proposition; vault; phrase; movement
schicken: to send
sich in etw. schicken–to adapt itself to
schicklich: fitting
das Schickliche: what is fitting; wherewithall
Schicksal: fate
Schickung: offering
das von-sich-her-Seiende: beings that arise on their own
Seinsgeschichte: history of being
Seinsgeschick: *Geschick* of being
Seinsverständnis: understanding of being

Sichentbergen: self-revealing
Sichentziehen: withdrawing; self-withdrawal
das Sichentziehende: what withdraws
Sicherheit: certainty
sichern: to secure
sicherstellen: to securely establish; secure
Sicherstellung: securing
Sicherung: safety mechanism; securing
Sichverbergen: self-concealing
Sichzuschicken: proffering
Spielraum: play-space
Sprache: language; words
sprachlich: literal
Spruch: saying; locution; verdict; fragment
Sprung: leap
Stand: stance; standstill
Ständigkeit: status
Standlose: without a stance
Stehen: standing; stand
das Stehende: something standing
Stelle: station
Stellen: presentation
stellen: to place; lodge (a claim)
die Sterblichen: mortals
das Steten: what is constant
Stetigkeit: constancy
Ton: pitch; tone
Tonart: tonality
tönen: to peal; intone
überliefern: to pass along; pass over
Überlieferung: tradition; legacy
übersetzen: to translate
Übersetzung: translation
übertragen: to transpose; convey
übertragenen: figurative
Übertragung: transposition
unerhört: unheard of; unprecedented
unterstellen: to impute; place under
das Unverborgene: what is unconcealed
verbergen: to conceal; harbor
Verbergung: concealment
verbleiben: to stay
das Verborgene: what is concealed
verklingen: to die away
Vermögen: faculty; capacity
vermögen: to be able; capable
vernehmen: to perceive; tune into
Vernunft: Reason
Verrechnung: reckoning up

versammeln: to assemble; gather
Verstand: understanding
verwahren: to preserve
verweilen: to linger; dwell
vollständig: complete
vor(-)denken: to think anticipatorily; think ahead; fore-thinking
vordenkend: anticipatorily
das Vorgestellte: what is represented; what is cognized
Vorgestelltheit: representedness
Vorliegen: presence; lying-present
vorliegen: to (lie, be) present
das Vor(-)liegende: what is ex-posed; what (lies, is) present
Vorliegenlassen: allowing-to-lie-present; letting lie present
Vorshein (zum V. kommen): to come to light
Vorstellen: cognition; representation; representational thinking
vorstellen: to represent; conceive; make something of
Vorstellung: idea; conception; notion; representation
das Währen: what is abiding
währen: to last; tarry
wahren: to preserve
walten: to reign; rule
das Weil: the while; the because
weil: because
weilen: to abide; to while
welten: to world
Wesen: essence; creature; being; essential nature; nature
wesen: come to be essential; essentially come to be
Wissen: knowing; knowledge
Wissenschaften: sciences
Wort: word
wörtlich: literal
Zeit-Spiel-Raum: temporal play-space
zeitigen: to temporalize
Zugehörigkeit: affiliation; belonging to
zureichen: to reach; accord; afford; provide; suffice
zurückdenken: to think back
zusammengehen: to converge
zusammengehören: to belong together
Zusammengehörigkeit: belonging together

Zusammenklang: accord
sich zuschicken: to proffer
Zuschickung: proffering
Zuspruch: appeal
zuständig: proper; qualified
zustellbar: available

Zustellbarkeit: renderability; availability;
    possibility of rendering
Zustellen: lodging
zustellen: to provide; render
Zuwerfen: throwing forth

ENGLISH-GERMAN

abide (v.): *weilen*
abiding (what is): *das Währen*
able (to be) (v.): *vermögen*
abrupt (what is): *das Plötzliche*
abyss: *Abgrund*
accord (v.): *zureichen*
account: *Rechenschaft; Rechnung*
account for (v.): *rechtfertigen*
adapt to (v.): *sich in etw. schicken*
address (v.): *ansprechen*
address; *Anspruch*
affiliation: *Zugehörigkeit*
afford (v.): *zureichen*
against: *gegen*
akin to grounds: *grundartig*
all-powerful (what is): *das Großmächtige*
allowing-to-lie-present: *Vorliegenlassen*
anticipatorily: *vordenkend*
appeal: *Zuspruch*
appoint (v.): *beschicken*
appropriate (what is): *das Geeignete*
appropriation: *Aneignung*
apropos (what is): *das Eigenen*
arise (v.): *aufgehen*
arising on its own: *aus ihm selbst Aufgehen*
arising-on-its-own: *aus-sich-Aufgehen*
ascertain (v.): *feststellen*
aspect: *Anblick*
assemble (v.): *versammeln*
assert (v.): *feststellen*
assessment: *Feststellung*
authority: *Herrschaft*
availability: *Beistellung; Zustellbarkeit*
available: *zustellend; zustellbar*
available (what is made): *das Beigestellte*
basis: *Boden; Grund*
because: *weil*
being: *Wesen; Sein*

beings that arise on their own: *das von-sich-her-Seiende*
belong to (v.): *gehören,*
belong together (v.): *zusammengehören*
belonging to: *Zugehörigkeit*
belonging together: *Zusammengehörigkeit*
bepower (v.): *machten*
bepower pervasively (v.): *durchmachten*
bepowering (what is): *das Machtende*
bepowering character: *das Machten*
bestow (v.): *beschicken*
bestowed ones: *die Beschickten*
bestowing: *Beschickung*
bring forward (v.): *herausstellen*
bring into view (v.): *erblicken*
calculability: *Berechenbarkeit*
calculable: *berechenbar*
calculation: *Berechnung; Berechnen*
calculative thinking: *rechnendes Denken*
capable (to be) (v.): *vermögen*
capacity: *Vermögen*
cast (v.): *prägen*
certainty: *Sicherheit*
claim (lay c. to) (v.): *beanspruchen*
claim: *Anspruch*
clear and light (v.): *lichten*
clearing and lighting: *Lichtung*
clearingly: *lichtend*
cognition: *Erkennen; Vorstellen*
cognized (what is): *das Vorgestellte*
come to be essential (v.): *wesen*
come to be present (v.): *anwesen*
come to light (v.): *zum Vorshein kommen;
    sich herausstellen*
commence (v.): *anfangen*
complete: *vollständig*
compute (v.): *errechnen*
conceal (v.): *verbergen; bergen*

concealed (what is): *das Verborgene*
concealment: *Verbergung*
conceive (v.): *begreifen; vorstellen*
concept: *Begriff*
conception: *Vorstellung*
configuration: *Gepräge; Prägung*
configured: *geprägte*
confirming: *Beständigung*
conform (v.): *richten*
conjunction: *Gegeneinanderüber*
constancy: *Stetigkeit*
constant (what is): *das Steten*
constant presence: *Bestand*
continues on toward us (what): *das An-währende*
converge (v.): *zusammengehen*
convey (v.): *beibringen, übertragen*
correspond (v.): *entsprechen*
count on (v.): *rechnen*
countenance: *Ansehen*
counter: *Gegen*
counter-throw: *Gegenwurf*
countering: *Entgegen*
creature: *Wesen*
decree: *Machtspruch*
demand: *Anspruch*
describe (v.): *darstellen*
destiny: *Geschick*
die away (v.): *verklingen*
discern (v.): *erkennen*
dominance: *Herrschaft*
dominion: *Machtbezirk*
during a given time: *jeweils*
dwell (v.): *verweilen*
emerge (v.): *aufgehen*
emerges-on-its-own (what): *von-sich-her-Aufgehende*
emerging-on-its-own: *das von-sich-her-Aufgehen*
encounter (v.): *begegnen, entgegenwarten*
engaged ones: *die Gebrauchten*
essence: *Wesen*
essential being: *Wesen*
essential nature: *Wesen*
essentially come to be (v.): *wesen*
establish firmly (v.): *feststellen*
estate: *Eigentum*
ex-posed (what is): *das Vor-liegende*
exacting claim: *Anspruch*
existence: *Dasein; Bestehen*

faculty: *Vermögen*
faculty of understanding: *Verstand*
fate: *Fatum; Schicksal*
fathomless: *Bodenlose*
figurative: *übertragenen*
figure (v.): *rechnen*
figure on (v.): *berechnen*
figure out (v.): *errechnen*
firmly establish (v.): *festellen*
fitting: *schicklich*
fitting (what is): *das Schickliche*
footing: *Boden; Grund und Boden*
fore-think (v.): *vor-denken*
form: *Prägung*
formulate (v.): *aufstellen*
found (v.): *begründen*
foundation: *Begründung*
fragment: *Spruch*
free (v.): *befreien*
free and open: *freie*
freedom: *Freiheit*
freedom and openness: *Freiheit*
fundamental: *grundsätzlich*
fundamental principle: *Grundsatz*
fundamental reason: *Grund*
furnish (v.): *einräumen*
gather (v.): *sammeln; versammeln*
gathering: *Sammlung*
genuine element: *das Eigentliche*
Geschick of being: *Seinsgeschick*
get to the bottom (v.): *ergründen*
glance: *Blick*
glance back: *Rückblick*
glimpse (v.): *erblicken*
go to ruins (v.): *zum Grunde gehen*
ground (v.): *gründen*
ground: *Grund*
ground-like: *grundhaft*
ground/reason: *Grund*
grounds (akin to): *grundartig*
guarantee (v.): *gewährleisten*
guarantee: *Gewähr*
harbor (v.): *verbergen, bergen*
has-been (what): *das Gewesene*
having a *Geschick*: *geschicklich*
hear (v.): *hören*
held under the sway: *durchwalten*
historical: *geschichtlich*
historicity: *Geschichtlichkeit*
history: *Geschichte*

history of being: *Seinsgeschichte*
hit bottom (v.): *zum Grunde gehen*
hold in the sway (v.): *durchwalten*
hold up (v.): *hinstellen*
idea: *Vorstellung*
impute (v.): *unterstellen*
in each case: *jeweils*
inaugural: *anfänglich*
incubation: *Incubation*
incubation period: *Incubationszeit*
individual: *jeweilig*
initial: *anfänglich*
injunction: *Machtanspruch*
insist (v.): *beanspruchen*
intonation: *Betonung*
intone (v.): *tönen*
intrinsic: *gehören*
keep (v.): *bewahren*
know (v.): *erkennen; wissen*
knowing: *Wissen*
knowledge: *Erkennen; Erkenntnis; Wissen*
language: *Sprache*
last (v.): *währen*
leap (v.): *springen*
leap: *Sprung; Satz*
leap from (v.): *abspringen*
leaping-off region: *Absprungsbereich*
leap-off: *Absprung*
legacy: *Überlieferung*
legend: *Sage*
letting lie present: *Vorliegenlassen*
liberating: *Befreien*
liberation: *Befreiung*
lie over against (v.): *gegenüberliegen*
lie present (v.): *vorliegen*
lies closest at hand (what): *das Nächstliegende*
lies present (what): *das Vorliegende*
lies under our nose (what): *das Nächstliegende*
linger (v.): *verweilen*
listen (v.): *erhören; hören*
literal: *wörtlich; sprachlich*
locale: *Ortschaft*
locution: *Spruch*
lodge (l. a claim) (v.): *stellen; Zustellen*
look: *Aussehen*
look at (v.): *anblicken*
look back: *Rückblick*
look upon (v.): *anblicken*

lookout: *Aussicht*
lying-present: *Vorliegen*
making available: *Bereitstellung*
make something of (v.): *vorstellen*
meaning: *Bedeutung*
metaphor: *Metapher*
metaphysics: *Metaphysik*
mighty (what is): *das Großmächtige*
mighty: *großmächtig, mächtig*
mold (v.): *prägen*
molding: *Prägung*
mortals: *die Sterblichen*
movement: *Satz*
mystery: *Geheimnis*
nature: *Wesen*
notion: *Vorstellung*
object: *Gegenstand*
Object: *Objekt*
objective: *gegenständlich*
objective (what is): *das Gegenständige*
objectless: *gegenstandlos*
objectness: *Gegenständigkeit*
obstancy: *Gegenstehen*
obvious (what is): *das Nächstliegendes*
offering: *Schickung*
only: *einzig*
opponent: *Gegner*
opposition: *Gegnerschaft*
orbit: *Machtbereich*
order (v.): *bestellen*
orient (v.): *beschicken; richten*
over-against: *Gegenüber*
overt (what is): *das Offenkundige*
particular: *eigentümlich, jeweilig*
pass along (v.): *überliefern*
pass over (v.): *überliefern*
passed on: *überliefert*
peal (v.): *tönen*
peculiar: *eigentümlich*
peculiar character: *das Eigentümliche*
peculiar to it (what is): *(sein) Eigenart*
perceive (v.): *vernehmen*
perspective: *Ausblick*
pertinent: *gehören*
phrase: *Satz*
pitch: *Ton*
place (v.): *stellen*
place under (v.): *unterstellen*
play-space: *Spielraum*
plot (v.): *darstellen*

point out (v.): *entgegnen*
portray (v.): *darstellen*
portrayal: *Darstellung*
possibility of rendering: *Zustellbarkeit*
power: *Macht*
presence: *Anwesen; Vorliegen*
presence (what comes to p.): *das Anwesende*
presence (what comes to p. on its own):
    das von-sich-her-Anwesende
presencing: *Anwesen*
present (to be) (v.): *anwesen; vorliegen*
present (what is): *das Anwesende;*
    Gegenwart; Vor(-)liegende
present (what lies): *das Vor(-)liegende*
present in its own right (what is): *das von*
    sich her Anwesende
presentation: *Stellen*
preserve (v.): *bewahren; verwahren; wahren*
Principle: *Prinzip*
principle: *Satz*
principle-reason: *Grund-Satz*
procuring: *Bereitstellung*
produce (v.): *herausstellen*
proffer (v.): *sich zuschicken*
proffered in the *Geschick* (what is): *das*
    Geschickliche
proffering: *Sichzuschicken; Zuschickung*
pronouncement: *Feststellung*
proper: *eigene; zuständig*
proper (what is most): *das Eigenste*
proper character: *das Eigene*
property: *Eigenschaft*
proposition: *Satz*
propriety: *das Eignene*
prove to be (v.): *sich herausstellen*
provenance: *Herkunft*
provide (v.): *beistellen; zureichen; zustellen*
province: *Gegend*
pursue (v.): *nachstellen*
qualified: *zuständig*
rational (what is): *das Grundartige*
reach (v.): *zureichen*
realm from which one leaps: *Absprungs-*
    bereich
reason: *Grund*
Reason: *Vernunft*
reasons: *Grund, Gründe*
reckon (v.): *rechnen*
reckoned (what is): *das Berechnete, das*
    Gerechnete

reckoning: *Rechnung*
reckoning up: *Verrechnung*
recollectively think(-)upon (v.): *andenken*
regard: *Ansicht; Rücksicht*
region from which one leaps: *Absprungs-*
    bereich
reign (v.): *walten*
render (v.): *zustellen*
renderability: *Zustellbarkeit*
rendering: *Zustellen*
reply (v.): *entgegnen*
reply: *Entgegnung*
represent (v.): *vorstellen*
representation: *Vorstellung; Vorstellen*
representational thinking: *vorstellendes*
    Denken; Vorstellen
represented (what is): *das Vorgestellte*
representedness: *Vorgestelltheit*
resonance: *Klang*
resound (v.): *anklingen*
respond (v.): *entsprechen*
response: *Entsprechung*
reveal (v.): *entbergen*
reverberate (v.): *hindurchklingen*
ring (v.): *klingen*
ring: *Klang*
ring out (v.): *erklingen*
roots: *Boden*
rule (v.): *walten*
safety mechanism: *Sicherung*
saying: *Sagen; Spruch*
sciences: *Wissenschaften*
secure (v.): *sichern; sicherstellen*
securely establish (v.): *sicherstellen*
securing: *Sicherstellung; Sicherung*
self-concealing: *Sichverbergen*
self-revealing: *Sichentbergen*
self-withdrawal: *Sichentziehen*
send (v.): *schicken*
sentence: *Satz*
set about (v.): *anschicken*
set up (v.): *aufstellen*
shaping: *Prägung*
singular: *einzig*
site: *Ort*
slavish: *hörig*
soil: *Grund*
sometimes: *bisweilen*
sound (v.): *klingen*
sovereignty: *Herrschaft*

speaking: *Sagen*
specific: *eigene*
spirit: *Geist*
stability: *Bestand*
stance: *Stand*
stand: *Stehen*
standing (what is): *das Stehende*
standing: *Stehen*
stands over against us (what): *das Gegenstehende*
standstill: *Stand*
station: *Stelle*
status: *Ständigkeit*
stay (v.): *verbleiben*
straighten up (v.): *einräumen*
stuff: *Bestand*
subsistence: *Bodenständigkeit*
sudden (what is): *das Jähe*
suffice (v.): *zureichen*
sufficiency: *Zureichen*
tarry (v.): *währen*
temporal play-space: *Zeit-Spiel-Raum*
temporalize (v.): *zeitigen*
terrain: *Boden*
think ahead (v.): *vor(-)denken*
think anticipatorily (v.): *vordenken*
think back (v.): *zurückdenken*
think upon (v.): *andenken*
throwing forth: *Entwurf; Zuwerfen*
throwing-over-against: *Entgegenwerfen; Gegenwurf*
tonality: *Tonart*
tone: *Ton*
tradition: *Überlieferung*
translate (v.): *übersetzen*
translation: *Übersetzung*
transpose (v.): *übertragen*
transposition: *Übertragung*

tune into (v.): *vernehmen*
unconcealed (what is): *das Unverborgene*
understanding of being: *Seinsverständnis*
understanding: *Verstand*
unheard of: *unerhört*
unique (what is): *das Einzigartige*
unique character: *Einzigartigkeit*
uniquely: *einzig*
uniqueness: *Einzigkeit*
unprecedented: *unerhört*
unthought (what is): *das Ungedachte*
usher (v.): *einräumen*
ushered ones: *die Eingeräumte*
utterance: *Sagen*
vault: *Satz*
verdict: *Spruch*
vicinity: *Nähe*
view: *Blick*
view (v.): *blicken*
view (bring into) (v.): *erblicken*
view (what can be brought into): *das Erblickbare*
vouchsafe (v.): *gewähren*
vouchsafed (what is): *das Gewährte*
warp and woof: *Gefüge*
whatever happens to be: *jeweils*
whereas: *dieweilen*
wherewithall: *das Schickliche*
while (v.): *weilen*
while (the): *das Weil*
withdraw (v.): *entziehen*
withdrawal: *Entzug*
withdrawing: *Sichentziehen*
withdraws (what): *das Sichentziehende*
without a stance (what is): *das Standlose*
word(s): *Wort; Sprache*
world (v.): *welten*

COGNATE WORDS

This glossary lists constellations of related words that are particularly important in Heidegger's text. These word groups suggest the rich textual resonances of the text.

schicken:
anschicken, beschicken, die Beschickten, Beschickung, entschicken, Geschichte, Geschick, geschicklich, das Geschickliche, schicken, sich in etwas schicken, das Schickliche, schicklich, Schicksal, Schickung, Seinsgeschick, Sichzuschicken, wegschicken, sich zuschicken

wahren/weilen:
bewahren, gewahren, gewahrleisten, verwahren, Verwahrnis, das An-währende, Gewähr, gewähren, Gewähren, das Gewährte, immerwähren, währen, während, bisweilen, dieweilen, jeweilig, jeweils, verweilen, weil, das Weil, weilen

machten:
bemächtigen durchmachten, großmächtig, das Großmächtige, Macht, Machtanspruch, Machtbereich, Machtbezirk, das Machten, machten, machtend, das Machtende, mächtig, Machtspruch

stellen:
aufstellen, Aufstellung, Beigestellte, beistellen, Beistellung, Bereitstellung, bestellen, darstellen, Darstellung, feststellen, Feststellung, Fragestellung, sich herausstellen, Herausstellen, hinstellen, Leitvorstellung, nachstellen, sicherstellen, Sicherstellung, Stelle, unterstellen, unvorstellbar, Vorgestellte, Vorgestelltheit, vorstellen, Vorstellung, Vorstellungsbereich, Vorstellungsverknüpfung, zustellen, Zustellung, zustellbar, Zustellbarkeit

stehen/stand:
bestehen, entstehen, gegenstehen, das Gegenstehende, stehen, das Stehenden, Bestand, Bestände, Beständigung, Gegenstand, Gegenstandbereich, gegenständig, das Gegenständige, Gegenständigkeit, gegenständlich, gegenstandlos, das Gegenstandlose, das Selbstverständliche, Stand, ständig, Ständigkeit, das Standlose, Standbild, Verstand, zuständig

eigen:
Eigenart, eigene, Eigenen, das Eigenliche, eigens, Eigenschaft, das Eigenste, eigentlich, Eigentum, das Eigentümliche

gegen:
Entgegen, entgegendrängen, entgegenwarten, Entgegenwerfen, entgegnen, Entgegnung, Gegen, Gegend, Gegeneinanderüber, Gegenstand, Gegen-stand, Gegenstandbereich, gegenständig, das Gegenständig, Gegenständigkeit, gegenständlich, gegenstandlos, Gegenüber, gegenüberliegen, Gegenwart, Gegenwurf, Gegner, Gegnerschaft

Address:
1st Front
II Re-jn. skept in 2300 yrs
118 - Tempelschlaf
12.9 reckoning (rechnen) → aufnehmen, vorne hinen, annehmen: vernehmen
     R. is a manner of perceiving
12 Sf transition to 2nd front
128 - doable imp   126 — Das Warum läßt kein Rule.
   - awakeness